Beer Lover's New York

First Edition

Sarah Annese & Giancarlo Annese

Guilford, Connecticut

FEB 2014

To buy books in quantity for corporate use
or incentives, call **(800) 962–0973**
or e-mail **premiums@GlobePequot.com.**

All the information in this guidebook is subject to change. We recommend that you call ahead to obtain current information before traveling.

All photos by Sarah Annese except photos on pages 20, 35, and 187 by Giancarlo Annese and photo on page 21 courtesy SingleCut Beersmiths.

Editor: Kevin Sirois and Amy Lyons
Project Editor: Staci Zacharski
Layout Artist: Casey Shain
Text Design: Sheryl P. Kober
Maps: Alena Joy Pearce © Morris Book Publishing, LLC

ISBN 978-0-7627-9199-6

Printed in the United States of America
10 9 8 7 6 5 4 3 2 1

Contents

Western New York 221

About the Authors

Husband-and-wife team Giancarlo and Sarah Annese are native New Yorkers who grew up on Long Island. They became immersed in craft beer culture after moving to New York City in the fall of 2008. Together they founded and run the NYC-centric website www.BeerUnion.com.

Sarah Annese began her writing career as a reporter at the historic *Brooklyn Eagle* newspaper. She and Giancarlo founded BeerUnion.com in 2009, and she is now a freelance writer specializing in beer and spirits. Sarah has contributed to *All About Beer* magazine, *Beverage World* magazine, and AlcoholProfessor.com.

Giancarlo Annese studied Classics and History at Union College and earned an M.A. in Medieval History at Fordham University. Through BeerUnion.com he and Sarah explore and write about craft beer culture in New York City. He works as the Senior Assistant Director for Student Accounts at Fordham University.

Acknowledgments

Researching and writing this book has been the most exciting and challenging project either of us has ever taken on. It would not have been possible without a lot of help and awesome people.

First and foremost we want to thank our families. To our parents—Mitch and Pam Tobol, Carlo Annese and Eileen Sheehy—thank you for everything, really. But more specifically, lending us your homes and your cars, your valuable insights and advice, and your unwavering willingness to try any beer we pour for you. To our siblings, Jake, Mary and Robin, for your enthusiasm and love. To our baby niece Audrey, who will not drink beer until 2034. To Grandma Tobol and Nana Rack. To Aunt Amy Tobol.

Big thanks and love to our amazing friends, who are always down for a beer. First to Mike Gallagher, for being an invaluable help to us with the homebrew recipes in these pages. And (in alphabetical order) Amelia Anderson, Kim Berlowitz, Hanna and Alex Donner, Ashley Gallagher, Emily and Matt Garland, Paul Hamill, Alison Holstein, Rich Leahy, Jessica Machado, Jackie and Mike Mangiolino, Caitlin McNamara, Phoebe Neidl, Arthur Rollin, John and Ally Traver, Jeff Williams, and Charlie and Natalie Wood.

Thank you to Mike Steger, who helped us iron out our very first book contract. Thank you John Holl and Jeff Cioletti, the best editors a freelancer could hope for. Thanks to John Kleinchester for helping us keep BeerUnion running throughout this process with your homebrewing columns.

To all the brewers we've met along the way, thank you for generously sharing your time and stories. To our fellow beer writers, thank you for your suggestions and thoughts. To the members of BrewYork, you're the most awesome beer geeks we know. Thanks for inviting us into your crew and sharing your beers.

And to the readers of BeerUnion.com. We wouldn't be here without you.

Introduction

New York doesn't get nearly the credit it should when it comes to craft beer. After traveling over 4,000 miles across the state and tasting hundreds of brews, we're not really sure why.

In every region we visited we found examples of brewers making quality traditional beers, and others using unique ingredients and innovative flavors. We tasted beers from brewers committed to English styles, and others who are adhering to the German Purity Law. Some brewers prefer to produce sessionable beers, others would rather make big, bold brews. And even though we came across some not-so-great libations, the majority of what we tasted was good or really good. And some of it was amazing.

There's rich beer history in this state, which at one time produced 90 percent of the country's hops. Utica is home to Matt Brewing Company, one of the oldest family-operated breweries in the country, founded by German immigrant F. X. Matt in 1888. Matt Brewing's Utica Club was the first beer officially sold after Prohibition. Genesee Brewing Company, located in the city of Rochester, was launched in 1878, and before it was purchased to become a division of North American Breweries (making it technically noncraft) was the fifth largest brewer in the United States.

Brooklyn Brewery, cofounded by Steve Hindy, a former Middle East War correspondent, has led the charge for craft beer growth in New York City since 1986. In 2012 Brooklyn Brewery was the 11th largest craft brewery in the country by sales volume.

As of mid-2013, there were over 130 breweries in New York State, with dozens more in planning. Everyone we met who had launched breweries in the past few years was passionate, driven, and collaborative. A common tale in New York is a startup brewer getting some much-needed hops from one that's more established. Or a group of breweries raising funds for another after a natural disaster nearly put it out of business.

We met brewers who've saved and pieced together money to build their own brewhouses, and others who use the valuable regional contract brewers as resources while they get off the ground. There are so many stories of brewers who have achieved widespread success by making their beers at Matt Brewing Company, Olde Saratoga Brewing Company, Butternuts Beer & Ale, or Custom BrewCrafters.

But if we put aside the history and personal stories, when it comes down to it, the beer speaks for itself.

In writing this book, we hope more people will take notice of the brewers in our state. Many new ones aren't yet able to distribute widely and require traveling to taste their offerings. If you're from New York or live here now, we hope to inspire you to visit your hometown brewery, and to seek out one nearby that you may not have previously heard of. Taste the local flavor, whether it's a Red Ale in the Adirondacks, a Cream Ale in Western New York, an IPA in the Finger Lakes, or a Sour in the Hudson Valley. Forget, for a while, about the imports available to you in New York City and try instead the beers from brewers who make the most out of tiny spaces.

Find out what New York beer tastes like.

How to Use This Guide

In the pages of this book you'll find a guide to the best and most interesting breweries and brewpubs in New York State. This book doesn't seek to list and review every single one, partly because they are opening at such a fast pace it wouldn't be possible, but also because we wouldn't suggest some of them.

Each brewery and brewpub listing will tell you its history, what's special about it, and why you'd want to visit. Each brewery listed in this book includes a **Beer Lover's Pick,** a look at one of their best or most interesting beers being produced, along with tasting notes. In many cases we've chosen beer that perfectly encapsulates the brewery that makes it, in other cases we've suggested a beer for you that is unique and so original that you'd be hard-pressed to find one like it anywhere else, and in some cases we've picked a beer that's part of New York's brewing history.

It's important to note here the difference between the breweries and brewpubs in this book. A brewery could have a public location to taste beers, or it might not. It could also have a restaurant attached to it. The main qualifier we used to differentiate between breweries and brewpubs is distribution: Breweries send their beer elsewhere, brewpubs don't.

We've also provided descriptions about the best beer bars in the state. Unfortunately there simply aren't enough pages in this book to detail every single beer bar in New York State, or even New York City. What we've given you are the special ones, the ones you'd be remiss if you didn't visit while you were in the area.

Brewery, brewpub, and bar descriptions make up the bulk of this book. But you'll also find secitons on the following:

Pub Crawls: If you're visiting a city and want to make the most of your time, check out these itineraries of some great pub crawls. Grab some friends and some good comfortable shoes to walk in and head out for a beer lover's adventure using these trip suggestions. A pub crawl is a great way to see multiple places in one day and allows you to do so safely, as long as you walk, take a cab, or find someone willing to be your designated driver.

Beer Festivals: A look at some of the biggest and most interesting beer festivals in the state that allow you to sample quite a large selection of beers from multiple breweries.

BYOB: Brew Your Own Beer: New York is one of the best states to be a homebrewer because of its great access to some amazing shops and fresh ingredients. Here you can find a handful of shops around the state to help you get started brewing, along with some clone recipes for those already familiar with brewing.

In the Kitchen: Beer is great on its own, but it can also make an amazing ingredient in food. In this section you'll find recipes you can make at home utilizing beer from around New York.

Glossary of Terms

ABV: Alcohol by volume—the percentage of alcohol in a beer.

Ale: Beer brewed with top fermenting yeast. Quicker to brew than Lagers, most craft beer is a style of Ale. Popular styles of Ales include Pale Ales, Amber Ales, Stouts, and Porters.

Altbier: A German style of Ale, typically brown in color, smooth, and fruity.

Barleywine: Not a wine at all but a high-ABV Ale that originated in England and is typically sweet. American versions often have large amounts of hops. These beers improve with age.

Barrel of beer: Production of beer is measured in barrels. A barrel equals 31 gallons.

Bitter: An English bitter is an English-style Ale, more hoppy than an English mild, but less hoppy than an IPA.

Bock: A German-style Lager, typically stronger than the typical Lager.

Bomber: Bombers are 22-ounce bottles. Most beers are packaged in 12-ounce bottles.

Brewpub: Typically a restaurant, but sometimes a bar, that serves house beers, often brewed on premises, but not distributed.

Cask: Also known as real Ales, cask Ales are naturally carbonated and either served with a hand pump or through gravity, rather than forced out with carbon dioxide or nitrogen.

Clone beer: A homebrew recipe based on a commercial beer.

Contract brewery: A company that does not have its own brewery and pays someone else to brew and bottle its beer.

Craft beer: High-quality, flavorful beer made by small, indepently owned breweries.

Craft beer bar: A bar that focuses on carrying craft or fine imported beers.

Double: Two meanings. Most often meant as a higher alcohol version of a beer, typically used in reference to a double, or imperial, IPA. Can also be used as an American translation of a Belgian *Dubbel,* a style of Belgian Ale.

ESB: Extra special bitter. A traditional malt-heavy English Pub Ale with low bitterness, often served on cask.

Gastropub: A beer-centric bar or pub that exhibits the same amount of care selecting its foods as it does its beers.

Growler: A half-gallon jug of beer.

Gypsy brewer: A company that does not own its own brewery, but rents space at an existing brewery to brew it themselves.

Hops: Flowers used in beers to produce aroma, bitterness, and flavor.

IBU: International bittering units, used to measure how bitter a beer is.

Imperial: A higher-alcohol version of a regular-strength beer.

IPA: India Pale Ale. A popular style of Ale created in England that has taken a decidedly American twist over the years. Often bitter, due to an emphasis on hops.

Kolsch: A light, effervescent German-style Ale.

Lager: Beer brewed with bottom-fermenting yeast. Takes longer to brew than Ales. Popular styles of Lagers include Black Lagers, Doppelbocks, Pilsners, and Vienna Lagers.

Malt: Typically barley malt, but sometimes wheat malt. Malt provides the fermentable sugar for the yeast and balanced the bitterness of hops in beers. The more fermentable sugar, the higher the ABV in a beer.

Nanobrewery: A brewery that brews four barrels or less of beer per batch.

Nitro draft: Most beers that are served on draft use kegs pressurized with carbon dioxide. Occasionally, particularly with Stouts, nitrogen is added, which helps create a creamier body.

Pilsner: A style of Lager that originated in the Czech Republic, usually light in color.

Porter: A dark Ale, similar to a Stout but with fewer roasted characters.

Quad: A strong Belgian-style Ale, typically sweet and high in alcohol.

Russian Imperial Stout: A Stout is a dark, heavy beer. A Russian Imperial Stout is a higher-alcohol, thicker-bodied version of a regular Stout.

Saison: Also known as a Belgian or French Farmhouse Ale. It can be fruity, and it can also be peppery.

Seasonal: A beer that is brewed only at a certain time of year to coincide with the seasons.

Session beer: A low-alcohol beer that you can imbibe several of in one drinking "session."

Stout: A dark-colored beer brewed with roasted malts.

Strong Ale: A style of Ale that is typically both hoppy and malty and can be aged for years.

Tap takeover: An event where a bar or pub hosts a brewery and has several of its beers on tap.

Triple (Tripel): A Belgian-style Ale, typically lighter in color than a Dubbel but higher in alcohol.

Wheat beer: Beers, such as Hefeweizens and Witbiers, are brewed using wheat malt along with barley malt.

Yeast: The living organism in beer that causes the sugars to ferment and become alcohol.

New York City

BARS

49	Adobe Blues
16	Alewife NYC
37	Alphabet Beer Co.
43	Barcade
20	Beer Authority
47	Bierkraft
29	Blind Tiger
1	The Bronx Ale House
33	Burp Castle
10	Cafe D'Alsace
38	The Diamond
6	Dive Bar
8	Earl's Beer and Cheese
46	4th Ave Pub
36	Idle Hands
7	Jacob's Pickles
34	Jimmy's No. 43
50	Killmeyer's Old Bavaria Inn
32	McSorley's Old Ale House
30	124 Rabbit Club
44	Pine Box Rock Shop
18	The Pony Bar—Hell's Kitchen
11	The Pony Bar—Upper East Side
38	Proletariat
13	The Queens Kickshaw
23	Rattle N Hum
42	Spuyten Duyvil
27	Taproom 307
9	Third Avenue Ale House
40	Torst

BREWERIES

14	Big Alice Brewing
39	Bridge and Tunnel Brewery
5	The Bronx Brewery
41	Brooklyn Brewery
3	Chelsea Brewing Company
25	City Island Beer Company
4	Harlem Brewing Company
2	Jonas Bronck's Beer Company
45	KelSo of Brooklyn
24	Radiant Pig Craft Beers
15	Rockaway Brewing Company
12	SingleCut Beersmiths
48	Sixpoint

BREWPUBS

31	508 Gastrobrewery
22	Heartland Brewery—Empire State Building
19	Heartland Brewery—Port Authority
17	Heartland Brewery—Radio City
21	Heartland Brewery—Times Square
28	Heartland Brewery—Union Square
26	La Birreria

New York City

It's an exciting time for craft beer in New York City. While not known for brewed offerings since the 1970s, the booming metropolis has recently seen a new wave of beer growth. Whether through contract brewing or a tiny setup in the basement of a restaurant, brewers are making things work in a city with sky-high real estate prices and millions of beer drinkers. The year 2012 saw the creation of the New York City Brewers Guild and the opening of three new breweries, all in Queens. In 2013 the newly formed Guild held the fifth annual NYC Beer Week, the craft beer and food festival Savor took place in the city for the first time, and even more new breweries opened in the outer boroughs.

New bars open practically every week with bigger and better tap lists, and in a city where restaurants are held to a high standard, craft beer is on the menu, increasingly treated on par with wine. And it isn't only the neighborhoods of Williamsburg or the East Village, even Midtown Manhattan and Kingsbridge in the Bronx are joining in.

Breweries

BIG ALICE BREWING

808 43rd Rd., Long Island City, NY 11101; (347) 688-BEER; BigAliceBrewing.com;
@BigAliceBrewing
Founded: 2013 **Founders:** Kyle Hurst, Scott Berger, Robby Crafton **Brewers:** Kyle Hurst,
Robby Crafton **Tours:** Yes **Taproom:** Yes; open Friday evening

While enjoying beers at the beer festival TAP NY in 2011, homebrewers Kyle Hurst, Scott Berger, and Robby Crafton decided to start their own brewery. The three of them work together at an air-conditioning company in Long Island City, Queens, and took inspiration from the borough to name their new venture. "Big Allis" is a large electric power generator, visible in the Queens skyline; "Big Alice" is

an homage to that distinctive feature. The three guys found a small brewery location just a few blocks away from their office and built it out to include a small taproom, where on Friday people can sample their beers. While imbibing, patrons can look through a window to see the small brewhouse.

Big Alice beers are made on a 10-gallon brewing system, which yields about 48 large format 750-milliliter bottles each batch. Because the beer is so limited, the trio have decided to take a different approach in structuring their brewery, and do so like a farm would a CSA. CSA stands for Community Supported Agriculture; to participate in a CSA, people purchase shares in a farm and in return receive regular installments of whatever the farm produces. Big Alice sells ninety beer shares per six-month period, in three increments: two, four, or six bottles a month. Bottles are also available to purchase and sample at the brewery's tasting room in Long Island City. Within a week of opening in June 2013, every share for the first six-month period was sold out.

Every beer from Big Alice Brewing is a one-off batch, not made previously and not to be made again. Many ingredients for the brews are sourced from local farmers' markets, and recipes often don't come together until the team takes a look at what they've found. The brewers discuss beer concepts and styles they like but craft the recipes as they obtain ingredients. Past beers include a Smoked Ale with peppercorns, an IPA with Buddha's Hand, a Belgian Red Ale with Cinderella pumpkin, and a Wheat Ale brewed with kumquats. The beers are brewed with the intention to be savored.

BRIDGE AND TUNNEL BREWERY
Maspeth, NY 11378; (347) 392-8593; BridgeAndTunnelBrewery.com
Founded: 2012 **Founder and Brewer:** Rich Castagna **Flagship Beer:** Angry Amel Dunkelweizen **Other Beers:** Tiger Eyes Hazelnut Brown Ale, Ol Gilmartin Milk and Oatmeal Stout, Red IPA **Tours:** No **Taproom:** No

Bridge and Tunnel Brewery is a real nanobrewery, a one-man operation started and maintained by Rich Castagna, a lifelong New Yorker who has been homebrewing for over 10 years.

Castagna's brewery and beer are a tribute to New York City, the outer boroughs especially. Each of his brews is named for a neighborhood story, person, or memory; events or people that may otherwise have been swept under the carpet. His **Angry Amel Dunkelweizen,** for example, recalls a crazy neighbor he had growing up, who would threaten to cut the ears off the children playing stickball and touch football in the street. The beer has flavors of clove, banana, and malt and comes in at 5.3

percent ABV. Castagna's **Tiger Eyes Hazelnut Brown** pours mahogany and got its name because the color is similar to that of the tiger's eye stone. Brewed in the English brown style, Tiger Eyes has strong malty flavors with notes of hazelnut, at 5.5 percent ABV.

Castagna built his brewery in a small space in Maspeth, and has made use of every inch of it to accommodate the 1.5-barrel system he built and put together himself. He makes his beer in the off-hours from helping his wife care for their three children and a full-time job arranging exports for a shipping company. Often Castagna starts brewing at 2 a.m., and he dedicates the nighttime and early morning

Ol Gilmartin Milk and Oatmeal Stout

Style: Sweet Stout

ABV: 5%

Availability: In the winter months, on draft only at bars in Queens, Manhattan, and Brooklyn

Ol Gilmartin is the first offering from Bridge and Tunnel Brewery, a tribute to the person who was originally slated to be Castagna's partner in the venture. The beer is a Milk Stout made with the addition of flaked oats in the mash. Malty and sweet, Ol Gilmartin is smooth with roasty flavors.

hours to making beer. He was inspired to start the brewery because he has always had an entrepreneurial spirit and likes the idea of creating something. Castagna is continuing to grow Bridge and Tunnel (with his wife helping deliver kegs) and hopes to eventually take on a partner. In the meantime his beers can be found on draft only at several bars in Queens and a few in Manhattan and Brooklyn.

THE BRONX BREWERY
856 E. 136th St., Bronx, NY 10454; TheBronxBrewery.com; @TheBronxBrewery
Founded: 2011 **Founders:** Chris Gallant, Damian Brown **Brewer:** Damian Brown
Flagship Beer: Bronx Pale Ale **Year-Round Beer**: Bronx Pale Ale **Seasonal/Specialty Beers:** Belgian Pale Ale, Rye Pale Ale, Black Pale Ale, Summer Pale Ale, Bourbon Barrel–Aged Pale Ale, Zinfandel Barrel–Aged Pale Ale, Gin Barrel–Aged Pale Ale **Tours:** No
Taproom: No

New York City's northernmost borough hasn't historically been known for fine craft beer, at least not since Rheingold shut down in 1960. Chris Gallant and Damian Brown sought to change that when they opened The Bronx Brewery in 2011. Since then they've taken on Sean McCain as a partner and sales director. The flagship **Pale Ale** was draft only at first and distributed by Gallant and Brown until the pair inked a deal with Union Beer Distributors in mid-2012. In April 2013 the brewery released its flagship brew in four packs of 16-ounce cans.

The mark of The Bronx Brewery is dedication to detail. Brewer Damian Brown has perfected his Pale Ale recipe, and each subsequent offering, seasonal or special, has been an interesting take on the flavor profile and spin of the flagship beer. In April 2012 the brewery released a **Bourbon Barrel–Aged Pale Ale,** then celebrated its first anniversary in September with a **Zinfandel Barrel–Aged Pale Ale.** The brewery's seasonal beers include a **Rye Pale Ale** in the fall, a **Black Pale Ale** in the winter, a **Belgian Pale Ale** in the spring and a **Summer Pale Ale** in the summer. The Pale Ale is malty and biscuity, and each subsequent beer has built on those characteristics with its own flavor profile. The Black Pale Ale has dark chocolate and roasted flavors, the Summer Pale Ale has crisp citrus notes, the Rye Pale Ale tastes of pine and herbs, and the Belgian Pale Ale is yeasty with a touch of citrus.

What's unique about The Bronx Brewery is that all of its beers are an expansion or play on their flagship Pale Ale. Brown is meticulous in producing his beer, working on bringing out the best aromas and flavor profile possible from each batch.

For the first couple of years the beers were contract brewed at Cottrell Brewing Company in Pawcatuck, Connecticut, with Brown performing a hands-on role. In February 2013 the team signed a lease for a location to build out a brewery in the Bronx. The new facility will include a taproom, beer garden, and outdoor dog run.

Bronx Pale Ale

Style: American Pale Ale

ABV: 6.3%

Availability: Year-round, on tap at many locations throughout New York and in 4-packs of 16-ounce cans at retail stores.

Brewer Damian Brown is a perfectionist about his Pale Ale. It is among the most consistent beers on the market. The combination of British, German, and American malts used give the beer a distinct biscuit flavor with some hints of caramel and a chewy full body. The Cascade and Centennial hops generate predominantly citrus and some floral notes in the aroma and a solid bitterness to balance out the sweetness of the malts.

BROOKLYN BREWERY

79 North 11th St., Brooklyn, NY 11249; (718) 486-7422; BrooklynBrewery.com; @BrooklynBrewery

Founded: 1988 **Founders:** Steve Hindy, Tom Potter **Brewer:** Garrett Oliver **Flagship Beer:** Brooklyn Lager **Year-Round Beers:** Brooklyn Lager, Brooklyn Brown Ale, Brooklyn East India Pale Ale, Brooklyn Pilsner, Brooklyn Pennant Ale, Brooklyn Blast!, Brooklyner Weisse, Brooklyn Radius **Seasonals/Special Releases:** Brooklyn Black Chocolate Stout, Brooklyn Winter Ale, Brooklyn Monster Ale, Brooklyn Dry Irish Stout, Brooklyn Summer Ale, Brooklyn Oktoberfest, Post Road Pumpkin Ale, Brooklyn Silver Anniversary Lager, Brooklyn Local 1, Brooklyn Local 2, Sorachi Ace, BAMboozle, Brooklyner-Schneider Hopfen-Weisse, Brewmaster's Reserve series of beers **Tours:** Yes **Taproom:** Yes

In the early 1980s Steve Hindy was a Middle East correspondent for the Associated Press, covering wars and assassinations. While there, he met American diplomats who brewed their own beer (alcohol was banned). Hindy moved back to New York with his family in 1984, and they found an apartment in Park Slope, where they met neighbor Tom Potter. The two bonded over homebrewing and teamed up to

start Brooklyn Brewery in Williamsburg. They launched in 1988 with their flagship Brooklyn Lager contract brewed at Matt Brewing Company upstate in Utica.

In 1994 the pair brought on Garrett Oliver as the brewmaster, and in 2011 expanded into the building next door to double in production size. In the 25 years since Hindy and Potter started the brewery, they have led not only the beer revolution in New York City, but also the dramatic revitalization of the surrounding Williamsburg neighborhood. Brooklyn Brewery beers can be found across the country and the world.

The brewery still produces its original **Brooklyn Lager,** which has since been joined by seven other year-round brews. Oliver's team brews a handful of seasonal offerings like the bold **Black Chocolate Stout** and the **Summer Ale,** as well as several specialty large bottles. The large bottle beers **Local 1,** a Tripel; **Local 2,** a Dubbel; and **Sorachi Ace,** a saison are the first Belgian styles in Brooklyn Brewery's lineup. Every few months Brooklyn Brewery releases an installment in its **Brewmaster's Reserve** series, a limited line of creative beers. The year-round beers and many of the specialty and seasonal releases are brewed up at Matt Brewing Company, while the Brewmaster's Reserve and other specialty beers are made in Brooklyn.

The brewery and taproom are open from Monday through Thursday for reservation-only Small Batch tours, Friday night for happy hour, and Saturday and Sunday for tastings and free tours. You can bring in food to enjoy along with your beers.

Beer Lover's Pick

Brooklyn Sorachi Ace
Style: Saison
ABV: 7.6%
Availability: Year-round,
    on draft and in
    large-format bottles

Sorachi Ace showcases the creativity at the heart of Garret Oliver's brew team. They combined the saison style native to Belgium and France with the Japanese hop Sorachi Ace. The hops lend a bit of lemon and grassiness to the aroma. The beer is refermented in the bottle and has an enjoyable, snappy effervescence. Sorachi Ace makes a great accompaniment to summer salads, seafood, or fried food.

CHELSEA BREWING COMPANY

Chelsea Piers, Pier 59, New York, NY 10011; (212) 336-6440; ChelseaBrewingCo.com; @CBCBeer

Founded: 1996 **Founder:** Pat Greene **Brewer:** Mark Szmaida **Flagship Beer:** Checker Cab Blonde Ale **Year-Round Beers:** Hop Angel IPA, Sunset Red Ale, Black Hole XXX Stout **Seasonals/Special Releases:** Alpha 5 Pale Ale, Sunset Red Ale, NY State of Mind (wet hopped IPA with New York State hops), Pumpkin Pie Ale, Blueberry Wheat **Tours:** Yes **Taproom:** Yes

Chelsea Brewing Company is among the few breweries in Manhattan that have been around for more than 10 years. Opened by Pat Greene in April 1996, Chelsea is one of the only survivors of the wave of brewpubs that opened in the borough in the 1990s and closed soon after. Located at the iconic Chelsea Pier, the 30-barrel brewhouse sits right on the Hudson River at 15th Street.

Russell Garret was the founding brewer who left after a year. His apprentice Chris Sheehan took the helm, with Mark Szmaida joining him later that year. The

Checker Cab Blonde
Style: Kolsch
ABV: 4.5%
Availability: Year-round
A crisp and easy drinking blonde ale styled after the traditional Kolsch beer from Cologne Germany, the Checker Cab Blonde is great for a relaxing summer afternoon or evening on the pier. Chelsea brews the beer with 10 percent wheat, giving it an easy mouthfeel, and Noble hops for some dryness and slightly grassy flavors. The manageable 4.5 percent ABV means you won't have to worry too much about enjoying more than one and navigating your way back to the subway.

two worked together to improve the recipes and create new ones, until Sheehan left in 2011, and Szmaida took over. Over 20 different styles of beer are made at Chelsea, a handful of which are distributed to bars throughout the city. The beer is draft only—the brewery closed its bottling line in 2001.

Chelsea produces a wide variety of beers, with flavors ranging from roasty to hoppy to sweet. Fans of Stouts won't be disappointed by the roasty **Black Hole XXX Stout** or the sweet **Chelsea Cream Stout.** Hop heads will be satisfied with the **Hop Angel IPA,** their sticky wet hop IPA.

The restaurant serves pizza and standard pub fare. The space is quite large, seating 275 diners and drinkers indoors and another 100 outside. While the brewpub is a fun atmosphere to enjoy some fresh brews indoors, it's particularly special to spend your time at Chelsea outside on the pier. Weather permitting, you'll stand right on the water, looking down at boats bumping against the dock, beer in hand.

CITY ISLAND BEER COMPANY
P.O. Box 76, Bronx, NY 10464; CityIslandBeer.com; @CityIslandBeer
Founded: 2011 **Founders and Brewers:** Paul, John, and Jeff Sciara **Flagship Beer:** City Island Pale Ale **Year-Round Beer:** City Island Pale Ale **Tours:** No **Taproom:** No

Many breweries begin with a passion for homebrewing and a desire to share that passion with others. City Island Beer Company is a great example. Brothers Paul, John, and Jeff Sciara are Bronx natives who began homebrewing in Paul's basement years ago and got so much positive feedback that they decided to go pro. City Island is one of only three breweries in New York City's northernmost borough, and they strive for their brand to be local, something others living in the Bronx can appreciate.

Taking inspiration from City Island's rich maritime history, the Sciaras founded the City Island Beer Company in 2011. They released their flagship Pale Ale in February 2013, at the opening party for NYC Beer Week. The trio constantly work to fine-tune the Pale Ale, which is contract brewed on a 20-barrel system at Paper City Brewing Company in Holyoke, Massachusetts, and aim for that beer to be the perfect image of their brand before moving on to any others.

City Island Pale Ale, an American-style Pale Ale, pours an amber color and is brewed with Magnum, Goldings, and Cascade hops, lending the beer the aroma of citrus, and Two-Row Pale Caramel malt. Citrus on the nose leads to more citrus tastes, combined with pine, bread, and a hop bitterness. Though the beer is brewed in Massachusetts, the brewery still calls the Bronx its home base. The Sciaras are looking for space to build out a full brewhouse in the borough. In the meantime the flagship pale ale is available on tap at bars, restaurants, and beer stores predominantly in the Bronx, but also in Manhattan, Queens, Brooklyn, and Westchester.

City Island Pale Ale
Style: American Pale Ale
ABV: 5.6%
Availability: Year-round
The City Island Pale Ale has a rounded body and some citrus flavors from the trio of hops: Magnum, Goldings, and a late addition of Cascade. This beer pours an amber color with a white, fluffy head. Bitter hops flavor mingles on the palate with grape-fruit, pine, and bread flavors. It's refreshing and drinks easy—you can just imagine sipping it while chowing down on some of City Island's famous seafood. At 5.6 percent it's not quite sessionable, but low in alcohol enough to enjoy more than one.

HARLEM BREWING COMPANY

360 W. 125th St., New York, NY 10027; (888) 876-2420; HarlemBrewingCompany.com
Founded: 2000 **Founder and Brewer:** Celeste Beatty **Flagship and Year-Round Beer:** Sugar Hill Golden Ale **Tours:** No **Taproom:** No

For Celeste Beatty, beer and music just go together. Her great-great-grandparents were ragtime musicians, and she always listens to music when she homebrews. Her family lived in the Sugar Hill area of Harlem, where she experienced influential jazz musicians. Beatty came up with the recipe for her **Sugar Hill Golden Ale** in her studio apartment in Harlem, where the kitchen and bathroom were so close that she was practically making beer in the bathtub. The beer is named after the Billy Strayhorn song "Take the A Train (up to Sugar Hill in Harlem)."

Beatty launched the Harlem Brewing Company in 2000, taking her recipe for Sugar Hill Golden Ale to Olde Saratoga Brewing Company, where she has contracted since then. Sugar Hill Golden Ale is available in six packs of 12-ounce bottles and on draft at select locations throughout New York City. She displays the connection between Sugar Hill and jazz right on the label of her bottles, which shows the catch-phrase "Taste the music" and incorporates a saxophone as part of the logo.

Beatty's goal is to bring her brewing operation to Manhattan. Mayor Bloomberg's office chose her as one of the original tenants for the CREATE @ Harlem Green, a commercial and industrial space being constructed in the former home of the Taystee Cake Bakery, a historic property that's been vacant and decaying since the

Beer Lover's Pick

Sugar Hill Golden Ale
Style: American Blonde Ale
ABV: 4%
Availability: Year-round, on draft and in
12-ounce bottles at select locations in
New York City

Medium bodied and drinkable, Sugar Hill
Golden Ale is inspired by the Sugar Hill area
of Harlem, where brewer Celeste Beatty's
family lived. Subtle citrus flavors mingle
with sweet tastes of biscuit and bread on
the palate. This balanced brew has a crisp
finish, and with 4 percent ABV is sessionable, perfect for a long evening listening to jazz.

1970s. The building, located on 125th Street in the heart of Harlem, is intended to
revitalize the neighborhood, and Beatty plans to take advantage of it by moving
her entire brewing operation there, offering tours, opening a taproom and brewing
museum, and growing hops on the roof. Beatty and Harlem Brewing Company hope
to be a key participant in the revitalization of Harlem.

JONAS BRONCK'S BEER COMPANY
260 East 239th St., Bronx, NY 10470; (347) 234-6860; BroncksBeer.com; @TheBroncks
Founded: 2011 **Founder and Brewer:** Steve Nallen **Flagship Beer:** Pelham Bay IPA
Other Beers: Pelham Bay IPA, Woodlawn Weiss, Kingsbridge Kolsch, Mott Haven Milk
Stout, Big Apple Cider **Tours:** No **Taproom:** No

Steve Nallen comes from a family who has been living and doing business in
the Bronx for six generations. For 30 years his father has owned a deli in the
Woodlawn neighborhood, where Nallen grew up. His passion for Bronx history and
good craft beer led him to create and launch Jonas Bronck's Beer Company, named
after the Swedish settler who gave the borough its name. Jonas Bronck arrived in
the area in the 17th century and established his farm just north of the Harlem River,

where he began brewing his own beer. It's reported that Bronck was the first person to brew outside the city limits.

Nallen, who had worked with The Bronx Brewery before splitting off to start his own venture, makes his beers as tributes to neighborhoods in his home borough. His first brew, **Woodlawn Weiss,** is named for the area where he resides. A German Hefeweizen, Woodlawn Weiss is fermented with a strain of traditional Bavarian yeast and brewed with 67 percent wheat grist. It's refreshing with lemon and orange aromas that carry over the flavor. Originally Woodlawn was a German community, which is why Nallen thought a German style would be perfect. Another German style Nallen brews that harkens back to the borough's early days is the **Kingsbridge Kolsch,** which pours a hazy blonde color and has flavors of sweet malt, grass, and hops.

Contract brewed at Butternuts Beer & Ale in Garrattsville, Jonas Bronck's beer is available at select bars and restaurants in New York City, mostly in its home borough.

Beer Lover's Pick

Pelham Bay IPA
Style: IPA
ABV: 5.8%
Availability: Year-round on draft at locations in New York City, mostly the Bronx

Pelham Bay IPA is Jonas Bronck's flagship brew, named after the Pelham Bay section of the borough. Brewed with English Marris Otter and Crystal malts and Magnum, Willamette, and Cascade hops, it has a balance between dryness and drinkability, pours golden orange, and is flowery with a hop bitterness. Its aromas of grapefruit lead to a balanced beer that's malty with caramel flavors. Pelham Bay IPA is drinkable at 5.8 percent ABV and isn't aggressively bitter.

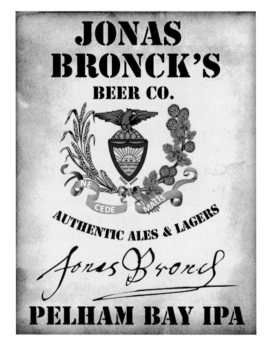

KELSO BEER COMPANY OF BROOKLYN

529 Waverly Ave., Brooklyn, NY 11238; (718) 398-2731; KelSoBeer.com; @KelSoBeer
Founded: 2006 **Founders:** Kelly Taylor, Sonya Giacobbe **Brewer:** Kelly Taylor **Flagship**
Beer: Nut Brown Lager **Year-Round Beers:** Nut Brown Lager, Pilsner, Pale Ale, IPA
Seasonals/Specialty Beers: Satisfaction, Octoberfest, Winter Lager, Flemish Red Ale,
Recessionator Doppelbock, Saison, Carrollgaarden Wit **Tours:** No **Taproom:** No

Accessibility may be the best way to describe KelSo Beer Company, the brainchild of Kelly Taylor and Sonja Giacobbe. Taylor began his brewing adventure in college, where he started homebrewing, and then apprenticed and worked his way up at breweries in California and Washington. While working at Pyramid Breweries in Seattle, where breweries are plentiful, Taylor met Giacobbe, a Northeast native. The couple moved to New York City and found only a handful of breweries in their new

Beer Lover's Pick

Flemish Red
Style: Flanders Red Ale
ABV: 5.5%
Availability: Fall
The recent sour beer trend has many brewers experimenting with some sort of wild fermentation or yeast strains that provide funky flavors. Among their most sought-after beers, KelSo's Flemish Red is one of the rare examples in the New York City area of a brewer blending different batches of sour beer. The beer is hard to find but worth seeking out to see what a fresh sour beer can taste like. Multiple batches of the beer are aged in oak barrels and blended to create the right balance of flavors. Batches can be aged up to two years in the oak barrels before they find their way into a finished product. The final beer carries vinegar flavors that have been mellowed by the oak aging and blending. An initial sweetness gives way to a pleasantly puckering tartness.

town. He got a job brewing for Heartland Brewery chain of restaurants, and in 2006 he and Giacobbe started KelSo Beer Company (an amalgamation of their names) at Greenpoint Beer Works, where Taylor contract brews and makes beer for Heartland, where he is now the brewmaster.

Seeing the increasingly intense and alcoholic beers coming from so many breweries, Taylor and Giacobbe struck out on their own path. They focused on flavorful beers that could be enjoyed with friends in a relaxed way without too much pretense. They launched with the **Nut Brown Lager** using Pilsner, Munich, and chocolate malt for a slightly sweet beer with hints of toffee. The Nut Brown Lager and their clean and slightly floral **Pilsner** have offered New Yorkers quality local beer options that are accessible to almost every palate. The husband-and-wife team also brew a line of seasonals that keep with their brewing philosophy. The **Winter Lager, Carollgaarden Wit, Kellerfest,** and **Saison** all clock in at 6 percent ABV or less.

In recent years the brewery has ventured outside its original focus on Lagers to introduce some bolder flavors and showcase its creativity. The **Industrial IPA** carries a whopping 10 percent ABV and a sticky 100 IBUs with big citrus aromas. Barrel-aged versions of the beer occasionally pop up at New York City bars. Among their most sought-after beers is the **Flemish Red,** a sour style that the brewery ages in oak barrels. Different batches are aged up to two years and blended to create just the right amount of tartness.

RADIANT PIG CRAFT BEERS
122 W. 27th St., Ste. 1022, New York, NY 10001; RadiantPigBeer.com; @RadiantPigBeer
Founded: 2012 **Founders and Brewers:** Rob Pihl, Laurisa Milici **Flagship and Year-Round Beer:** Junior IPA **Tours:** No **Taproom:** No

For Rob Pihl and Laurisa Milici, partners both in business and in life, beer is an art form. Avid homebrewers who decided to turn their passion into a business, the pair launched Radiant Pig Craft Beers in 2012. After three years of planning and perfecting, their flagship and first offering, **Junior IPA,** hit New York City in the first half of 2013. While the brewery is based in Manhattan, Pihl and Milici make their beer through an arrangement at Thomas Hooker Brewing Company in Bloomfield, Connecticut. A tenant brewing setup, rather than a contract brewing situation, allows the pair to actually brew the beer themselves, using Thomas Hooker's 40-barrel system, which they do about once a month.

Future plans include releasing more beers and finding a physical location somewhere in New York City, probably not Manhattan due to space and financial constraints. But in the meantime the duo will focus on perfecting and distributing

Beer Lover's Pick

Junior IPA
Style: IPA
ABV: 5%
Availability: Year-round on draft throughout New York City

The first offering from Radiant Pig Craft Beers, Junior was named such because "if an IPA and a Pale Ale had a baby, Junior would be it." Clocking in at around 5 percent ABV, Junior is a relatively sessionable IPA. On the nose you'll detect citrus, tropical fruit, and floral aromas. Refreshingly hoppy, Junior is earthy and not too bitter. Radiant Pig's Junior pairs well with barbeque—and not just because of its name.

Junior, which is available on draft only throughout the five boroughs, mostly in Manhattan and Brooklyn. Pihl and Milici aim for Junior to be drinkable. Floral and bitter notes contribute to an earthy taste in this sessionable beer, brewed with Columbus and Falconer's Flight hops.

As for the quirky name: Jean-Michel Basquiat is Pihl and Milici's favorite artist, and he was known as the "Radiant Child." Pig stands for "People in Gastropubs" and is an homage to New York City and the plethora of food and drink available just at their fingertips. The pair, who are also graphic designers, view beer as their own artistic medium.

ROCKAWAY BREWING COMPANY

5-01 46th Ave., Long Island City, NY 11101; (347) 504-1591; RockawayBrewCo.com;
@RockawayBrew
Founded: 2012 **Founders and Brewers:** Ethan Long, Marcus Burnett **Flagship Beer:** Rockaway ESB **Year-Round Beers:** Old School IPA, Black Gold Stout, Sez John Saison
Tours: No **Taproom:** Yes

Until 2012 there were no breweries in Queens. Three opened that year, with Rockaway Brewing Company leading the trend, started by friends and home-brewing partners for three years, Marcus Burnett and Ethan Long. Both are California

transplants who were surprised by the lack of local beer when they came to New York. The two met and became good friends at their summer houses at the Bungalows of Rockaway. One summer they took a road trip through Northern California with their wives and children. When they returned to New York City, they decided to remedy the lack of local beer by opening a brewery in tribute to their summer neighborhood. Their namesake neighborhood was destroyed by Hurricane Sandy, but their brewery, located in Long Island City, came out virtually unscathed, save for a few feet of floodwater that ruined some of their pumps.

Their first brew—also Rockaway's flagship—was an **Extra Special Bitter (ESB),** and they've since made an **IPA,** a **Black Gold Stout,** and a **Saison,** among other, experimental one-off brews. The pair took an American twist on the traditionally English ESB, using an American yeast. The Black Gold Stout has smoky, roasted flavors with distinct coffee and chocolate notes, coming in at 5.6 percent ABV. Each batch of Rockaway beer is brewed by hand, allowing the team to tinker with and tweak the recipes.

Long and Burnett, who have both kept their jobs as a set designer and cinematographer, respectively, open the doors to their small taproom—located in a former meat packing plant—Thursday and Friday in the evening and Saturday during the day. At the brewery you can take a peek at the two-barrel brewing system and taste their newest beers. While enjoying some fresh brews listening to tunes coming from a vintage record player in the corner, examine the vintage beer can collection on one of the walls.

Rockaway ESB
Style: ESB
ABV: 5.2%
Availability: Year-round, on draft throughout New York City

The ESB is part of the Rockaway's year-round rotation and with good reason. There is some bitterness to the ESB style, but it usually isn't overpowering, and this example is very drinkable and balanced. A sweet toffee malt character is tapered by some slight hop bitterness and dryness. The beer is a manageable 5.2% ABV, so you won't have to worry too much about having a couple. It's also good for introducing new craft beer drinkers to an easy-drinking but accessible beer.

SINGLECUT BEERSMITHS

19-33 37th St., Astoria, Queens, NY 11105; SingleCutBeer.com; @SingleCutBeer
Founded: 2012 **Founder and Brewer:** Rich Buceta **Flagship Beer:** 19-33 Queens Lagrrr **Year-Round Beers:** Jan Olympic White Lagrrr, 19-33 Queens Lagrrr, Pacific NW Dean Mahogany Ale, BIlly 18-Watt IPA, Billy Half Stack IPA **Seasonals/Special Releases:** Hank The Strand Lager, Rudy Rum Barrel Aged Double Umlaut Lagrrr, Neil Ol'Blackie IPA, Derek Honey Koolsch, Keith SW4 English Pale Ale, Le Von Le Citron Saison, John Michael Dark Lyric Lagrrr, Martin Brown Sound Ale, Western Chet IPA, Calme Ale George D'Abbaye, BOB Sunburst Finish Lagrrr, Eric More Cowbell! Milk Stout, Billy Full Stack IIPA **Tours:** Yes **Taproom:** Yes

SingleCut Beersmiths is the third brewery to open in Queens (three launched in 2012). Founder Rich Buceta was frustrated with some of the breweries in New York City that don't actually brew in the city and choose instead to contract brew at another facility. He set out to open a place in Queens that served beer made in Queens—a "true local beer."

In December 2012 SingleCut opened its 30-barrel brewhouse and taproom and started distributing its beers on draft throughout the city. Specializing in Lager production, the flagship **19-33 Queens Lagrrr** is named for the year Prohibiton ended. A Czech Pilsner, 19-33 has bready, grassy flavors with herbal notes and a lingering bittery taste. Buceta is a musician—SingleCut refers to a type of guitar he likes to play—the tap handles are shaped like guitars, and many of the beer monikers are in tribute to rock heroes. The Lagrrr spelling refers to Riot Grrrl, and Buceta's **Billy 18-Watt IPA** and **Billy Half Stack IPA,** for example, are inspired by Billy Duffy, guitarist for The Cult. There's a stage at SingleCut's taproom that provides the setting for live music.

Buceta isn't afraid to push the boundaries, even aging his **Double Umlaut Lagrrr** in rum barrels, producing sweet rum aromas and flavors. SingleCut's taproom is open Thursday from 5 to 10 p.m., Friday from 5 to 11 p.m., Saturday from 1 to 11 p.m., and Sunday from 1 to 8 p.m. The drinking area is open and airy; patrons can sit on stools at long wooden tables. In addition to brews, visitors can enjoy meat pies or plates of cheese or meat and cheese.

Jan Olympic White Lagrrr
Style: Pale Lager
ABV: 5.2%
Availability: Year-round

Jan Olympic White Lagrrr is a light-bodied and cleaner-tasting alternative to Belgian Witbiers and is a great brew for summer days. The beer is a Lager brewed with coriander, orange peel, chamomile, and peppercorns. It's lightly hopped for some balance against the sweetness that is upfront in the taste. The spices lend an herbal tone to the beer that lingers at the end. At 5.2 percent ABV, Jan Olympic White Lagrrr is drinkable and just low enough in alcohol that you can enjoy a few without falling out of your chair.

SIXPOINT

40 Van Dyke St., Brooklyn, NY 11231; SixPoint.com; @SixPoint
Founded: 2004 **Founder:** Shane Welch **Brewmaster:** Jan Matysiak **Year-round Beers:** Sweet Action, Righteous Ale, Bengali Tiger, The Crisp, Resin, Brownstone **Seasonals/ Special Releases:** Harbinger, Apollo, Autumnation, Diesel, 3Beans, Gorrilla Warfare, Otis, Signal, Redd, Old Redhooker, The Incredible Mild, The Mad Scientist Series, The Spice of Life Series **Tours:** No **Taproom:** No

Based out of Red Hook, Brooklyn, Sixpoint has brought an intense passion for brewing traditions and unique ingredients to New York City's brewing community. It was awarded the 2013 F.X. Matt Memorial Cup for the best brewery in New York State at TAP NY. Founder Shane Welch and brewmaster Jan Matysiak have sought to explore a wide variety of classic styles and an experimental combination of ingredients. They've brewed beers like **Apollo,** a German Kristallweizen, and **Signal,** a hoppy American IPA that is made with smoked malt. Their mainstays **Sweet Action, Righteous Rye, The Crisp,** and **Bengali Tiger IPA** have been converting

Beer Event

Beer for Beasts

Each spring Sixpoint and beer review website Beer Advocate collaborate on Beer for Beasts, a charity event benefiting the New York Humane Society. The brewery teams up with local businesses and homebrewers to brew over 30 distinct small-batch beers for the event.

new craft beer drinkers for the past seven years. These four beers, along with the recently added sticky **Resin,** the popular **Brownstone,** and bitter and roasty seasonal **Diesel,** have found their way into the "nano-kegs" (cans) brewed by The Lion Brewery in Wilkes-Barre, Pennsylvania for Sixpoint.

The Red Hook facility is the brewsite for Sixpoint's draft beers including its **Mad Scientist** line, which allows the brewers to push their creative boundaries. Produced in small batches, the Mad Scientist beers have made use of local coffee, hops sourced from upstate New York, shisho leaves from rooftop gardens in Brooklyn, and Massachusetts cranberries. Sixpoint has also joined the trend of releasing a single-hop series of beers; theirs is dubbed the **Spice of Life Series.** Each month a new beer highlights the distinct flavors of a different hop variety.

Sixpoint was one of several New York breweries impacted by the forceful floods of Hurricane Sandy in October 2012. The brewery reported over eight feet of water in the facility but took the opportunity to double its capacity while rebuilding. Sixpoint came back with **Three Beans,** a collaborative Stout brewed with Stumptown Coffee, cocoa from Mast Brothers, and Romano beans.

Autumnation

Style: Pumpkin/Wet Hop Ale

ABV: 6.7%

Availability: Fall

One of the only fall seasonals actually released in the fall instead the end of the summer, Autumnation is a unique beer. Until 2013, the beer featured fresh pumpkin (canned pumpkin purees are commonly used in fall beers) and wet hops. The result was unforgettable with the dank but beautiful stickiness of fresh wet hops sitting on top of a sweet backbone. In 2013 Sixpoint changed the Autumnation recipe. While it originally was a pumpkin beer made with wet hops, the pumpkin was eliminated, making the beer a wet-hopped ale. Autumnation is available on draft and in cans beginning in early fall. One of the hops is a "fan choice," chosen from a poll on the brewery's blog.

New York City

Brewpubs

508 GASTROBREWERY

508 Greenwich St., New York, NY 10013; (212) 219-2444; 508NYC.com; @508Gastro
Brewery
Founded: 2008 **Founders:** Jennifer Hill, Anderson Sant'Anna de Lima **Brewer:** Chris
Cuzme

Space is a hot commodity in Manhattan, which is why if you have some, it's important to make the most of it. 508 GastroBrewery, located in Tribeca, is a perfect example of economizing space. The two-barrel brewing system was built by founding brewmaster Anderson Sant'Anna de Lima, across several rooms in the basement of the restaurant. The brewpub's proximity to the Hudson River led to six feet of water in the basement from Hurricane Sandy, which occurred just as current brewmaster Chris Cuzme was about to take over the helm. Cuzme's first task as brewer was to clean and reorganize the equipment, getting the system back in working order.

A homebrewer at heart, Cuzme's brewing style is creative and original. He often brews one-off batches and collaborative beers with homebrewers and other local breweries. He's used Szecuan peppercorns in a saison, pomegranate tea in a Pale Ale, and local honey to brew his version of the White House Honey Porter. Cuzme's creativity extends to his beer names. Some memorable ones have been **Saxual Healing,** a Russian Imperial Stout; **Beauty Booty Blonde,** an American blond ale; and **Nug Bug Stout,** an Irish Dry Stout.

508 wouldn't be a brewpub without the cuisine, imagined by Chef and Owner Jennifer Hill, a graduate of the Institute of Culinary Education. The menu is billed as "Rustic Mediterranean-American" and features sliders, artisanal pizza, house-made pasta, and burgers. As one of the three brewpubs in Manhattan, 508 is a great place to enjoy delicious food and fresh brews.

HEARTLAND BREWERY

35 Union Square West, New York, NY 10003; (212) 645-3400; HeartlandBrewery.com;
@HeartlandBrew
Founded: 1995 **Founder:** Jon Bloostein **Brewers:** Kelly Taylor (brewmaster) **Year-
Round Beers:** Farmer Jon's Oatmeal Stout, Red Rooster Ale, Indiana Pale Ale, Harvest
Wheat Beer, Cornhusker Lager, Indian River Light **Seasonals/Special Releases:** Bavarian
Black Lager, Greatful Red Lager, Mother's Milk Maibock, Old Red Nose Ale, Smiling
Pumpkin Ale, Imperial Pumpkin Ale, Stumpkin, Summertime Apricot Ale, Full Moon
Barleywine, Not Tonight Honey Porter, Empire Premium Beer, NY State Wildflower Wheat,
Belgian Pale Ale, Extra Special Bitter, Good Grain Gluten-Free Ale

Opened in 1995 by Jon Bloostein, Heartland Brewery has helped maintain a presence of good beer in Manhattan for almost 20 years. The original location still operates in Union Square and has since been joined by six new locations scattered among iconic sites in Midtown Manhattan like the Empire State Building, Radio City, and Times Square. Each restaurant has a different theme, like a chophouse, rotisserie, and burger joint. Most locations are quite large and are good places for large groups looking for fresh beer.

Beer used to be brewed on site, primarily at the original Union Square location (which is why Heartland is in the brewpub category), but running a brewing operation at several different locations across Manhattan was difficult. Now the brewing equipment at the restaurants is purely decorative, and the beer is brewed by Kelly Taylor over at Greenpoint Beer Works in Brooklyn to ensure consistency of product.

Over the course of a year, Taylor will brew up to 20 beers. Six beers make up the core offerings: **Farmer Jon's Oatmeal Stout, Red Rooster Ale, Indiana Pale**

Ale, Harvest Wheat Beer, Cornhusker Lager, and Indian River Light. Seasonals include beers like Summer Apricot Wheat and Smiling Pumpkin Ale. Stumpkin, a combination of Farmer Jon's Oatmeal Stout and Smiling Pumpkin Ale, has become a seasonal favorite. Taylor even brews Good Grain, a gluten-free beer using sorghum, buckwheat, beet sugar, honey, and the popular citra hops.

The South Street Seaport location was severely damaged in Hurricane Sandy and is currently under repair. An eighth, non–New York City location is planned for Port Chester, north of the city.

LA BIRRERIA

200 5th Ave., New York, NY 10010; (212) 937-8910; Eataly.com/Birreria; @EatalyBirreria
Founded: 2011 **Founders:** Mario Batali, Joseph Bastianich, Sam Calgione, Teo Musso, Leonardo di Vincenzo **Brewer:** Peter Hepp **Year-Round Beers:** Wanda, Gina, **Seasonals/Special Releases:** Calabrona, Sofia, Ruby, Nerone, Patrizia, Garlic Breadth

On the roof of gourmet Italian marketplace Eataly, a treasure trove of some of the best Italian food and drink in New York City, sits La Birreria, a brewpub offering fresh beers, bottled beers, and gourmet eats. It's the ambitious brainchild of

Mario Batali, Joseph Bastianich, Sam Calgione (of Dogfish Head), Teo Musso (of Birra Baladin), and Leonardo di Vincenzo (Birra del Borgo).

The restaurant and bar are enclosed by a retractable glass roof, making the spot ideal in almost any type of weather. Drinkers can savor their beers with some unique views of the tallest buildings in Midtown Manhattan—the Flatiron building is just across the street. Even during slow times of day, the wait for a table can be up to 45 minutes, so reservations are recommended. Unless you're interested in hanging out in the bar area.

Peter Hepp runs the brewing operation, which pumps out Ales that the restaurant serves on cask. The beers make use of unique ingredients like chestnuts (**Wanda**), thyme (**Gina**), and even yeast from the bowels of hornets (**Calabrona**). Alongside their own beers, La Birreria serves up American craft and many of the finest brews from Italy, where an exciting beer revolution is in full swing. It is one of the few places in New York that you can find so many beers from Italian brewers like Loverbeer, Birra del Borgo, Birra Baladin, and Birradamare. The American craft available is usually from creative brewers like Allagash, Dogfish Head, and Captain Lawrence.

Among the food offerings are skirt steak, pork shoulder, lamb chops, and salads. You can also partake of cheese and meat plates.

New York City

Beer Bars

ADOBE BLUES

63 Lafayette Ave., Staten Island, NY 10301; (718) 720-2583; @AdobeBlues
Draft Beers: 5 **Bottled/Canned Beers:** 200

Due to lack of a subway line that connects it to Manhattan, Staten Island often gets overlooked. And located on a quiet residential street in the New Brighton neighborhood of the borough, Adobe Blues could be easily passed by. But this bar/restaurant offers Tex-Mex food and more craft beer choices than you can even imagine. Walking inside the bar, you know you're in a special place. Opened in 1992 by theatrical set designers Jim Stayoch and Ken Tirado (who owns Killmeyer's, also on Staten Island), the interior is filled with Southwestern-style furnishings and decorations. Stayoch is now sole owner of the restaurant, which is managed by beer expert Ryan Barker.

An extensive menu featuring tasty eats such as enchiladas, tacos, fajitas, and burgers complements an astounding beer list with over 200 options, 5 on draft. The brews are characterized by style and have each beer's *Beer Advocate* rating listed next to it. If you need additional suggestions, Barker and the bar staff are knowledgeable and helpful.

The (free) Staten Island Ferry docks 2 miles from Adobe Blues, which can be reached on foot or by a 15-minute bus ride. In addition to great beer and food, the venue is periodically home to live music, normally blues or jazz. It's a comfortable, relaxed place to spend a weekend day enjoying practically any beer you could think of, alongside Southwestern-inspired food.

ALEWIFE NYC

5-14 51st Ave., Long Island City, NY 11101; (718) 937-7494; AlewifeQueens.com; @AlewifeNYC
Draft Beers: 29 including 1 cask **Bottled/Canned Beers:** Over 80

One stop into Queens from Manhattan on the 7 train, Alewife NYC is a towering space with a second floor and a sunny terrace for warm weather days. The bar area is usually busy, but you can often find a spot at one of the tables on the first or second floor. There are large communal picnic-style tables and high-tops for group seating on the ground level, and a few couches and a pool table on the second floor.

Beer Event

aPORKalypse

The cleverly named aPORKalypse is an annual festival of craft beer and pork, two products that have passionate followings in the foodie culture of New York City. With 10 pigs and dozens of beers, the festival has seen rare brews like Founders CBS (Canadian Breakfast Stout) and Anchorage Brewing the Tide and Its Takers.

The beer list is chock-full of high-quality American craft beer and sought-after imports, especially Belgians. Some of the smallest local brewers like Rockaway, Port Jeff, and Blind Bat are often available. With Patrick Donagher of Get Real Presents, a company that runs beer and food festivals in New York City, as the bar manager, Alewife is often the venue for events that combine fine beers with creative eats.

The food menu changes regularly, with interesting dishes ranging from brussel sprouts in a harissa buffalo sauce to pan-seared venison. Burgers, pizza, and fried chicken are also available for those who aren't feeling adventurous.

ALPHABET BEER CO.
96 Avenue C, New York, NY 10009; (646) 422-7103; ABCBeer.co; @ABCBeerCo
Draft Beers: 12 **Bottled/Canned Beers:** Over 350

Alphabet Beer Co's location on Avenue C in the Alphabet City neighborhood is off the beaten path but well worth the visit. The bottle shop, bar, and food shop won recognition in 2013 from *Time Out New York* as the Best New Bar in New York City.

The dimly lit bar is welcoming, small, and cozy with armchairs and couches. For drinking in the shop, 12 draft beers are served from American craft brewers like Victory and Smuttynose and New York brewers like Peekskill and Wagner Valley. Draft beers are available in full, half pints, or in growlers to take home. In addition to enjoying a couple of pints at the store, there are over 350 bottled beers available to purchase and bring home.

Servers are friendly and willing to help beer novices find their way to new craft beers. Sandwiches, meat plates, and cheese plates are available to help sop up your beer. Alphabet Beer Co. is a great destination for those who want the feel, but not the craziness, of Manhattan.

BARCADE
388 Union Ave., Brooklyn, NY 11211; (718) 302-6464; barcadebrooklyn.com; @barcadebrooklyn
Draft Beers: 24 on tap, 1 on cask

Awesome craft beers plus vintage arcade games. It's this winning combination that makes Barcade such a fun place to visit. Opened in a former metal shop in Williamsburg in 2004, Barcade is the brainchild of four longtime friends: brothers Kevin and Scott Beard, Pete Langway, and Paul Kermizian.

Classic games line the walls of the expansive bar, favorites like Ms. Pacman, Contra, Donkey Kong, Tetris, and Frogger, among many others. There's also Tapper, a video game produced by Anheuser-Busch, that challenges players to serve as many pints as possible in the time allotted. Tapper is likely Barcade's most popular game and often has a long wait, so if it's open, play it. Any of the arcade games can be played for the incredibly reasonable price of one quarter.

Of course, Barcade wouldn't be as special without the beer. Twenty-four brews on tap and one on cask (no bottles or cans) are all American craft. Local mainstays like Barrier and Captain Lawrence share a menu with craft favorites like Dogfish Head, Harpoon, and Sierra Nevada. The bar often holds special tap takeover events from breweries like Peekskill, Perennial, and Founders. The bartenders are very knowledgeable, and brews are always served in their proper glassware. Barcade can get pretty crowded, especially on weekend nights and during tap-takeover events.

With their first venture so successful, the owners of Barcade opened two more locations in 2011, one in Jersey City, New Jersey, and one in Philadelphia. A fourth location is being planned for Manhattan's Chelsea neighborhood. The Barcade team also owns The Gutter, a bar and bowling alley in Williamsburg.

BEER AUTHORITY
300 W 40th St., New York, NY 10018; (212) 510-8415; BeerAuthorityNYC.com; @BeerAuthNY
Draft Beers: 80 **Bottled/Canned Beers:** Over 100

Let's face it: No one in his or her right mind really wants to go to Times Square, or the area nearby. The sidewalks are overcrowded, and it's overstimulating. But it's unavoidable. Maybe you're playing tour guide to tourist friends, maybe you're seeing a Broadway show, or maybe you're meeting someone for drinks who works in the area. This is where Beer Authority is a saving grace amidst the craziness. It has a huge selection of beers across many different styles and types. Standard pub foods like mac and cheese, sandwiches, and Buffalo wings share the menu with charcuterie, mussels, and crab cakes.

You won't find many rare beers here, but you will find a different brew for every taste. You'll see beers from local breweries like Blue Point and Brooklyn to others from American craft breweries like Dogfish Head and Oskar Blues. And yes, there are some macros on the list too. If you aren't into beer, Beer Authority has a full bar and a selection of wine.

Beer Authority is an enormous space, with two floors (a bar on each floor) and a rooftop patio. The place can get pretty busy, but on a weeknight it can be a great place to get away from the Midtown bustle.

BIERKRAFT

91 5th Ave., Brooklyn, NY 11215; (718) 230-7600; Bierkraft.com; @Bierkraft
Draft Beers: 14 on tap, 2 on cask **Bottled/Canned Beers:** Over 100

Bierkraft has a bit of everything: beer bottle shop, bar, sandwich shop, and recently, brewpub. The bottle selection features some of the best local beers as well as rare bottles that beer geeks run out to snatch up, like Founders KBS or offerings from Cantillon. The place even has a temperature-controlled beer cellar for aging, releasing the beers for purchase when the staff believe they are at their peak. There are 14 rotating taps and space for 2 casks. Local beers from breweries like Captain Lawrence, Brooklyn Brewery, Barrier, Blue Point, and Greenport dominate the taps. All bottles are priced for on-site consumption, making them more expensive than other bottle shops but cheaper than most restaurants or some bars. Growlers are available for most beers on tap. In 2013 Bierkraft started putting together a one-barrel system sandwiched between the bottle cases and the bar.

Bierkraft doesn't only do great beer, they also serve up top-notch cheese, charcuterie, and some of the best sandwiches in the neighborhood, all served on fresh crunchy bread.

Owner Ben Granger has worked tirelessly to advance Brooklyn's beer community since opening Bierkraft. Every Tuesday night, patrons are led through free educational beer tastings by either Bierkraft staff members, brewers, or brewery representatives. Brewery events are held every Thursday except the last of every month, which is reserved for IPA night.

Annual Cask Festival and Local Oyster Shuck

Bierkraft sets up several casks predominately from local brewers (an Oyster Stout from KelSo Beer Company of Brooklyn is a special find at this event) on the back patio to serve while the staff shucks countless fresh local oysters. The event is held the last weekend of April.

BLIND TIGER

281 Bleecker St., New York, NY 10014; (212) 462-4682; BlindTigerAleHouse.com; @BlindTigerNYC

Draft Beers: 28 on tap, 3 on cask **Bottled/Canned Beers:** Over 50

Blind Tiger is an iconic bar and craft beer institution. As one of the oldest bars serving craft beer in New York City, it not only has a great beer list but also a great story. After moving to its current location in 2006, Blind Tiger struggled to get the required licensing to reopen as a bar and briefly operated as a coffee shop in the meantime. Once the licensing came through, Blind Tiger converted back to a bar. As one of the best-known craft beer bars around, the list often features the most limited, sought-after beers and is a favorite spot for brewers from out of town while they are visiting the city.

The bar can get packed and loud, especially for special events, which are best to get to as early as possible. Very Special Keg and brewery tap takeover events, which are chock-full of rare and unusual beers, usually begin by 3:30 p.m. Each Wednesday Blind Tiger holds a beer and cheese night, with a selection of complimentary cheeses

from another Village institution, Murray's Cheese. Each July, Blind Tiger has a "Christmas in July" night, offering Christmas and winter beers from the previous year.

THE BRONX ALE HOUSE

216 W 238th St., Bronx, NY 10463; (718) 601-0204; BronxAleHouse.com; @BronxAleHouse
Draft Beers: 16 on tap, 1 on cask **Bottled/Canned Beers:** Over 30

The Bronx Ale House is a rare bright spot in the sparse collection of beer bars in the Bronx. Located in the Kingsbridge neighborhood, one block from the 238th Street stop on the 1 train, the place is surprisingly easy to get to from the West Side of Manhattan. Grab a seat near the front of the bar during good weather, when the windows are thrown open for some fresh air.

The bar can be dimly lit and a bit loud, but it carries a solid selection of craft beer served with free popcorn and a solid pub-style food menu. The 16 taps hit a wide variety of beers, a well-curated bottle list includes some large format bottles,

and there's even a rotating cask. A few rare beers are always available on draft or in bottles, think Firestone Walker Double DBA or Allagash Curieux.

Tap takeovers can be especially good at the Bronx Ale House, and it's a great place to grab a Bronx Pale Ale from The Bronx Brewery or an Oskar Blues Dale's Pale Ale with one of the enormous and delicious pulled pork sandwiches. Wednesday night is can night, with craft cans and a burger offered for $10.

BURP CASTLE
41 E. 7th St., New York, NY 10003; (212) 982-4576; BurpCastleNYC.wordpress.com; @BurpCastle
Draft Beers: 10 **Bottled/Canned Beers:** 40

Really great beer deserves to be imbibed in an environment that respects its quality with proper reverence. Opened in 1992, Burp Castle is such an environment. The bar bills itself as a "temple of beer worship," offering fine and rare Belgian brews, on tap and in bottles. You'll most likely see Chimay and Duvel, and you might find Corsendonk or Boon on draft (beers you can normally find in bottles).

The bar is practically hidden on East 7th Street in the East Village behind a wrought iron fence blanketed with ivy (situated next to Standings sports bar and above Jimmy's No. 43, the three are known as the "Brewmuda Triangle"). Subtle letters and an awning made to look like the top of a castle are the only indications that you've come upon anything out of the ordinary.

Burp Castle is a small space, with only beer offered—no wine or spirits. The walls are covered with medieval-esque paintings, and soft Gregorian chants fill the air. You'll sit at dark wood tables in dim lighting. But don't let your conversations get too loud; signs suggest that patrons should keep their voices to a whisper, and bartenders will emit a loud "sssssshhhhhh," if the volume gets too high.

Though Burp Castle doesn't sell food, on Sunday, Monday, and Wednesday at 5 p.m., free fries are offered from Pommes Frites, the Belgian fry place around the block. Ever friendly to the beer community, Burp Castle opens its doors once a month for the New York City Homebrewers Guild to hold its meetings.

CAFE D'ALSACE

1695 2nd Ave., New York, NY 10128; (212) 722-5133; cafedalsace.com; @CafeDAlsace
Draft Beers: 8 **Bottled/Canned Beers:** 80

A French restaurant on the Upper East Side of Manhattan might not be the first place you would look for one of the most selective beer lists in the city, but under the direction of beer and wine sommelier Gianni Cavicchi, Cafe D'Alsace has cemented its place among the best places for a beer and food pairing in the area. The tap list keeps some local standards like The Bronx Brewery Pale Ale and seasonal offerings, but also rotates in brewers like Stillwater Artisanal Ales and Stone Brewing. The bottle list is treated like a wine list, with a variety of beers of different flavors and prices all stored at proper temperatures along with the restaurant's wine in the cellar. Th strength of this list's lies in Belgian beers from Cantillon, Rodenbach, St. Feuillien, and others.

The restaurant serves high-quality French dishes with a focus on the region of Alsace in the east of France, like duck sausage and stews that are expertly paired with beer and wine by Cavicchi. Occasionally Cavicchi and the restaurant's chef Phillipe Roussel put together beer-pairing dinners that focus on themes like French beers or dishes featuring duck. During spring and fall there are regular "Firkin Friday" events that have showcased creative casks from American brewers and even rare casks from Germany.

Cafe D'Alsace has a romantic atmosphere similar to a French bistro. It's a nice place to enjoy a cozy meal in the colder seasons, or to dine outside during the warmer months, watching passersby on Second Avenue.

THE DIAMOND

43 Franklin St., Brooklyn, NY 11222; (718) 383-5030; TheDiamondBrooklyn.com
Draft Beers: 7 **Bottled/Canned Beers:** Over 25

Greenpoint is the northernmost neighborhood in Brooklyn and is sometimes not so easy to get to. But taking the G train (the only Brooklyn-Queens subway line) to get to The Diamond is totally worth it. The plain black painted exterior is no indication of the laid-back fun you can experience inside. The decor of the bar has sort of a beachy, California vibe. The tables and chairs don't feel cramped, and alongside the wall opposite the curved bar is a shuffleboard table. The outdoor patio has an actual cable car that you can sit in to enjoy your beers.

One of the best features of The Diamond is its beer menu, organized not by style or region but by ABV. Session beers lead to middleweight beers lead to strong beers. While many bars list the ABV next to all the beers they carry, you may or may not take notice. This way, you know what you're drinking, and if you have two or three high-alcohol beers, it's on purpose.

You'll find an assortment of styles and regions on the menu. There's also a curated wine list. As for food offerings, The Diamond carries savory pies, chili, and meat and cheese plates. It's a great place to spend the day drinking session beers and playing shuffleboard.

DIVE BAR

732 Amsterdam Ave., New York, NY 10025; (212) 749-4358; www.divebarnyc.com; @DiveBarNYC
Draft Beers: 33 **Bottled/Canned Beers:** over 60

Normally craft beer enthusiasts avoid dive bars, but the Dive Bar group of spots on the Upper West Side of Manhattan turns the term on its head with the decor. Dive Bar isn't divey, per se, but instead takes its name from the scuba diving equipment, aquariums, and fishing paraphernalia that adorn its walls. Owners Lee Seinfeld and Jim Peterson opened the bar in the late 1980s, and recently Lee's son Nick has taken the lead on the beer selection. In addition to the location on Amsterdam near 96th Street, the group has added locations on Broadway at 101st Street and on 75th Street between Columbus and Amsterdam Avenues.

The beer list boasts over 30 draft options that hit a wide range of brews from American craft beers to popular imports. Dive Bar keeps small local brewers like the Hudson Valley's Newburgh Brewing in regular rotation, and along with its sister bars are the only three places in New York City that carry Chatham Brewing. Dive Bar keeps beers from the big brewing corporations like Guinness and Hoegaarden on draft for those who are new to beer and looking for something familiar. There's also a house beer on tap: Dive Bar Unfiltered Amber Ale, made by Chatham Brewing. Regular brewer tap takeovers from regional and local brewers like Cisco and Brooklyn Brewery keep the events calendar interesting. The food menu covers most of your standard pub food, with sandwiches, burgers, and salads, but Dive Bar also serves breakfast all day.

EARL'S BEER AND CHEESE

1259 Park Ave., New York, NY 10029; (212) 289-1581; earlsny.com; @earlsnyc
Draft Beers: 4 **Canned Beers:** 6 or 7

The concept for Earl's Beer and Cheese came about through a happy accident. Owners Mike Cesari and Adam Clark originally wanted to open a bar, but in order to get a liquor license they needed to serve food. So they brought on chef Corey Cova, whose imaginative and unique creations make Earl's a clear win.

Earl's can be found in a tiny storefront on the Upper East Side, long considered to be a craft beer desert. A picnic table and two small bars—one at the front window and one on the left wall—are the only places to sit at this bar/restaurant, which has less than 20 seats. Arrive early, because the place can get packed quickly, but there's always reliable turnover. As you walk in and to the back to order, you'll observe rustic decorations: taxidermy deer heads and a mural of a forest on the wall to the right.

American craft beers are offered on tap and in cans, from breweries like 21st Amendment, KelSo, Sixpoint, and Keegan. The food menu at Earl's is small but filled with unexpected deliciousness. A Calabro mozzarella grilled cheese has pickles, chips, and miso mayo, all on a toasted English muffin. A scallion pancake taco contains pork shoulder, queso fresco, shredded cabbage, raddish, and cilantro. Beer cheese made with New York cheddar and Lager is served with toast. Other menu items include mac and cheese, tomato soup, and other grilled cheeses.

4TH AVENUE PUB
76 4th Ave., Brooklyn, NY 11217; @FOURTHAVEPUB
Draft Beers: 24 **Bottled/Canned Beers:** 60

Fourth Avenue Pub is one of the best bars in the Park Slope neighborhood of Brooklyn, an area full of quality beer spots. The beer list, written on a chalkboard hanging to the right of the doorway, is jam-packed with quality craft options. The majority are American craft beers from brewers as far as Firestone Walker and as close as Sixpoint, but there are also a decent amount of imports, especially on the bottle list.

There are usually a couple of sour beers on the tap menu, like Rodenbach Grand Cru or Peekskill Simple Sour. Despite the high-quality beer, the bar is remarkably unpretentious and even maintains Budweiser on the menu for those who aren't into craft. The bottle list includes a few large bottles for sharing, like a 22-ounce Stone Ruination IPA for $10 or a 25-ounce Gouden Carolus Grand Cru for $20.

The patio, out the back of the bar and down a flight of stairs, takes bar greenery to a new level and is crawling with hop bines. There are several wood picnic tables for larger groups. While there's no food menu, you can enjoy some free popcorn. 4th Avenue Pub is also easy to get to, located a few blocks from Brooklyn's Atlantic Avenue/Barclays Center subway hub, where almost 10 subway lines and the Long Island Railroad converge.

IDLE HANDS BAR

25 Avenue B (downstairs), New York, NY 10009; (917) 338-7090; IdleHandsBar.com;
@IdleHandsBar
Draft Beers: 8 **Bottled/Canned Beers:** 35

When he was a teenager, David "The Rev" Ciancio's father would tell him that opening a bar would be the coolest thing for him to do. So 25 years later, he did, opening Idle Hands as a "rock and roll speakeasy," in a large basement-level space on the Lower East Side of Manhattan.

As you descend into the bar, you start to hear rock and roll tunes and see concert posters all over the walls. Idle Hands has an extensive beer collection that changes almost daily and over 80 unique types of bourbon. The bartenders are serious and knowledgeable about their beer. The tap list always has a few local brews from places like The Bronx Brewery or Greenport Harbor mixed in with some craft classics like Stone IPA. Cans of 21st Amendment Bitter American and Oskar Blues Dale's Pale Ale share the menu with bottles like Founders Breakfast Stout or Stone Smoked Porter.

In 2013, Idle Hands expanded, taking over the space upstairs.

The bar is a nice size and can accommodate large groups. It's a fun and funky place to visit or take out-of-towners. On Wednesday night the bar offers drinkers guided $10 tastings that include three beers, a spirit, and tater tots. The events are often focused on specific breweries, like Port Jeff Brewing Company or SingleCut Beersmiths, and occasionally even pair the beers with songs from bands like Guns N' Roses or Iron Maiden.

JACOB'S PICKLES

509 Amsterdam Ave., New York, NY 10024; (212) 470-5566; jacobspickles.com; @jacobspickles
Draft Beers: Over 20

The biscuits at Jacob's Pickles on the Upper West Side of Manhattan are drool-worthy. Moist and slightly sweet, they're served alongside maple butter, with three small squeeze bottles of "fixins": strawberry preserves, orange marmalade, and clover honey. The pickles at Jacob's Pickles are also pretty delicious. House made, your choices include sour cucumbers, dill kosher cucumbers, green beans, sweet and spicy carrots, and sour green tomatoes, all of which you can enjoy at the restaurant or take home. The food menu is largely Southern inspired, with offerings such as catfish tacos, shrimp and bacon grits, and fried chicken.

Jacob Hadjigeorgis opened his paradise of beer, biscuits, and pickles in 2012. It's a hip, trendy spot in a not-so-trendy neighborhood. With high ceilings and dark wood features, Jacob's Pickles is a comfortable place to eat and drink. The beer list (draft only) showcases American craft organized by region. While you'll find brews from all across the country, New York is represented the most on the menu. Brews from city breweries like SingleCut, Brooklyn, and Bronx have been on tap alongside other New York operations such as Greenport, Ommegang, and Ithaca. Order beers by the pint or in flights, and for an extra two bucks you can add some bacon.

It's not only pickles and biscuits you can take to go, either. Fill up (or purchase) growlers at Jacob's Pickles, and even bring home a bag of those amazing biscuits.

JIMMY'S NO. 43

43 E. 7th St., New York, NY 10003; (212) 982-3006; JimmysNo43.com; @JimmysNo43
Draft Beers: 13 on tap, including 1 cask ale **Bottled/Canned Beers:** 40

After owning a restaurant for a number of years, Jimmy Carbone decided to branch into bar ownership. He found a space in the East Village of Manhattan and took it as-is, turning it into a bar within four weeks. Carbone didn't name the place, instead relying on the address for identification purposes—putting a 43 sign outside—and it organically evolved to become Jimmy's No. 43.

Carbone serves a full, rotating menu because he believes food makes for a better place. Menu items could range from burgers and beer sausage to Bahn Mi hot dogs and sauteed kale. Jimmy's is the setting for regular beer pairing dinners and special beer nights that showcase beers of a certain style or from a particular brewery.

In his eight years in business, supporting the local craft beer community has been paramount. Beers made in New York City and the surrounding areas are always on tap, especially ones from new or up-and-coming brewers. Jimmy's was the first Manhattan bar to put brews from Rockaway Brewing Company on tap, and during 2013's NYC Beer Week he hosted a "Bridge and Tunnel" night, featuring beers from brand-new breweries in Queens.

In 2008 Carbone started the Good Beer Seal as a way to highlight the best and most special bars in New York City that serve great beer. He also launched Beer Sessions Radio, an online radio station on Heritage Radio Network that promotes beer in New York.

Jimmy's is situated below two other mainstays of East Village craft beer: Standings sports bar and Burp Castle. Together they are known as the "Brewmuda Triangle" and even share a beer refrigerator.

KILLMEYER'S OLD BAVARIA INN
4254 Arthur Kill Rd., Staten Island, NY 10309; (718) 984-1202; Killmeyers.com; @Killmeyers
Draft Beers: 9 (inside), 12 (outside) **Bottled/Canned Beers:** Over 100

You may not realize it, but New York City has some of the richest German heritage in the United States. Nineteenth-century New York was practically bursting at the seams with Germans looking for opportunities in America. They brought many traditions with them, and among the most important (for our purposes) was a love for beer. Not much of this history is still visible in a city where buildings and businesses are constantly in flux or change hands, but there are still a few holdovers, like Killmeyer's Old Bavaria Inn.

Killmeyer's is located at the end of Staten Island farthest from Manhattan and is surrounded by trees. Walking into the bar, you feel transported back to nineteenth-century New York City, or even Germany itself.

Nicholas Killmeyer bought the building in 1855, selling it to the Simonson family in 1945. The Simonsons renamed it a couple of times before selling it to the Tirados in 1995. The building's current owner, Ken Tirado, has restored much of its character, including the original name.

Bavarian lodge–style decorations abound at this bar/restaurant/beer garden, and it's perfectly normal for an accordion player dressed in lederhosen to entertain the crowd in the early afternoon on a Sunday. The most striking feature may be the ornately carved mahogany bar with the inscription KILLMEYER'S 1890. Killmeyer's is also home to one of the few true beer gardens in the city, with communal seating and lots of shady trees.

The beer list focuses on German beer, with traditional styles available on tap and in bottles. Beers like Hofbräu Dunkel, Reissdorf Kolsch, and Kostritzer Schwartzbier dominate the eight tap lines. The food is traditional German fare like pretzels, wurst, sauerbraten, and Wiener schnitzel. Grab a refreshing Kolsch and relax in the beer garden during the summer or drink a Dunkel while eating some sauerbraten or goulash in the winter.

McSORLEY'S OLD ALE HOUSE

15 E. 7th St., New York, NY 10003; (212) 473-9148
Draft Beers: 2

McSorley's Old Ale House exudes history, from the sawdust covered floor to every bit of memorabilia on the walls. The bar claims to have opened in 1855 and served the likes of Abraham Lincoln, Theodore Roosevelt. and Boss Tweed. Despite all the changes to the city over the years, the owners have treated the bar as a sort of working museum of old New York. This extends beyond the newspaper clippings and photos on the walls, to the wishbones that hang over the bar (although health inspectors recently had the owners dust the bones). According to legend, soldiers heading out to serve in Europe during the First World War left the bones, and they were to be picked up upon their return home.

Bits of history and legend have helped to make McSorley's a tourist destination for those looking to capture a bit of old New York in the dusty floors and no-nonsense service. In addition to the relatively harmless bits of history, McSorley's also gained notoriety as one of the last bars in New York City to allow only men, holding out until 1970 when a court order forced the establishment to admit women.

Your beer options at McSorley's are limited to their house beers, "light" and "dark," brewed by Pabst. If you order one beer, it's served in two small mugs. The "dark," brewed in the Irish black Lager style, has a touch of roast and a light body, while the "light" is a quaffable Pale Ale. Don't expect anything too interesting on the food menu, the cheese plate here is American and cheddar cheese with saltines and raw onions. The intense mustard takes things up a notch for dishes like the liverwurst sandwich and the burger.

124 RABBIT CLUB

124 Macdougal St., New York, NY 10012; (212) 254 0575
Draft Beers: 6 **Bottled/Canned Beers:** 60

A basement-level bar in Manhattan's Greenwich Village, 124 Rabbit Club is easy to miss. The only indicator that you're there is the waist-high yellow rabbit painted on the black exterior. The bar does not have a website. All of these factors contribute to a feeling of mystery and intrigue, like you're the only one who knows about this secret place (even though that's clearly not true).

This is a long, narrow bar, with tables in the front and couches in the back. The bartenders are helpful and knowledgeable, a plus because the beer list is also extensive, mostly in bottles. Dark and dingy with low ceilings, some might perceive 124

Rabbit Club as a bit of a hole in the wall. But that contributes to its charm. Rabbit decorations, decals, and paintings are sprinkled around here and there; you may not notice them all until you've been sitting there awhile.

The beer list is divided into three sections: Belgian, English, and German. You're likely to see some rare and obscure finds at this spot. The bar doesn't serve food, but being in Greenwich Village, there are plenty of fun and funky nearby places to choose from if you're hungry.

PINE BOX ROCK SHOP

12 Grattan St., Brooklyn, NY 11206; (718) 366-6311; pineboxrockshop.com; @pinebox rockshop
Draft Beers: 16 on tap, 1 on cask **Canned Beers:** 5

One of the first things you'll notice when you sidle up to the bar at Pine Box Rock Shop is that the bar itself is lined with concert tickets encased in resin. Located in Bushwick in a former casket factory, Pine Box Rock Shop is a large minimalist space with high ceilings. The interior feels a bit casketlike (but not too morbidly so), with the walls covered in repurposed shipping pallets.

What you definitely wouldn't notice when visiting Pine Box Rock Shop is that it's a vegan bar. Owners Heather and Jeff Rush—a husband-and-wife team from

Seattle—are committed to serving booze with only plant-based ingredients, evidenced in the house-made, soy-based Irish cream. Many beers are inherently vegan, though some do contain animal products such as gelatin, honey, or lactose. Just because the bar's vegan friendly doesn't mean the beer isn't good, though. Brews such as Ithaca Flower Power, KelSo Pilsner, Long Ireland Pale Ale, and He'Brew Hop Manna IPA could be found on the draft list. You can also choose from a handful of canned beers like Brooklyn Lager and Oskar Blues Dale's Pale Ale.

Trivia night is Wednesday, and there's karaoke on Thursday. Heather and Jeff are musicians, so you're likely to hear some great tunes while there. Pair your beers with a selection of vegan empanadas or potato chips.

THE PONY BAR

637 10th St., New York, NY 10036; (212) 586-2707; 1444 1st Ave., New York, NY 10036; (212) 288-0090; theponybar.com; @ThePonyBar
Draft Beers: 20 on tap, 1 or 2 on cask at each location **Bottled/Canned Beers:** Just two: Budweiser and Bud Light

Dan McLaughlin opened The Pony Bar in Manhattan's Hell's Kitchen neighborhood in 2009. Three years later, in 2012, he opened a second location on the Upper East Side (UES). The Pony Bar UES is almost exactly like the original, in a slightly larger space. The bars take their name not from horses, but from small "pony" beers. All the beers on tap and cask (over 20 in total) are American craft. Loyal Pony Bar patrons (of which there are many) can join the All-American Club. If you drink and rate 100 unique beers at Pony—keeping track with a smart phone app—you earn a button-down shirt with the Pony logo.

Beers at The Pony Bar are some of the most affordable in Manhattan, where it's commonplace to pay upward of $8 a pint. Each brew is $6, except during the hour from 4:20 to 5:20 p.m. Then they're $5. When a draft beer kicks at The Pony Bar, one of the bartenders rings a loud bell, and everyone inside shouts "New beer!" It's these traditions that make The Pony Bar such a crowd favorite among New York City beer aficionados. You'll only find craft beer on draft at Pony, where the bottles are Budweiser and Bud Light. Beers are displayed on an electronic tap list, which is updated in real time on the bars' websites.

Both Pony Bar locations feature a full menu with comfort foods such as meatball sandwiches, grilled cheese, burgers, and soft pretzels with beer mustard, and other hearty eats like gumbo, chili, roast chicken, and fried oysters. Both Pony Bar locations can get pretty busy, but the crowds are worth it for high-quality American craft at such low prices.

PROLETARIAT

102 St. Marks Place, New York, NY 10009; (212) 777-6707; ProletariatNY.com;
@ProletariatNY
Draft Beers: 12 **Bottled/Canned Beers:** Over 25

One of the coolest things about drinking in Manhattan is the chance to visit a speakeasy. There's something awesome about going to a bakery and opening a door in the back to find a veritable beer paradise. Such was the case when Proletariat opened in the East Village in 2012. The pint-size bar could be found through a door at the back of Jane's Sweet Buns. The bar has since taken over the bakery space and is no longer a speakeasy, but it retains its old feel. Exposed brick, vintage photos, and dim lighting contribute to a cool and comfortable vibe. You really could spend the whole day at this bar.

Proletariat is known by some as one of the best bars in the city to satisfy your inner beer geek. The bartenders are knowledgeable and friendly. If you're unsure about what you may want to drink, they'll make suggestions for you based on what styles you normally enjoy. The beer list is manageable but well curated, with highly touted Belgian beers like the sour Tilquin Gueze and gypsy brewers like Evil Twin rubbing shoulders with local favorites like The Bronx Brewery's special release beers. Beer cocktails are also offered on tap.

Manhattan's East Village is ripe with good beer bars, but Proletariat might have the best list. Though it can get pretty crowded, it's worth a visit. At Time Out New York's annual Food and Beverage Awards, it took home the Best Pint Size Brew Shrine award.

THE QUEENS KICKSHAW

40-17 Broadway, Astoria, NY 11103; (718) 777-0913; thequeenskickshaw.com;
@QueensKickshaw
Draft Beers: 4 **Bottled/Canned Beers:** Over 30

In the bustling Astoria neighborhood of Queens, nestled in between a Subway and a Mexican restaurant that looks like it's been there for years, is a small, unassuming storefront that's home to The Queens Kickshaw. Husband-and-wife team Ben Sandler and Jennifer Lim opened the place in 2011 and decided on the name because Sandler owns three vintage kick-started scooters. The Queens Kickshaw has seven tap lines—one dedicated to Kombucha, one to cider, one to cold brew coffee, and four to beer.

When Sandler and Lim opened up they wanted to never serve the same beer twice, and have largely stuck to that goal. In addition to 4 draft options and over

30 bottled and canned brews, the duo offer beer that comes in large-format bottles by the glass. They are able to keep the beer fresh in the bottles after pouring a glass by using a custom-made system, originally developed for Champagne, that fills the space of opened bottles with carbon dioxide and repressurizes them when resealed. It's nice to be able to enjoy just one glass of beer that's only available in 750-milliliter bottles, such as beers made by Big Alice Brewing.

The space is long and slim, with the bar in the front and long family-style tables in the back. Dinner and a late-night menu are offered daily, with breakfast and lunch on weekdays and brunch on weekends and holidays. Soon after opening, The Queens Kickshaw became known for grilled cheese. A Gouda grilled cheese with black bean hummus, guava jam, and pickled jalapenos is most popular. Other grilled cheese options include a gruyére, a manchego and ricotta, a cheddar and mozzarella, and a Great Hill blue.

RATTLE N HUM

14 E. 33rd St., New York, NY 10016; (212) 481-1586; www.rattlenhumbarnyc.com; @RattleNHumBarNY
Draft Beers: 40 **Bottled/Canned Beers:** Over 100

As a general rule Midtown Manhattan isn't really the best place to visit for craft beer. But bars like Rattle N Hum and its sister bar Beer Authority are changing the landscape. With 40 taps, regular casks, and a deep bottle and can list, Rattle N Hum is a great stop before a Rangers or Knicks game at the nearby Madison Square Garden. As is to be expected for the neighborhood, Rattle N Hum can be pricey, with pints climbing to well over $10, but during happy hour and on "Kick the Keg Sundays" select drafts are $5.

America's top brewers, such as Dogfish Head and Firestone Walker, are regulars on the tap list, along with locals like Brooklyn Brewery and Captain Lawrence. The bottle list is a mix of small and special, large-format bottles like Maine Beer Company and Ithaca's Excelsior Series. The menus are helpful for beer experts and beginners alike, with directions on how to taste beer and the beer style, ABV, and flavor profiles listed for each draft option. Events frequently feature some of the most popular brewers like Founders Brewing and Green Flash Brewing.

The chalkboard-painted walls display brewery signs and a map of the country with brewers on it. Beyond the long and usually crowded bar, there are tables and a few booths if you're interested in a meal with your beers. The food menu features classics like bratwurst and sliders but also the popular IPA fries that the bar brines in an IPA before cooking.

SPUYTEN DUYVIL

359 Metropolitan Ave., Brooklyn, NY 11211; (718) 963-4140; SpuytenDuyvilNYC.com; @SpuytenDuyvilNY
Draft Beers: 6 on tap, 1 on cask **Bottled/Canned Beers:** Over 1,000

From the outside, Spuyten Duyvil may not seem like a craft beer destination. Covered by red metal bars, the facade could easily be the entrance to a coffee or sandwich shop. Located on a bustling street in Brooklyn's Williamsburg neighborhood, Spuyten Duyvil is a top-flight beer bar specializing in imported beer and rare American craft beer that opened in 2003. The eight constantly rotating tap lines often feature unique beers from Germany, Italy, and France alongside revered Belgian beers that the bar focuses on. While the draft beers are consistently delicious, you can find some real gems on the bottle list.

The decor in the bar is eclectic, with some unique throwback chairs and other vintage finds. You can enjoy your tasty brews outside on a small patio, accompanied by a meat or cheese plate or Brooklyn-made pickles.

Spuyten Duyvil—which loosely translated into Dutch means "in spite of the devil"—has garnered a cultlike following, with beer fans visiting from all over to partake of the rare finds from breweries like Cantillon, De Dolle, and De Ranke.

TAPROOM 307

307 3rd Ave., New York, NY 10010; (212) 725-4766; www.taproom307.com; @taproom307
Draft Beers: 40 **Bottled/Canned Beers:** Over 60

Just northeast of the Union Square buzz, Taproom 307 combines a gastropub experience with the feel of the surrounding Gramercy neighborhood. Beer sommelier Hayley Jensen, a veteran of Daniel Boulud's DBGB, teams up with her husband Stephen Durley, the restaurant's chef, to pair the extensive beer selection with a fun and creative food menu. Jensen's tap list often has a local focus, with New York City–based brewers like The Bronx Brewery and SingleCut Beersmiths alongside regional brewers like Victory and Wandering Star.

The bottle list extends into more obscure and creative imported beers like the highly regarded German smoked beers from Aecht Schlenkerla or the Italian Birrifico Baladin. Popular and sought-after American beers like Dogfish Head's 120 Minute IPA and the Founders Brewing Backstage Series also appear among the bottles.

The food menu has standards like a pulled pork sandwich and fish and chips but also creative dishes like beer-brined burrata cheese and tiger shrimp hush puppies. Tuesday night is trivia night, and there is a craft beer event every Wednesday night, which could be brewery tap takeovers, beer and food pairings, or beer cocktail selections. Regulars can join the bar's rewards program to accumulate points to spend on free beers, growler fills, beer classes, and eventually the "beer baptism ceremony," where the drinker is presented with a certificate and has his or her head dipped in beer.

Taproom 307 has a long bar area and booths and tables that can accommodate large groups. The bar can get packed on weekends and big game nights; reservations are recommended, unless you are stopping in during odd hours or for lunch on a weekday.

THIRD AVENUE ALE HOUSE
1644 Third Ave., New York, NY 10128; (646) 559-9131
Draft Beers: 26 on tap, 1 on cask **Bottled/Canned Beers:** Over 30

Until recently the Upper East Side of Manhattan was considered by many to be a craft beer desert full of overpriced Irish-style pubs and dive bars. Lately things have started to change, and with bars like Third Avenue Ale House, which opened in December 2012, the neighborhood is showcasing great craft beer alongside affordable food menus.

The beer list at Third Avenue Ale House has a wide variety of American craft beer. You can usually count on brews from Founders, Avery, and Tröegs being on the list with local breweries like Peekskill, Barrier, and Greenport. The food menu is mostly pub style with sandwiches, burgers, nachos, and hummus.

The bar area has more space than others with several high-top tables available in the front to help alleviate some of the crowding and a second room in the back that provides ample seating. In the summer the bar sets up tables out on the street (a good way to do some people watching while enjoying a tasty brew).

TØRST
615 Manhattan Ave., Brooklyn, NY 11222; (718) 389-6034; TorstNYC.com; @TorstNYC
Draft Beers: 21 **Bottled/Canned Beers:** 200

Yes, you can drop $150 on a bottle of a 14-year-old Belgian Lambic at Tørst. While featuring some of the most expensive and rare beers in the city, this bar also has one of the best and most carefully curated beer lists in New York State. The bartenders are helpful and happy to indulge any beer geek's desire for a trendy sour beer or a beer novice looking for an approachable but flavorful craft option.

The draft list features several beers from Evil Twin Brewing Company brewed by the gypsy-brewing Jeppe Jarnit-Bjergsø, who also manages Tørst's beer operation with beer sommelier John Langley. The draft list shows off rare international beers like BFM Abbaye de Saint Bon-Chien or Alvinne Wild Undressed. Each draft beer is served at its proper temperature into a freshly cleaned glass through a system that allows the bar to control each tap line's temperature, dubbed the "flux capacitor." Most pours are either 8 or 14 ounces and range from $4 to $10.

The bottle list is an overwhelming compilation of rare American craft beer and the highest-quality imports available from brewers such as California's The Bruery, Italy's Loverbeer, or the Belgian De Dolle. The bar serves small side dishes like local radishes with butter and meat and cheese plates. Luksus, a small restaurant headed by Daniel Burns formerly of NYC hotspot Momofuku, is located in the back of the bar and serves inventive and seasonal food. The bar itself is clean marble with geometric wood paneling on the walls and tables, contributing to a romantic, eclectic atmosphere.

Pub Crawls

A pub crawl is a great way to see multiple places in one day and allows you to do so safely, as long as you walk, take a cab, take subway, or find someone willing to be your designated driver.

East Village, Manhattan

The East Village has one of the highest concentrations of good beer bars in Manhattan. More than most neighborhoods you can experience the old guard of beer bars and the newest trends in bars.

Jimmy's No. 43, 43 E. 7th St. (basement level), New York, NY 10003; (212) 982-3006; JimmysNo43.com

Jimmy Carbone has made Jimmy's No. 43 the unofficial meeting place for the city's beer community with beer dinners, release parties, and tastings. The newest and smallest breweries in New York City, the Hudson Valley, and on Long Island are usually on tap. The subterranean bar is dimly lit and has a tasty menu; try the grilled cheese or some sausage.

Standings, 43 E. 7th St., New York, NY 10003; (212) 420-0671; StandingsBar.com

Walk upstairs from Jimmy's No. 43 to Standings, one of the best sports and beer bars in the city. The 12 taps feature craft beer and the 8 TVs play every big game. There is even free pizza on Friday night and bagels on Sunday during football season.

Burp Castle, 41 E. 7th St., New York, NY 10003; (212) 982-4576; BurpCastleNYC .Wordpress.com

Just next door to Standings is Burp Castle, where Belgian Krieks, Dubbels, and Tripels rule the draft lines. The small bar has a quiet rule that bartenders enforce with shushing to keep conversation at a more level more conducive to beer worship.

Proletariat, 102 St Marks Place, New York, NY 10009; (212) 777-6707; ProletariatNY .com

Walk a few blocks to Proletariat, where the motto "Rare and Unsual Beers" is taken to heart. You can explore some of the highest-quality beers you never heard of under the guidance of the helpful bartenders. Some of the bottles at Proletariat are quite rare; keep an eye on their social media accounts for beer announcements. The bar is small and can get very packed, so try to get there early and grab seats at the bar.

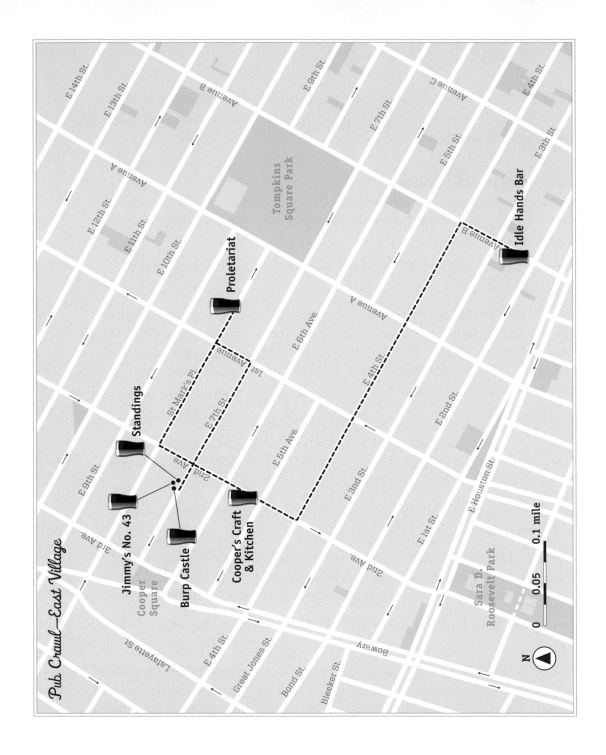

Pub Crawl—East Village

Cooper's Craft & Kitchen, 87 2nd Ave., New York, NY 10003; (646) 606-2384; CoopersNYC.com

Just down Second Avenue is Cooper's Craft & Kitchen, where 22 taps regularly feature the newest and freshest beers from local brewers like The Bronx Brewery or Radiant Pig. There is also an extensive food menu that includes sandwiches and a mean mac n' cheese.

Idle Hands Bar, 25 Avenue B, New York, NY 10009; (917) 338-7090; IdleHandsBar .com

Walk two blocks to the south and three to the east to get to Idle Hands Bar. This basement rock bar is one of the best ways to end a night in New York City. Rocking music is accompanied by a great selection of craft beers and whiskies.

Upper East Side, Manhattan

The Upper East Side of Manhattan used to be a craft beer desert. You might find a few pubs and dive bars offering beers like Budweiser and Coors, but that was about it. Now the Upper East Side is a beer (and food) destination.

Earl's Beer and Cheese, 1259 Park Ave., New York, NY 10029; (212) 289-1581; EarlsNY.com

Earl's Beer and Cheese doesn't have an extensive beer list, but it's well curated. And most important, Earl's is where you can get some of the best grilled cheese around. Stop here on Saturday or Sunday right when it opens at 11 a.m. to get a great start on your beer day.

A.B.V, 1504 Lexington Ave., New York, NY 10029; (212) 722-8959; ABVNY.com

Right around the block from Earl's is its sister bar A.B.V. You'll find a beer menu with local and imported offerings, as well as a selection of artisanal sodas in case you'd like to take a beer break.

Merrion Square, 1840 2nd Ave., New York, NY 10128; (212) 831-7696; MerrionNYC.com

Two blocks south and two blocks east of A.B.V. is Merrion Square, the diviest bar on this crawl. But it's got a great beer selection. If you order a pint, you get a burger for free. If you order a pitcher, you get an order of wings for free.

Third Avenue Ale House, 1644 3rd Ave., New York, NY 10128

Pub Crawl—Upper East Side

Central Park

Jacqueline Kennedy Onassis Reservoir

East River

Carl Schurz Park

Lighthouse Park

John Jay Park

Central Park

Earl's Beer and Cheese

A.B.V

Merrion Square

Third Avenue Ale House

Jones Wood Foundry

The Pony Bar

Madison Ave.

Park Ave.

1st Avenue

FDR Drive

2nd Ave.

Lexington Ave.

East Dr.

5th Ave./Museum Mile

Madison Ave.

Park Ave.

3rd Ave.

2nd Ave.

1st Avenue

York Ave.

East End Ave.

FDR Drive

Main St.

E 105th St
E 104th St
E 103rd St
E 102nd St
E 101st St
E 100st St
E 99th St
E 97th St
E 96th St
E 95th St
E 94th St
E 93rd St
E 92nd St
E 91st St.
E 90th St.
E 89th St.
E 88th St.
E 87th St.
E 86th St.
E 85th St.
E 84th St.
E 82nd St.
E 81st St.
E 80th St.
E 79th St.
E 78th St.
E 77th St.
E 76th St.
E 75th St.
E 74th St.
E 73rd St.
E 72nd St.
E 71st St.

3rd Ave.
2nd Ave.
1st Avenue

N

0   0.05   0.1 mile

Walk two more blocks south and one west to Third Avenue Ale House for a selection of draft brews from local and other American craft breweries like Brooklyn, Bronx, Peak Organic, and Oskar Blues. If you didn't eat at Merrion Square, there's a full menu here with upscale pub fare.

Jones Wood Foundry, 401 E. 76th St., New York, NY 10021; (212) 249-2700; JonesWoodFoundry.com

After Third Avenue Ale House, you can walk for about a half an hour, or head over to Second Avenue and take the M15 bus down to 75th Street (15 minutes) and walk east a couple of blocks. Jones Wood Foundry is designed as an English-style public house with a tap and bottle list that features beers from the United Kingdom, organized by light, medium, and dark.

The Pony Bar, 1444 1st Ave., New York, NY 10021; (212) 288-0090; ThePonyBar.com

Just around the corner from Jones Wood Foundry is The Pony Bar, where you can top off your pub crawl with $6 drafts from American craft brewers, and join in the chorus of patrons who yell "NEW BEER!" when a keg is kicked.

Park Slope, Brooklyn

Brooklyn's Park Slope neighborhood, specifically Fourth and Fifth Avenues, is a great place to visit and spend the day. Scores of boutiques, restaurants, and bars line these two streets.

Bierkraft, 191 5th Ave., Brooklyn, NY 11211; (718) 230-7600; Bierkraft.com

Bierkraft is a great start to any pub crawl, even one that takes you across multiple neighborhoods. This spot has delicious sandwiches, great draft beers—many of which are local—and an extensive bottle and can selection for consumption on premises. Brewing equipment for Bierkraft's own house beers sits right next to the bar.

The Gate, 321 5th Ave., Brooklyn, NY 11215; (718) 768-4329; TheGateBrooklyn .blogspot.com

Walk down Fifth Avenue to The Gate, home to one of the best patios in the neighborhood, where you can watch the notorious Park Slope strollers roll by while you enjoy your beer. Keep an eye out for vintage kegs from breweries like Founders and Brooklyn that occasionally show up on the menu.

Pub Crawl—Park Slope

Bergen St.
3rd Ave.
Pacific St.
Wyckoff St.
Dean St.
Atlantic Ave.
Baltic St.
Douglass St.
Hoyt St.
Nevins St.
Butler St.
Pacific Standard
4th Avenue Pub
Warren St.
St Marks Pl.
Flatbush Ave.
Union St.
Bond St.
Degraw St.
4th Ave.
5th Ave.
Prospect Pl.
6th Ave.
Park Pl.
Sackett St.
Sterling Pl.
1st St.
Carroll St.
St John Pl.
2nd St.
Gowanus Canal
Mission Dolores
Bierkraft
Union St.
Lincoln Pl.
Berkeley Pl.
1st St.
7th Ave.
3rd St.
President St.
2nd Ave.
6th St.
3rd Ave.
4th Ave.
Garfield Pl.
Carroll St.
8th St.
7th St.
The Gate
6th Ave.
2nd St.
8th Ave.
9th St.
5th Ave.
4th St.
1st St.
3rd St.
11th St.
9th St.
Owl Farm
6th St.
7th Ave.
5th St.
13th St.
12th St.
10th St.
8th St.
Prospect Park West

N

0   0.1   0.2 miles

The Owl Farm, 297 9th St., Brooklyn, NY 11215; (718) 499-4988; TheOwlFarmBar
.com

A few blocks down on Ninth Street is the relative newcomer to the neighborhood,
The Owl Farm. Opened in 2012 by the team behind Mission Dolores (your next stop
in this pub crawl) and Bar Great Harry, The Owl Farm has an extensive beer list
characterized by style.

Mission Dolores, 249 4th Ave., Brooklyn, NY 11215; (347) 457-5606; MissionDolores
Bar.com

Retrace your steps up Fifth Avenue and cross over to Fourth at Carroll Street to find
Mission Dolores, a no-nonsense bar with a tap list that always has a solid variety.
Take in some fresh air out in the courtyard or play some vintage arcade games
indoors.

Pacific Standard, 82 4th Ave., Brooklyn, NY 11217; (718) 858-1951; PacificStandard
Brooklyn.com

Walk down Fourth Avenue a ways to happen on the last stops of your pub crawl,
Pacific Standard and 4th Avenue Pub, a few doors apart. Pacific Standard is a bar that
stays focused on West Coast beer. A home away from home for those who've migrated
over to the East Coast, Pacific Standard often has some rare and hard-to-find brews.

4th Avenue Pub, 76 4th Ave., Brooklyn, NY 11217; (718) 643-2273

On the same block as Pacific Standard is 4th Avenue Pub, where craft beer, free
popcorn, and a hop-covered back patio make the perfect combination. Conveniently
located just a few blocks from the Barclay's Arena, home of the Brooklyn Nets,
and Atlantic Terminal, you can grab most subway lines or hop on the Long Island
Railroad to head home.

Williamsburg, Brooklyn

Brooklyn's Williamsburg neighborhood is well-known for its craft beer, thanks largely
to Brooklyn Brewery, which helped usher in the craft beer resurgence throughout
the entire city. Not surprisingly, awesome craft beer hotspots have cropped up near
the brewery.

Brooklyn Brewery, 79 N. 11th St., Brooklyn, NY 11249; (718) 486-7422; Brooklyn
Brewery.com

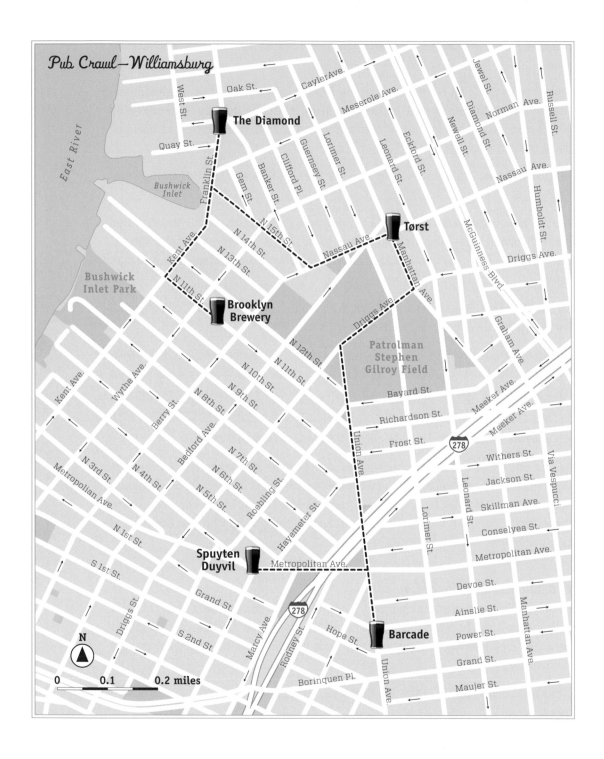

Pub Crawl—Williamsburg

East River

Bushwick Inlet

Bushwick Inlet Park

The Diamond

Tørst

Brooklyn Brewery

Patrolman Stephen Gilroy Field

Spuyten Duyvil

Barcade

N

0   0.1   0.2 miles

The best time to visit the Brooklyn Brewery is Saturday or Sunday at noon, right when its doors open. Purchase drink tokens to enjoy some high-quality brews and hop on the 1 p.m. free tour.

The Diamond, 43 Franklin St., Brooklyn, NY 11222; (718) 383-5030; TheDiamond Brooklyn.com

A short walk from the Brooklyn Brewery is The Diamond, which opens at 2 p.m. on weekends (5 p.m. during the week). Beachy decor and great food contribute to an awesome atmosphere to try some good beers, helpfully organized by ABV. Make sure to at least take a peek outside, where you'll see a cable car gondola.

Tørst, 615 Manhattan Ave., Brooklyn, NY 11222; (718) 389-6034; TorstNYC.com

Brooklyn's newest hottest beer bar, Tørst has one of the best and most carefully curated beer lists in the city. Beers are temperature regulated by a system under the bar dubbed the "Flux capacitor" and served in fine glassware. Hop on the G train at the nearby Nassau Avenue stop to get to your next spot.

Barcade, 388 Union Ave., Brooklyn, NY 11211; (718) 302-6464; BarcadeBrooklyn .com

One stop on the G train to Metropolitan Avenue will put you out near Barcade. Combination craft beer bar and vintage arcade, it's not hard to see why this is such a popular destination. If there isn't too long of a wait, try your hand at the beer-themed video game Tapper.

Spuyten Duyvil, 359 Metropolitan Ave., New York, NY 11211; (718) 963-4140; SpuytenDuyvilNYC.com

A short walk away from Barcade is Spuyten Duyvil, which loosely translated from Dutch means "in spite of the devil," a bar that specializes in imported beer and rare American craft. While away the evening inside or out on the back patio, enjoying a meat or cheese plate with your brew.

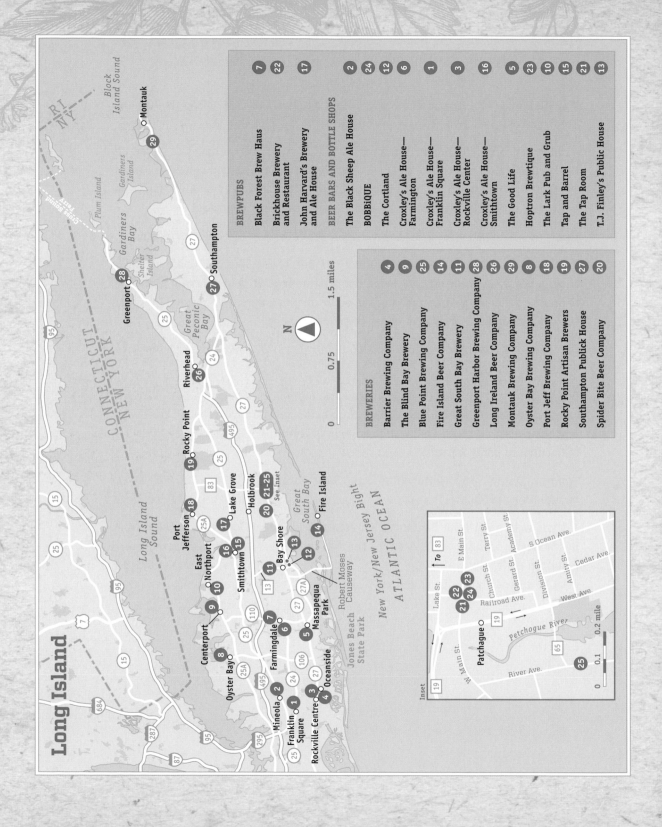

Long Island

BREWERIES

- 4 Barrier Brewing Company
- 9 The Blind Bay Brewery
- 25 Blue Point Brewing Company
- 14 Fire Island Beer Company
- 11 Great South Bay Brewery
- 28 Greenport Harbor Brewing Company
- 26 Long Ireland Beer Company
- 29 Montauk Brewing Company
- 8 Oyster Bay Brewing Company
- 18 Port Jeff Brewing Company
- 19 Rocky Point Artisan Brewers
- 27 Southampton Publick House
- 20 Spider Bite Beer Company

BREWPUBS

- 7 Black Forest Brew Haus
- 22 Brickhouse Brewery and Restaurant
- 17 John Harvard's Brewery and Ale House

BEER BARS AND BOTTLE SHOPS

- 2 The Black Sheep Ale House
- 24 BOBBiQUE
- 12 The Cortland
- 6 Croxley's Ale House—Farmington
- 1 Croxley's Ale House—Franklin Square
- 3 Croxley's Ale House—Rockville Center
- 16 Croxley's Ale House—Smithtown
- 5 The Good Life
- 23 Hopton Brewtique
- 10 The Lark Pub and Grub
- 15 Tap and Barrel
- 21 The Tap Room
- 13 T.J. Finley's Public House

Long Island

In the early 2000s, Long Island's nascent brewing community looked very much like other parts of the state and country: A few brewpubs and bars dotted the Island, and most of the population had yet to discover or appreciate craft beer's potential. Since then the region has seen numerous breweries and bars open, fueled by an enthusiasm and passion that are quickly making the island a craft beer destination.

Breweries like the popular Greenport Harbor Brewing Company are expanding to increase their reach and add bottling, while brewers like Rocky Point Artisan Brewers are perfectly content to remain an ultra-local nanobrewery. The brewers have formed the Long Island Craft Brewers Guild and established Long Island Craft Beer Week in May. At the TAP NY beer festival, brewers from Long Island brought home the F.X. Matt Memorial Cup for the Best Brewery in New York State two years in a row, with Barrier Brewing Company in 2011 and Spider Bite Beer Company in 2012.

With the recent explosion of brewers, there has also been a resurgence in hop farming. Several farms on eastern Long Island have begun growing this essential beer ingredient. With new harvests of hops, brewers will have an opportunity to brew more limited wet-hopped beers with fresh ingredients.

Breweries

BARRIER BREWING COMPANY

3001 New St., Unit 2a, Oceanside, NY 11572; (516) 594-1028; BarrierBrewing.com;
@BarrierBrewing

Founded: 2009 **Founders and Brewers:** Evan Klein, Craig Frymark **Beers:** Antagonist ESB, Barnacle American Brown, Beech St. Belgian Spiced Wheat, Belgian 1 Belgian Pale Ale, Bittersweet American Pale Ale, Bulkhead India Red Ale, Bumble Wheat IPA, Caddywompus English Pale Bitter, Cairn Scotch Ale, Craven Belgian Red Ale, Cycle Petite Saison, Dubbel Down Belgian Dubbel, Dunegrass Double IPA, Evil Giant Rye IPA, Frau Blucher German Rauchbier, Greenroom American Pale Ale, Gosilla German Goze Bier, Hopfen Blasten German IPA, Icculus German Kolsch, Imposter Czech Pilsner, Le Pete Belgian Smoked Wheat, Lights Out Stout, Oblong Dark Strong Rye, Oil City India Black Ale, Mare Undarum Belgian IPA, Medulla English IPA, Mollycoddle English Dark Mild, Money IPA, Moochelle Milk Stout, Morticia Imperial Stout, red Button Imperial Red, Rembrandt Robust Porter, Riprap Baltic Porter, Ruckus IPA, Saazquash Butternut Squash Ale, Saisoff Saison, Simple California Common, Spelunker Dark Saison, Undertow Dunkel Rauchbier, Unimperial IPA, Vermillioin Red Saison, Zythossaurus Imperial Pale Ale, Barrier Relief, Surge Protector IPA **Tours:** Yes; the brewery and taproom are in the same space; you can clearly see the equipment **Taproom:** Yes

Evan Klein and Craig Frymark were homebrewers who met when they had jobs at Brooklyn's Sixpoint Brewery in the mid 2000s, but always wanted to start their own venture. In 2009 Klein made the first step and founded Barrier Brewing Company—named after the Long Beach Barrier Island were he resides—with Frymark joining him shortly thereafter. They began brewing on a 1-barrel system in Oceanside, expanding to 30 barrels in 2012. Klein and Frymark enjoy many different styles of beer, and brew all of them.

Since its launch, Barrier has made its name by being innovative and experimental, quickly establishing itself as one of New York's most sought-after breweries. The pair's beers are available throughout New York City and Long Island, and many are draft only, while some are sold in bottles. **Caddywompus** is an English Style Bitter, low in alcohol at 4.3 percent. The brew is full of flavor and great for summer, with a bready, biscuity malt character and an earthy hoppiness. Barrier's **Unimperial IPA** is a citrus, bitter hop bomb at only 4 percent ABV, so hop heads can enjoy more than a couple.

Klein and Frymark have experienced their share of challenges along the way. At the end of October 2012, Hurricane Sandy struck Barrier Brewing and destroyed the 30-barrel brewhouse they had just built, forcing them to cease production for several

Delayle
Style: Berliner Weisse
ABV: 4.5%
Availability: Limited
Brewed with oak-smoked malt,
Delayle has a smoky and bacon-
like aroma. The flavor is made up
of a delicious puckering sourness
of lemons. Completely drinkable,
Delayle (while hard to pronounce)
is a refreshing offering for summer,
or any other time of year, if you can
find it.

months, and at the time it was unclear when they would be able to reopen. The beer community in New York State rallied around Klein and Frymark, with Simon Thorpe, CEO of Brewery Ommegang, inviting the duo to brew at his facility. The resulting beer, **Barrier Relief,** raised money to rebuild. Blue Point Brewery invited Barrier to join other Long Island breweries on a collaborative brew, **Surge Protector IPA,** made with one ingredient donated from each and brought in $29,000 for Barrier, and also $29,000 for Sandy relief.

THE BLIND BAT BREWERY
420 Harrison Dr., Centerport, NY 11721; (631) 891-7909; BlindBatBrewery.com; @BlindBatBrewer
Founded: 2008 **Founder and Brewer:** Paul Dlugokencky **Flagship Beer:** Hellsmoke Porter **Year-Round Beers:** Vlad the Inhaler, Hellsmoke Porter **Seasonals/Special Releases:** Honey Basil Ale, Long Island Potato Stout, Mild Mannered Ale, Beached Blonde, Hell Gate Golden Ale, Ceci N'est Pas Mild Ale, Long Island Pale Ale, Eye Chart Ale, Mild-Mannered Ale, Honey and Basil Ale, Harborfields Hefeweizen **Tours:** No **Taproom:** No

You don't hear of too many licensed breweries that operate out of a garage. Paul Dlugokencky launched The Blind Bat Brewery in 2008, at the time a $^1/_3$-barrel system in his 350-square-foot carport at his home in Centerport on Long Island. In 2010 he upgraded to a 3-barrel system. The Blind Bat is named in homage to speakeasies during Prohibition, which were called "Blind Pigs" or "Blind Tigers." Since "Blind Tiger" was already the name of a longtime well-known New York City bar, Dlugokencky decided on Blind Bat, since he is also near-sighted and colorblind.

Dlugokencky is experimental and innovative with his brews. He makes a selection of wood-smoked beers, such as the **Hellsmoke Porter,** which is brewed with English pale malt, some of which has been smoked over alder and applewood. The beer is roasty, with chocolate flavors balancing out the smokiness. Blind Bat beers are often given whimsical names, such as **Vlad the Inhaler,** a Grodziskie, which is a smoked-wheat ale hopped with Saaz hops. The wheat and barley that make up Vlad are smoked over oak for two hours before mashing. **Beached Blonde,** a Belgian-inspired Blonde Ale, is spiced with cardamom and coriander. In a commitment to community and locally sourced ingredients, Dlugokencky launched a **Farm-and-Garden** series of beers, including **Long Island Potato Stout** and the **Honey & Basil Ale,** brewed with Catskill honey and organic basil, giving the beer a floral, earthy taste.

The Blind Bat is slated to expand to a larger facility in mid 2014. To help along the expansion, Dlugokencky launched The Blind Bat Brewery Club, where members can choose one of five levels to participate in, and by paying a membership price either get discounts or discounts and a quarterly allotment of beer.

Long Island Potato Stout

Style: Irish Dry Stout

ABV: 3.9%

Availability: Limited, on draft and in
large-format bottles

The first beer in The Blind Bat's Farm-
and-Garden series of brews using local
ingredients, Long Island Potato Stout is
made with Long Island–grown, organic
Yukon Gold or Keuka Gold potatoes. The
spuds are boiled, mashed, and added to
the mash of grains, making the Stout
extra dry. This beer is malty and crisp with
a light mouthfeel. Slightly sweet, Long
Island Potato Stout has flavors of chocolate and caramel. It pairs well with oysters, steak, burgers, or sharp cheese.

BLUE POINT BREWING COMPANY

161 River Ave., Patchogue, NY 11772; (631) 475-6944; BluePointBrewing.com;
@BluePointBrewer

Founded: 1998 **Founders:** Peter Cotter, Mark Burford **Brewer:** Christian Ryan **Flagship
Beer:** Toasted Lager **Year-Round Beers:** Toasted Lager, Hoptical Illusion, Blueberry Ale,
RastafaRye Ale, Pale Ale, Oatmeal Stout, White IPA **Seasonals/Special Releases:** Spring
Fling, Summer Ale, Oktoberfest, Pumpkin Ale, Winter Ale, Double Blonde, Golden Ale, Old
Howling Bastard, No Apologies, Sour Cherry Imperial Stout, Toxic Sludge, Double Pilsner,
ESB **Tours:** Yes **Taproom:** Yes

Peter Cotter and Mark Burford started Blue Point Brewing Company in 1998. Both
avid homebrewers, Burford had opened a homebrew shop in Franklin Square in
the early 1990s, then worked as the brewmaster at the now-defunct Long Island
Brewing Company.

Blue Point Brewing Company is Long Island's oldest craft brewery and has become
one of the most recognizable. The draft beer is made at the Patchogue brewery, while

the bottles and cans are brewed in Rochester, New York, at North American Brewers. After the brewery's founding in 1998, beers were brewed on a 25-barrel system that used a brick brew kettle with open flames. After 10 years on the brick system, the brewery upgraded to a new system and has added a bottling line at the Long Island Brewery for 22-ounce bottles. Cotter and Burford have grown Blue Point from a small brewer available only on Long Island to one of the region's larger craft brands, producing over 30,000 barrels a year with distribution as far as Florida.

Blue Point steadily produces beers like the versatile **Toasted Lager** and a bold black IPA called **Toxic Sludge.** The flagship Toasted Lager is copper colored with a pillowy white head. The aroma is bready and followed by a biscuity sweetness and minimal bitterness. The Toxic Sludge, originally brewed to benefit Tri-State Bird Rescue and Research in the wake of the infamous BP oil spill of 2010, pours inky black and layers intense hop bitterness over dark roasted malts.

The brewery's taproom, located in Patchogue, is larger than most, with a long bar and plenty of seating. Drinkers can sample core brand beers, seasonals, and specialty brews.

Beer Lover's Pick

Spring Fling
Style: Copper Ale
ABV: 5.2%
Availability: Spring, on draft and in bottles

Blue Point's Spring Fling is a great spring seasonal, available from February through April. The copper-colored Ale is slightly sweet with flavors of caramel and toffee and a bit of nuttiness. The light body and touch of hops balance out the sweetness and keep the beer refreshing, perfect for outdoor imbibing on a warm spring day.

Blue Point Brewing's Cask Festival

Blue Point's Cask Festival, originally held during a January blizzard in 2006, has since moved to the more appropriate weather of April and draws a large crowd of drinkers who love cask ales. Brewers from around the region bring casks to serve outdoors rain or shine.

FIRE ISLAND BEER COMPANY

P.O. Box 546, Ocean Beach, NY 11770; (631) 482-3118; FireIslandBeer.com; @FireIslandBeer

Founded: 2012 **Founders:** Tom Fernandez, Bert Fernandez, Jeff Glassman **Brewer:** Tom Fernandez **Flagship Beer:** Red Wagon IPA **Year-Round Beers:** Red Wagon IPA, Fire Island Lighthouse Ale **Seasonals/Special Releases:** Frozen Tail Pale Ale, Sea Salt Ale, Pumpkin Barrel Ale **Tours:** No **Taproom:** No

When Tom and Bert Fernandez were in their late teens, their father, Tom Sr., leased a concession stand called The Shack at Atlantique Beach on Fire Island, an island off the south shore of Long Island. The brothers and their cousin Jeff Glassman worked the stand and took over in their early 20s. After a day at the beach selling hot dogs and hamburgers, the guys would go back to their beach house to barbeque and brew beer. This passion for brewing grew and continued after they gave up the lease on the stand, and in 2009 they launched the Fire Island Beer Company as a tribute to their summertime home.

In the beginning they contracted out the beer to Olde Saratoga Brewing Company, recently moving production of the recipes—all formulated by brewer Tom—to Two Roads Brewing in Stratford, Connecticut. With a focus on sessionable, balanced brews, their year-round offerings are the **Lighthouse Ale** and **Red Wagon IPA,** available on draft and in 12-pack bottles across Long Island, and at locations in Westchester and New York City. The Lighthouse Ale is a slightly sweet Amber Ale,

Red Wagon IPA
Style: American IPA
ABV: 7%
Availability: Year-round

The Red Wagon IPA is named so to recall the car-less lifestyle on Fire Island, whose inhabitants have been known to bring belongings in red wagons. With flavors of floral hops, toasted biscuits, and burnt caramel, this crisp IPA has a medium mouthfeel and pours an amber color with a foamy white head. The beer is balanced with 7 percent ABV and has slight notes of citrus.

with malty flavors and flowery characteristics from the hops, while the Red Wagon IPA is a balanced, crisp brew with notes of bitter hops and subtle caramel. Fire Island recently expanded to produce several seasonal beers, most notable of which is the **Sea Salt Ale,** a Blonde Ale brewed with the addition of Atlantic sea salt. The **Frozen Tail Ale,** a winter warmer, is a blend of five different types of hops and four malts that give the brew caramel and toffee flavors.

Next up, the trio plans to find a permanent location on Long Island. Due to the logistics and the sewer system on Fire Island, building a brewery there wouldn't be feasible. But the beers will remain a tribute to their summertime memories.

GREAT SOUTH BAY BREWERY

25 Drexel Dr., Bay Shore, NY 11706; (631) EZ-AT-GSB; GreatSouthBayBrewery.com; @GreatSouthBay

Founded: 2009 **Founder and Brewer:** Rick Sobotka **Flagship Beer:** Massive IPA
Year-Round Beers: Massive IPA, Blood Orange Pale Ale, Robert Moses Pale Ale, Blonde Ambition Blonde Ale **Seasonals/Special Releases:** Snaggletooth Stout, Splashing

Pumpkin Ale, Kismet Saison, Sleigh Ryed Winter Ale, Hoppocratic Oath Imperial IPA, Great South Bay Lager, Marauder Bourbon Barrel Aged Scotch Ale, Conscious Sedaison Saison, Bayliner Weisse **Tours:** No **Taproom:** Yes

In the growing trend of startup breweries, when Rick Sobotka launched Great South Bay Brewery on Long Island, he had limited space and brewed on a one-barrel system, while the majority of his beer was contracted out, in his case to Kelly Taylor's Greenpoint Beer Works in Brooklyn. In 2012 Sobotka moved his brewery to a new building, upgrading from 2,000 to 39,000 square feet, from 1 barrel to 30. In mid-2013, production of all his beers was out of the new facility, a gutted office building. In early fall-2013, Great South Bay's taproom was completely renovated and a bottling line put into use.

A homebrewer for two decades who learned from his father, Sobotka apprenticed at the San Diego Brewery and has started and maintained his brewery while also working as an anesthesiologist. When he began planning Great South Bay Brewery in 2009, Sobotka asked his friend, former Blue Point brewer Greg Maisch, to come

on board. While looking for their first space, the guys worked out of Sobotka's basement, creating the original Great South Bay lineup of beers, taking influence from American, German, and Belgian styles of brewing.

Great South Bay's beers are incredibly drinkable. Its **Massive IPA,** which took home the Bronze Medal for Best Craft Beer in the state at the 2012 TAP NY Awards, is made in the East Coast IPA style and brewed with two types of malt and Centennial, Simcoe, Cascade, and Chinook hops. The "massive" hop character is provided by a hop-backing technique, where boiling wort is pumped over fresh hops on its way to fermentation. **Blonde Ambition** is an easy-drinking American blonde ale with toasty aromas and flavors, which combine with notes of honey and apricots.

The logo, beer labels, and names for Great South Bay are nautically inspired because of Sobotka's deep love for the water. He lives on the Great South Bay, rents a home on Fire Island in the summer, and enjoys spending time on his boat—and drinking beer.

Beer Lover's Pick

Blood Orange Pale Ale
Style: American Pale Ale with Blood Orange Extract
ABV: 5%
Availability: Year-round, on draft and in 12-oz bottles

There's a certain trepidation when you hear about fruity beers. So many of them are too sweet and unbalanced. Not so with Great South Bay's Blood Orange Pale Ale. Notes of orange are strong and pleasant on the nose, but take a backseat on the palate. Crisp and drinkable, the Blood Orange Pale Ale pours a light orange color and is slightly bitter, with notes of sweet orange on the back end.

Bay Fest

Each year starting in 2013, on the first Saturday of Long Island Craft Beer Week, Great South Bay hosts a Bay Fest kick-off event. The festival showcases beers from all of the Long Island breweries, in addition to many beers from other New York breweries.

GREENPORT HARBOR BREWING COMPANY

234 Carpenter St., Greenport, NY 11944; (631) 477-6681; HarborBrewing.com; @GreenportBrew

Founded: 2009 **Founders:** John Liegley, Rich Vandenburg **Brewer:** DJ Swanson
Flagship Beer: Harbor Pale **Year-Round Beers:** Harbor Pale Ale, Black Duck Porter, Otherside IPA, Hopnami, Gobsmacked IPA **Seasonals/Special Releases:** Summer Ale, Leaf Pile Ale, Anti-Freeze, Canard Noir, Spring Turning Rye Saison, Havre Rouge, Triton, Weesh'd Scotch Ale, Big TIPA, Black IPA, Unsinkable, Ahtamatic IPA, Baltic Porter, Citrus IPA, Chinook'red, Belgian IPA, Hammer and Sickle, Hoppy Stout, Maibock, Old Yenne Cott, Scotch Ale, Supeh Freak, Strong Ryeland **Tours:** No **Taproom:** Yes

While the North Fork of Long Island is well-known as a destination for wineries, Greenport Harbor Brewing has captured the focus of locals as well as tourists visiting the picturesque town on the water near Shelter Island. Founders John Liegley and Rich Vandenburg started the brewery out of an old firehouse just a block off of Main Street.

Brewer DJ Swanson, who at one point was head brewer at the Long Island location of John Harvard's Brewery and Ale House, has created a lineup of flavorful beers that are accessible yet stay true to the innovation of the craft beer community. The flagship **Harbor Pale** uses 30 percent wheat and a blend of Warrior, Glacier, and Cascade hops for a well-balanced and drinkable Pale Ale that weighs in at a manageable 5.3% ABV. Their fall seasonal, **Leaf Pile Ale,** is especially popular in the New

York City area for its balance and restraint, not usually common for a spiced autumn beer, with ginger, cinnamon, allspice, and nutmeg.

The taproom on the second floor of the brewery is nautical themed and overlooks part of Main Street. You can peruse the art that depicts sperm whales or admire the classic harpoon on the wall while you make your way through the brewery tasting. The $8 tasting includes a pint glass and small tastes of all the year-round beers and any specialty or seasonal beers available at the time. Beforehand or when you're done sampling beers, you can walk several blocks through the town of Greenport directly to the water.

The brewery plans to open a larger production facility in nearby Peconic, where large batches will be brewed and bottled. The original location will remain in use for making specialty and limited-release beers.

Black Duck Porter
Style: Porter
ABV: 4.7%
Availability: Year-round

In a craft beer world that witnesses the regular release of Imperial Stouts and Porters, it's refreshing to see a brewer showcase the full flavors of a Porter while keeping the ABV as low as 4.7% so that drinkers can enjoy more than one pint at their leisure. The beer pours black with a beige head. The aroma is sweet with cocoa and vanilla notes, and the flavor emphasizes its malt background with roasted coffee, chocolate, and notes of caramel. It's a great beer for a rainy afternoon or to pair with dessert. In the summer try using the Black Duck Porter for a beer float with vanilla ice cream.

LONG IRELAND BEER COMPANY

817 Pulaski St., Riverhead, NY 11901; (631) 403-4303; LongIrelandBrewing.com; @LongIrelandBeer

Founded: 2009 **Founders:** Dan Burke, Greg Martin **Brewer:** Dan Burke **Flagship Beer:** Celtic Ale **Year-Round Beers:** Celtic Ale, Breakfast Stout, IPA, Pale Ale **Seasonals/ Special Releases:** Raspberry Wheat, Pumpkin Ale, Winter Ale, Summer Ale, Black Friday Russian Imperial Stout, Collaboration Saison, Double India Pale Ale, ESB, Wet Hopped Pale Ale **Tours:** Yes **Taproom:** Yes

Dan Burke and Greg Martin were friends and coworkers who hated their boss. A shared passion for homebrewing, Martin recently recovering from a rare form of bone cancer and losing friends on September 11, and Burke feeling like he needed a new challenge, caused them to strike out on their own. The pair interned for a year

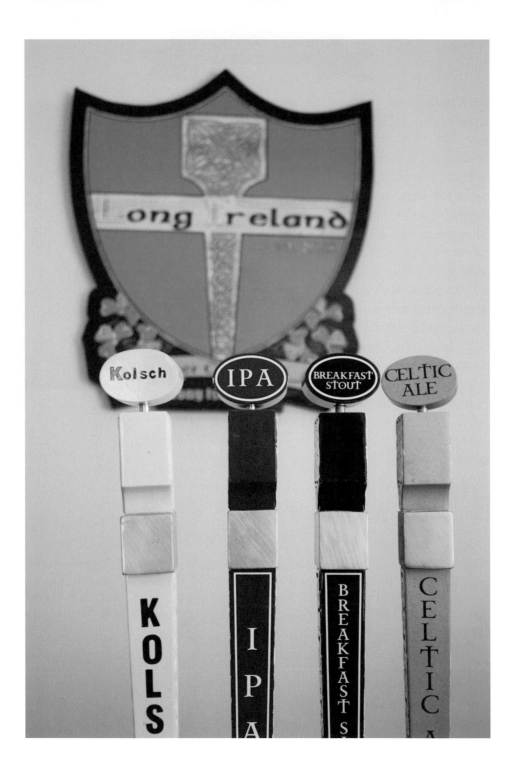

Long Ireland Breakfast Stout
Style: Breakfast Stout
ABV: 3.5%
Availability: Year-round

Sessionable isn't a word you normally associate with Breakfast Stouts. Yet clocking in at 3.5 percent ABV, Long Ireland's version of the style is exactly that. This beer was a happy brewing accident, when Head Brewer Dan Burke looked up a recipe for a Milk Stout, but when he tasted it, found it entirely too sweet. The result was undrinkable, so he decided to add chocolate and coffee in an attempt to experiment before dumping the batch. Long Ireland Breakfast Stout was born. Balanced, and incredibly easy drinking, Breakfast Stout has aromas and flavors of coffee, with a hint of chocolate. The beer is roasty and pours a deep brown color.

at New England Brewing Company, making beer for their friend and brewery owner, Rob Leonard. In 2009 Burke and Martin brewed their first batch of beer, the **Celtic Ale,** as the Long Ireland Beer Company. While neither of them has been to Ireland, they used to listen to the Dropkick Murphys and Flogging Molly while homebrewing. Their logo takes its inspiration from the Burke family crest, to give a feeling that when you drink this beer you're in the family.

Long Ireland beer was first brewed at New England Brewing Company, then contracted through Olde Saratoga Brewing. When Burke and Martin expanded to their current location in 2010, they acquired a 20-barrel system, which they purchased on eBay sight unseen. It turned out to be the very first brewing system Leonard started on at New Haven Brewing Company in 1992. Since 2010 Long Ireland beer has been brewed at the Riverhead brewery.

Burke decided to launch with the Celtic Ale because at the time everyone was making an IPA. The beer was a homebrew recipe and provided an easy transition for anyone who enjoyed Heineken, Amstel, or Budweiser. An Irish Red style beer, Celtic Ale is slightly malty with a hint of caramel sweetness and subtle bitterness. Long Ireland's **ESB** is hop forward, with grassy tastes combining with a caramel malt flavor on the palate. Every year on Black Friday, Long Ireland releases an **Imperial Stout,** and in the fall the brewery produces a **Pumpkin Ale** from fresh pumpkins. In 2013 Long Ireland became a licensed Farm Brewery under new legislation.

MONTAUK BREWING COMPANY
62 South Erie Ave., Montauk, NY 11954; (631) 668-8471; MontaukBrewingCo.com; @Montauk_Brewing
Founded: 2012 **Founders:** Vaughan Cutillo, Eric Moss, Joseph Sullivan **Brewer:** Eric Moss **Flagship and Year-Round Beer:** Driftwood Ale ESB **Seasonals/Special Releases:** The Helmsman Hefeweizen, East Bound Brown Ale, Arrowhead Red, Off Land IPA **Tours:** No **Taproom:** Yes; open Friday through Sunday

When longtime friends Vaughan Cutillo, Eric Moss, and Joseph Sullivan returned to Long Island after college, they began homebrewing together. Former classmates at East Hampton High School, they were inspired by Eric's experience in the Colorado beer scene during his college years. Writing a business plan and starting a brewery seemed a natural next step. Montauk Brewing Company officially launched at the end of June 2012.

To represent their brewery and differentiate it from other breweries on the waterfront, the guys had a logo featuring an arrowhead designed, inspired by an arrowhead artifact a family member had given Cutillo when he was younger. The logo is also a throwback that pays respect to the Montauk Native Americans.

Moss is the lead brewer and formulates all the recipes, though all three often brew together, on their pilot, one-barrel system. The majority of their beers, draft only and distributed on the East End of Long Island, are brewed upstate at Butternuts Beer & Ale. At their tasting room in Downtown Montauk, the team offers up samples and growler fills of their beers. When brainstorming beers to start with and be known for, Moss decided on an ESB to be named **Driftwood Ale,** harkening back to the ubiquitous material found throughout Montauk. Montauk beers aim to be drinkable and accessible, and eventually will incorporate local ingredients.

The team at Montauk Brewing is slowly adding seasonal beers to their lineup, including the **Helmsman,** a wheat-forward Hefeweizen with a banana finish for summer, and a chocolatey, nutty **East Bound Brown Ale** for fall. Licensing for a full brewery in Montauk was approved in mid-2013, and the three brewers will eventually build a seven-barrel brewhouse.

Driftwood Ale
Style: ESB
ABV: 6%
Availability: Year-round

The flagship and year-round offering from Montauk Brewing Company pours a light amber color. On the nose, this ESB has aromas of malt and herbal hops. Tastes of caramel and malt combine with herbal notes and a slight hop bitterness in this medium-bodied brew. Many of Montauk's beers are inspired by its namesake town, and this is no exception. Driftwood is often found on the sandy beaches.

Long Island

OYSTER BAY BREWING COMPANY

76 South St., Oyster Bay, NY 11771; OysterBayBrewing.com; @OysterBayBrewin
Founded: 2013 **Founders and Brewers:** Gabe Haim, Ryan Schlotter **Flagship Beer:** IPA **Other Beers:** IPA, Wheat, Amber Ale, Stout and Raspberry Wheat **Tours:** No **Taproom:** Yes

Friends and coworkers at Rallye BMW in Westbury, Gabe Haim and Ryan Schlotter were looking for a business to start together. When they came up with the idea for a brewery, they knew it was the right way to go and began homebrewing together and thinking about where to establish the business. Longtime residents of Long Island, Haim and Schlotter knew Oyster Bay was the perfect location for them because it has a rich history and attraction. Teddy Roosevelt's estate Sagamore Hill is about a mile from the brewery, and Billy Joel is a well-known resident of the town. It's also a seaside clamming and oyster village.

Located in a former Mexican restaurant and sharing a building and address with a baseball-card shop, Oyster Bay Brewing Company operates on a three-barrel system in a room big enough for expansion. Two walls that face outdoors are covered with windows, providing a bright, open space that fits the custom bar and brewery, which visitors can see while enjoying the beers.

Haim and Schlotter launched in 2013 after two years of planning, with an **IPA** and an **Amber Ale.** It's important to them to make drinkable, approachable beers that will appeal to a wide array of people. The IPA is balanced with a nice floral character in the nose from the hops, while the Amber is easy drinking, with a bit of a bite on the back end and some notes of coffee and toast.

The brews are available for sampling and growler fills at the Oyster Bay location, and will eventually be seen in bars and restaurants on Long Island's Gold Coast.

IPA
Style: IPA
ABV: 9%
Availability: Year-round
The IPA from Oyster Bay Brewing Company is one of the brewery's first two offerings. With a hop-forward floral aroma, this IPA has flavors of citrus and pine on the palate, with resin on the finish. This fresh brew would make a good companion to seafood and salads you're bound to see in the harbor town on Long Island's north shore.

PORT JEFF BREWING COMPANY

22 Mill Creek Rd., Port Jefferson, NY 11777; (877) 475-2739; PortJeffBrewing.com; @portjeffbrewing
Founded: 2011 **Founder and Brewer:** Mike Philbrick **Flagship Beer:** Schooner Ale
Year-Round Beers: Schooner Ale, Port Jeff Porter, Low Tide Black IPA **Seasonals/Special Releases:** Boo Brew, Whites Beach Wit, Dead's Ryes Ryes-N-Bock, Runaway Smoked Ferry Imperial IPA, H3 (Trippel H), Starboard Oatmeal Stout (SOS) **Tours:** Yes; Saturday 12 to 4 p.m. **Taproom:** Yes

Among the recent boom in Long Island breweries since 2010, Port Jeff Brewing Company is a prime example of local brewers tapping into their community culture while giving an American twist to classic styles. Brewmaster Mike Philbrick started Port Jeff after homebrewing for 10 years and graduating from the World Brewing Academy at Siebel Institute in Chicago.

Port Jeff Brewing's nautical theme fits perfectly within the bustling town of Port Jefferson on the northern shore of Long Island. The bar in the small taproom is made to look like the front of a boat, and the large windows look onto the sparkling, custom-made brewhouse. Drinkers can taste samples of the eight beers on tap or buy bottles and growlers to take home.

The beers run a full range of popular styles spanning roasty Stouts to bitter IPAs. The seven-barrel brewhouse produces three year-round beers, four seasonals, and a few special-release beers during the year. Port Jeff beer can be found at bars, restaurants, and stores throughout Long Island and in select locations in New York City and Westchester County.

The slightly sweet **Starboard Oatmeal Stout** pours inky black and is brewed with flaked oats, brown sugar, and raisins but still has a manageable 5.4% ABV. Their **Low Tide Black IPA** combines Black Patent malt, Citra hops, and a bit of sea salt for a well-rounded version of the popular style with a combination of grapefruit and dark chocolate. The **Port Jeff Porter,** which is brewed to be a traditional example of the style, is sweetened with local organic honey. Made with Maris Otter, Black Patent, Caramel, and Chocolate malts, along with Fuggles and Northdown hops, the Porter is smooth and dark.

Schooner Ale
Style: English-style Pale Ale
ABV: 6.5%
Availability: Year-round, on
draft or in 22-ounce bottles

Schooner Ale, a nicely balanced
beer that is easy to pair with
food, won the silver medal at
the 2012 US Open Beer Championship. The light amber beer
brings British and American Pale
Ale styles together with the use
of Maris Otter malt for a biscuity
backbone that is balanced out
by citrus aroma from Columbus
hops and the earthy bitterness
of Kent Golding hops. Schooner
Ale is continuously hopped dur-
ing its boil and dry hopped throughout fermentation.

ROCKY POINT ARTISAN BREWERS

56 Hallock Landing Rd., Rocky Point, NY 11778; (631) 848-2261; Beer.DonovanHall.net;
@theangler
Founded: 2012 **Founders:** Donavan Hall, Mike Voigt **Brewers:** Donavan Hall, Mike
Voigt, Yuri Janssen **Year-Round Beers:** Hefeweizen, Pilsner, Calypso Red Saison, Altbier
Seasonals/Special Releases: Belgian Wheat, Edel-Hell Maibock, Irish Porter, Irish Red,
Cimarron, Erta Ale, Doppel Bock, Winter Warmer Ale, Ardennes Tripel, Oktoberfest, Doppel
Schwarz, Oktoberweisse, June Bock **Tours:** No **Taproom:** No, but samples are available at
the Rocky Point Farmers Market, open Sunday

Mike Voigt and Donavan Hall are longtime homebrewers who began making
beer together in 2006. Because they felt theirs was better than the average
brew, the pair brought on fellow homebrewer Yuri Janssen and built a nanobrewery
in Voigt's late father's home. They decided to calculate how much money each of

Altbier
Style: Altbier
ABV: 4.8%
Availability: Limited

Rocky Point's Altbier pours an amber color and has aromas of toast and malt. Made in the traditional German style, the beer is fermented with ale yeast. Clean and crisp, malty and fruity flavors mingle on the palate. Alt in the name means "old" in German and refers to the old method of brewing.

them spent on beer each month, which worked out to $200 to $300. They vowed to drink their own beer instead and pool the savings for brewing equipment.

Unlike many start-up breweries, Rocky Point plans to stay small and always brew on a nano scale, with a 1.5-barrel capacity. The word *artisan* in the name is meant to indicate to others that the beer is handcrafted, with each batch turning out a little differently than the last. Rocky Point doesn't have a flagship, because the team doesn't want to pigeonhole the brewery into being known for only one thing. They lean toward Belgian and German styles, but will also make Porters. The bottom line: Voigt, Hall, and Janssen brew what they like to drink and what they're proud of. Their **Pilsner,** one of only several year-round offerings, puts a spin on a traditional Bavarian-style recipe, with hoppy, malty flavors and an effervescent mouthfeel. The Maibock, a Bock beer released each May, goes by the name **Edel-Hell** to refer to the noble hops (*Edel* means "noble" in German) that give the beer a distinct hop bitterness. The brewers release an **Irish Porter** for St. Patrick's Day, which is dark, roasty, and sweet with a subtle bitterness.

Rocky Point beers are available in draft form only at select restaurants and beer stores on Long Island. The trio is on hand every Sunday at the Rocky Point Farmers' Market, which they currently dub the "tasting room," while they look for a space to build a proper taproom in Rocky Point's business district.

SOUTHAMPTON PUBLICK HOUSE

40 Bowden Sq., Southampton, NY 11968; (631) 283-2800; Publick.com; @SPH40
Founded: 1996 **Founder:** Don Sullivan **Brewer:** Evan Addario **Flagship Beer:** Double
White **Year-Round Beers:** Burton India Pale Ale, Keller Pils, Southampton Double
White, Altbier, Montauk Light, Grand Cru, Saison Deluxe, Cuvee des Flowers, Abbot 12
Seasonals/Special Releases: Pumpkin Ale, Imperial Porter, Biere De Mars, Russian
Imperial Stout **Tours:** No **Taproom:** Yes

Among the oldest of Long Island's breweries, Southampton Publick House made
a name for itself under former brewmaster Phil Markowski (now brewmaster at
Two Roads Brewing in Connecticut). The beers focused on European styles like the
earthy and bitter **English Burton IPA** or the malty but balanced **Altbier,** a German
style that isn't often seen on this side of the Atlantic. Evan Addario, Markowski's
apprentice for eight years and an engineer by training, took over in 2012 and has
continued his mentor's tradition.

In addition to beers offered in standard 12-ounce bottles, the brewery also
brews several beers in 750-milliliter large-bottle format. Most are the brewery's take

Double White
Style: Witbier
ABV: 6.7%
Availability: Year-round, on draft and
    in bottles

Among Southampton Pulick Houses's
most popular beers is the slightly
sweet and effervescent Double White.
A bigger, more flavorful version of
the ubiquitous unfiltered Belgian Wit
style, the Double White is brewed with
the classic orange peel and coriander
for a citrusy aroma and slight spice in
the taste. The spice and citrus are enough to balance out the sweet creaminess from
the wheat. The beer is available year-round but is among the best Long Island beers
to enjoy during summer months.

on Belgian styles. **Abbot 12** is a Belgian Quadrupel style with strong flavors of dark
fruit like figs and grapes and an assertive effervescence from bottle conditioning
to help balance out the sweetness. Clocking in at 10.5% ABV, the brewery suggests
Abbot 12 as an after-dinner beer. Southampton brings a strong floral aroma to its
Saison Cuvee des Fleurs by adding lavender, chamomile, calendula, and rose hips.
The result is a clever surprise for the copper-colored Saison and a great spring and
summer beer.

The beers served at Publick House itself are brewed at its Southampton location,
while the beers distributed are brewed off-site. Southampton's beers find themselves
throughout Long Island and New York City. The brewery is in the process of moving
their operation from Olde Saratoga to a new facility in Pennsylvania.

Publick House itself is large, with separate bar and restaurant areas. There is
a large outdoor space with a porch and lawn for enjoying your brew outside. The
menu is mostly made up of pub food—sandwiches, wings, and salads. The brewpub is
located within walking distance from Downtown Southampton. After a day of shop-
ping in the posh town, you could stop in for a round of fresh beers.

SPIDER BITE BEER COMPANY

920 Lincoln Ave., Holbrook, NY 11741; (631) 942-3255; SpiderBiteBeer.com;
@SpiderBiteBeer
Founded: 2008 **Founders:** Larry Goldstein, Anthony LiCausi **Brewer:** Larry Goldstein
Flagship Beer: First Bite Pale Ale **Year-Round Beers:** First Bite Pale Ale, Eight Legged
RyePA, Eye Be Use Imperial IPA **Seasonals/Special Releases:** White Bite Wheat Ale,
Boris the Spider Russian Imperial Stout **Tours:** No **Taproom:** No

Friends and neighbors Larry Goldstein and Anthony LiCausi incorporated Spider Bite Beer Company in 2008 and released their first beer, **First Bite Pale Ale,** in November 2011. Goldstein had been passionate about craft beer and homebrewed for almost two decades. While the two brewed together in LiCausi's driveway, they experienced too many bug bites, which lead to their brewery name. Most of the beers are named along the spider theme. Just a year after its launch, Spider Bite received the F.X. Matt Memorial Cup for Best Brewery in New York at the TAP NY festival.

Goldstein and LiCausi only brew beers that they like to drink, which lean toward the hoppy side, and many of them are big in terms of alcohol content. Their Russian

Beer Lover's Pick

White Bite Wheat Ale
Style: American Wheat
ABV: 4.5%
Availability: Summer
White Bite Wheat Ale is Spider
Bite's summer seasonal offering. Crisp, light, and refreshing,
White Bite is brewed with about
50 percent wheat malt. Coriander, lemon, and pepper compliment toasty flavors. It's a great
beer to enjoy while lounging
on a patio or beach during the
summer—of course while avoid-
ing those pesky spiders.

Imperial Stout, **Boris the Spider,** clocks in at 10 percent ABV and is a tasty example of the style. Very dark, almost black in color, Boris the Spider has notes of chocolate, coffee, and licorice on the palate, with hints of sweetness. Spider Bite's Rye beer, **Eight Legged RyePA,** has bold flavors of pine, cracked pepper, and bitter hops.

Since they launched, Goldstein and LiCausi have contracted their beer out to Cooperstown Brewing Company on its 20-barrel system in Milford, New York. Spider Bite currently doesn't have a public location, but the pair hopes to soon open a pilot brewery and tasting room. Its beers are available on draft and in bottles on Long Island, in Manhattan and Brooklyn, and throughout Westchester

Brewpubs

BLACK FOREST BREW HAUS

2015 New Hwy., Farmingdale, NY 11735; (631) 391-9500; BlackForestBrewHaus.com
Founded: 1998 **Founder:** Privatbrauerei Hoepfner of Karlsrue, Germany **Brewer:** Joseph
Hayes **Year-Round Beers:** Pilsner, Hefe-Weizen, Helles, Amber, Rye Steam **Tours:** No
Taproom: Yes

Located in an industrial section of Farmingdale, you may not have high hopes when observing the old, plain exterior of Black Forest Brew Haus. However, when you sit and read through a menu, you'll find that this Long Island brewpub was actually opened by a German brewery, Privatbrauerei Hoepfner, located in Karlsrue. The "mother" brewery, operating since 1798, shares all knowledge and expertise with Black Forest, including recipes and equipment.

The beers are—you guessed it—German styles, made by Brewmaster Joseph Hayes, who graduated from the brewing program at UC Davis, and worked at a German-themed brewpub while there. In 2006 the **Amber Lager** won the F.X. Matt Memorial Cup at TAP NY for Best Beer in New York State. An Oktoberfest-style Lager, the Amber pours a red color with a beige head. Malt sweetness is the primary aroma, with toffee and caramel flavors following in the taste. Some light hop character balances the beer out and keeps it from being too sweet.

The menu is full of authentic German dishes like Weiner schnitzel, sauerbraten, goulash, and spaetzle. You'll even find some dishes made with beer, such as the Lager Fondue, made from a blend of cheeses and the Amber Lager, served with homemade pretzels. Beer-battered chicken tenders and beer-battered onion rings are also available.

BRICKHOUSE BREWERY AND RESTAURANT

67 W Main St., Patchogue, NY 11772; (631) 447-2337; BrickhouseBrewery.com; @BHBBrickBrew
Founded: 1996 **Founders:** Thomas Keegan, George Hoag, Jim McPeak **Brewer:** Charles Noll **Year-Round Beers:** Street Light, Hurricane Kitty, Nitro Boom Stout, Boy's Red **Seasonals/Special Releases:** Beowulf IPA, Mother Chugga, Anarchy, Smokin Betty, May Bock, 21 Club, Pale Ryder, Main Street Coffee Porter **Tours:** No **Taproom:** Yes

The city of Patchogue has fast become a craft beer destination on Long Island, with the recent influx of businesses on Main Street. But before Hoptron Brewtique or BOBBiQUE, there was BrickHouse Brewery and Restaurant, started by George Hoag, Jim McPeak, and Thomas Keegan (father of Tom Keegan, founder and brewer of Keegan Ales in Kingston, New York). As you might expect, the building is made of red brick. The brewery's equipment sits right in the front window, giving everyone a look before making their way to their seats. Inside the brewpub you'll find dim lighting, chalkboard beer lists, and a long wooden bar.

Brewmaster Charles Noll brews a wide variety of beers that are meant to pair up with the food menu. Their maltier beers like **Boy's Red,** a Red Ale, and **Mother Chugga,** an Amber Lager, are easily accessible beers that go well with the sandwiches at the restaurant. If you like Medieval references and hops, look out for their **Beowulf IPA,** an English-styled IPA that packs a punch with a 7% ABV and **Grendel,** an Imperial IPA weighing in at 9% ABV.

Out back the brewpub has a patio with plenty of seating, lined by a hop garden. In the late summer you can bask in the sun and admire the growth of the hop bines. The hops even find their way into their brew kettle, so watch for some of their beers

brewed with their homegrown ingredients. The full food menu includes salads, sandwiches, pastas, and pizzas.

JOHN HARVARD'S BREWERY AND ALE HOUSE

2093 Smithhaven Plaza, Lake Grove, NY 11755; (631) 979-2739; JohnHarvards.com; @JohnHarvards

Opened: 1997 **Brewer:** David Deturris **Beers:** Mo'Bay Stout, Nut Brown Ale, John Harvard's Pale Ale, Atomic Espresso Stout, Oktoberfest Lager, Strawberry Wheat, Dunkelweizen, Weizen Bock. Pinstripe Porter, Red Ale, Pumpkin Ale, 'Ohana Coconut Brown Ale, Long Island Light, Vienna Lager, Altbier, Black Hole IPA, Amarillo Anonymous, Kattenstoet Tripel, Kolsch **Tours:** No **Taproom:** Yes

John Harvard's Brewery and Ale House in Lake Grove opened in 1997 as part of the Cambridge, Massachusetts–based chain that has locations in several states across the northeast. This is not a cookie-cutter brewery pumping out the same exact beers as the original, however. The beers are brewed on-site and each brewer has creative license with recipes. This keeps each location unique and tied to their locale.

The beers at the Lake Grove John Harvard's, brewed by David Deturris, are a mix of styles that are easy to pair with classic American dishes. German styles like the **Alt,** a hybrid of an Ale and Lager, and **Southern Belle,** a honey Ale brewed with Columbus hops, are approachable for novice beer drinkers and interesting enough for longtime beer lovers to enjoy. The **Pumpkin Ale** brewed seasonally for the fall is the most popular and served in glasses rimmed with cinnamon sugar.

Deturris does get a chance to do some experimentation with beers like **'Ohana,** a coconut brown Ale he brewed in early 2013. The food menu is focused on American pub food like chicken potpie and burgers. The pizzas are made with the spent grain from the brewing process.

Beer Bars

THE BLACK SHEEP ALE HOUSE

78 2nd St., Mineola, NY 11501; (516) 307-1280; BlackSheepAleHouse.com;
@BlackSheepAH
Draft Beers: 25 on tap, 1 on cask **Bottled/Canned Beers:** Over 75

Located a short walk from the Mineola Long Island Rail Road Station, the Black Sheep Ale House serves up some of Long Island's best beers. Owner Vince Minutella, who ran the bar when it was known as Donnelly's, changed the name to The Black Sheep Ale House in an attempt to make the bar more personal for drinkers. The atmosphere and beer list appeal to craft beer fans and non-craft beer fans alike.

While you can find beer from all over the country, local breweries like Barrier, Port Jeff, and Blue Point are regulars on the tap list. The bottle list also features rare beers from New York brewers like Hops N' Roses from Captain Lawrence, along with European classics like the Trappist Rochefort and the Yorkshire Brewer Samuel Smith. The bar also took a lead role in Long Island Craft Beer Week and hosts regular events with brewers. Free hot dogs are available to help you sop up your beer.

BOBBIQUE

70 W Main St., Patchogue, NY 11772; (631) 447-7744; Bobbique.com; @Bobbique
Draft Beers: 12 **Bottled/Canned Beers:** Over 50

Beer and barbecue is a classic combination but BOBBiQUE takes it to another level. Award-winning Chef and Owner Eric Rifkin was inspired to start an "authentic pit barbeque" after coming home from a trip to Memphis, Tennessee. In 2006 Rifkin opened BOBBiQUE to combine his passions for southern-style barbecue, blues, bourbon, and beer. He named his new temple of barbeque after his daughter Bobbi.

While many barbecue places stick to standard macro adjunct Lagers, BOBBiQUE offers a long list of American craft beer. Well-known breweries like Stone, Anchor, Rogue, and Sierra Nevada make up a significant portion of the list, along with regional breweries like Brooklyn, Victory, and Tröegs. Long Island brewers like Rocky Point, Blue Point, and Spider Bite also appear on the list.

The beers are the perfect pairing for classic barbecue like St. Louis–style ribs, Memphis-style pulled pork, and chopped brisket. Blues bands perform several nights a week, usually starting around 9 p.m. While walking down Main Street in Patchogue, you'll know you're getting close to BOBBiQUE—you can smell the mouthwatering barbeque from a block away.

THE CORTLAND
27 W. Main St., Bay Shore, NY 11760; (631) 206-2220; TheCortland.com; @TheCortland
Draft Beers: 4 **Bottled/Canned Beers:** Over 30

Usually a couple of local beers on tap are enough for a bar to get a reputation for supporting local brewers. The Cortland in Bay Shore takes things a step further by only serving beers from New York State. There are so many great beers in the state, definitely enough to sufficiently fill a high-quality beer list.

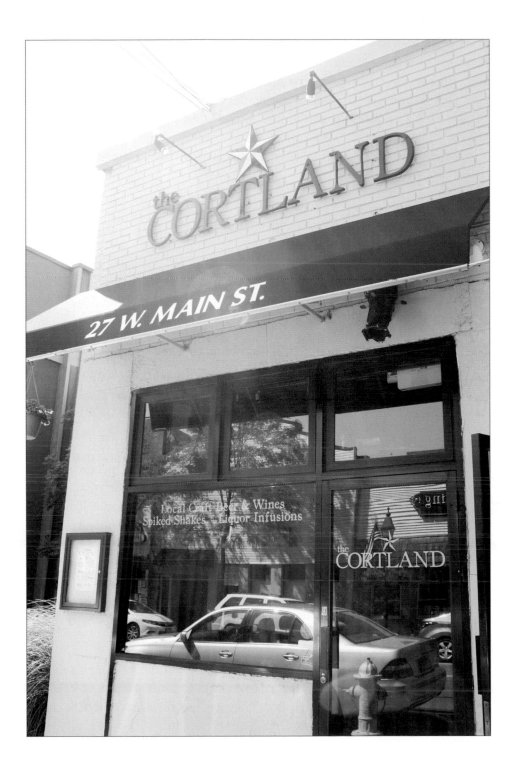

This focus on New York beers makes The Cortland stand out in a town that is fast becoming a craft beer destination for Long Island. There are only four taps, but they keep drinkable beers like Bronx Pale Ale and Barrier Caddywompus on rotation. The bottle list features several large-format bottles from Brooklyn and Ommegang. The bar also has a slew of smaller bottles from Ithaca, Blue Point, and Captain Lawrence, and cans from Butternuts and Sixpoint.

The food menu offers fun takes on classic pub food like smoked Gouda mac n' cheese and soy chili wings.

CROXLEY'S ALE HOUSE
129 New Hyde Park Rd., Franklin Square, NY 11010; (516) 526-9542; Croxley.com
Draft Beers: 60 **Bottled/Canned Beers:** 50

With five locations, four of which are on Long Island, and a sixth in Brooklyn in planning, Croxley's Ale House is a fixture on the Long Island beer scene. Started in 1992 by friends Jeff Piciullo and Chris Werle in Franklin Square on New Hyde Park Road, the original Croxley's has expanded from 18 to 60 draft lines and proudly declares "Brands we do not carry: Bud, Coors, Miller."

As you might expect with 60 draft lines, the beer list is eclectic with brews from all over the country. Classic craft beers like Brooklyn Lager and Harpoon IPA are regulars. but the list also includes unique beers from brewers like Dogfish Head and a large number of British beers such as Belhaven, Boddington's, and Newcastle. The bottle list is also deep and full of special beers in 22-ounce and 750-milliliter bottles. When the sixth location opens in Brooklyn, it is expected to bring the total tap lines across all Croxley's bars to 344, including the staggering 80 at the Smithtown location.

The original Croxley's in Franklin Square serves American classics like potpie and meatloaf. The 10-cent wing specials are particularly well-known and available at the other locations. The other locations are focused on particular styles and cuisines. Smithtown has a German theme in both beer and food.

THE GOOD LIFE
1039 Park Blvd., Massapequa Park, NY 11762; (516) 798-4663; TheGoodLifeNY.com
Draft Beers: 24 **Bottled/Canned Beers:** Over 70

Opened in 2010 by Peter Mangouranes and brothers Paul and Anthony Olivia, The Good Life in Massapequa Park took home the 2013 Golden Tap Award for Best Beer Bar in Nassau County. Its doorway, constructed to resemble a life-size classic red London phone booth, recalls an English-style pub.

The bar and restaurant space is large, with a spacious bar area, big round tables in the dining area, and even a room for events. The 24 taps serve beers from many different breweries, such as Oskar Blues and Dogfish Head to Gulden Draak and Wynchwood. You'll find some more traditional British beers on the bottle and can list from Boddington's, Innis & Gunn, and Samuel Smith, to name a few.

A fun and comfortable atmosphere and good service make The Good Life a great place to drink, eat, or hang out. The large food menu features both pub food and entrees that add to the English-pub theme, such as Olde English clam chowder pot-pie, Shepard's pie, fish-and-chips, and bangers and mash. If you're not into classic English dishes, there are plenty of other options, like burgers, skirt steak, chicken tikka masala, seared tuna, and cold and hot sandwiches. On the second Tuesday of every month the restaurant used to host a four-course beer dinner showcasing a brewery for $40, which have been moved to Jam, The Good Life's sister restaurant.

HOPTRON BREWTIQUE

22 West Main St., Patchogue, NY 11772; (631) 438-0296; HoptronBrewtique.com; @HoptronBrewtq
Draft Beers: 16 **Bottled/Canned Beers:** Over 290

Great beer towns need a great bottle shop, and Hoptron Brewtique is an awesome bottle shop. Owners Amanda Danielsen and Sue Elizabeth opened on Main Street in November 2012 and have since been offering a large and well-curated selection of bottled and canned craft beer with a local focus.

Danielsen and Elizabeth run the store with an eye toward educating new craft beer drinkers and making great beer accessible without an atmosphere of snobbery. They have succeeded with a friendly staff, regular live music, and Home Brew 101 classes. It's a huge shop with ample table space. While sitting and enjoying a beer, you can ogle the giant selection of bottles and cans.

Painted on one wall, a brightly colored map of Long Island features each brewery's logo on its geographical location. Usually these breweries occupy half of the 16 taps. They are also featured heavily in the bottle selection, where you can find some of Long Island's most popular beers, like Blind Bat's Long Island Potato Stout, Barrier's special releases, and Southampton's Saison. Draft beers are available as growlers to go, pints to stay and enjoy, and flights to be paired with cheese, popcorn and pretzels. When you walk in the door of Hoptron, you'll find a display of a good amount of home-brewing equipment.

THE LARK PUB AND GRUB

93 Larkfield Rd., East Northport, NY 11731; (631) 262-9700; TheLarkPubAndGrub.com
Draft Beers: 20 **Bottled/Canned Beers:** 50

Northport is a small town, but it is home to two Long Island craft beer destinations: Karp's Homebrew Shop and The Lark Pub and Grub, just down the road from each other. If you're heading to Karp's for home brew supplies, don't skip out on grabbing a pint or two at The Lark.

Long and narrow, The Lark is a vibrant beer bar, with over 70 craft selections available on tap and in bottles. You'll find the draft list on a chalkboard over the bar, proudly displaying offerings from Southern Tier, Oskar Blues, and Dogfish Head. Local brewers keep a sizeable presence on the tap list with beers from Greenport, Spider Bite, and Fire Island.

Usual pub dishes are featured on the food menu, with nachos and quesadillas for appetizers and burgers and pizzas making up most of the main courses. You'll also find some unique options like mashed potato egg rolls, Thanksgiving egg rolls, and a variety of mac and cheeses. Every Wednesday night you can play trivia while enjoying your fine craft beer.

TAP AND BARREL

550 Smithtown Bypass, Smithtown, NY 11787; (631) 780-5474; 52Taps.com; @Tap_and_Barrel
Draft Beers: 52 **Bottled/Canned Beers:** Over 70

When you walk into Tap and Barrel in Smithtown, you immediately realize you're going to have a hard time choosing what to drink. Tap handles run the length of the bar, and the list is split up on two chalkboards, full of great beers. It can be overwhelming.

Established American craft brewers including Dogfish Head and Firestone Walker can usually be found along with local Long Island breweries like Port Jeff and Spider Bite. Tap and Barrel is also one of the locations to carry beer from Rocky Point Brewing Company, a tiny nanobrewery in Rocky Point. European classics such as Gaffel Kolsch and Hofbrau Original, and even sour beers like Boon Kreik and Petrus Aged Pale, can also be found on the list.

While the tap list is definitely the star of the show at Tap and Barrel, the bottle and can lists are impressive as well, featuring some of the most highly sought-after beers. You might see cans of Alchemist Heady Topper and large bottles of sour beers from Cascade Brewing and The Bruery. While drinking your beers you can play some classic arcade games or shoot some pool.

THE TAP ROOM

114 W Main St., Patchogue, NY 11772; (631) 569-5577; TheTapRoomLI.com
Draft Beers: 28 **Bottled/Canned Beers:** 20

The Tap Room is an integral part of the thriving beer scene in Patchogue. Just down the street from Hoptron Brewtique, BOBBiQUE, and BrickHouse Brewery and Restaurant, The Tap Room is focused on a high-quality draft list and getting local beer into the hands of Long Islanders.

Beers from nearby Blue Point are regularly on the list, as are beers from other Long Island brewers, including Montauk Brewing Company and Port Jeff Brewing Company. To entice more drinkers to pick Long Island beers, the bar runs half-off Long Island taps on Monday. For those not looking for local beers, The Tap Room also offers brews from Allagash, Chimay, and Victory, to name a few.

The bar has also established itself as one of the best spots for watching soccer while enjoying a pint. Matches are projected onto a screen that is lowered down from the ceiling on game days. The bar publishes the schedule of games it will show on its website. The kitchen, which mostly serves bar food like sandwiches and burgers, stays open at least until midnight and even 3 a.m. on Friday and Saturday nights. During happy hour, Monday through Friday 4 to 7 p.m., Mussels are $5 (normally $10).

T.J. FINLEY'S PUBLIC HOUSE

42 E Main St., Bay Shore, NY 11706; (631) 647-4856; TJFinleys.com; @TJFINLEYS
Draft Beers: 26 on tap, 1 on cask **Bottled/Canned Beers:** Over 50

Sure, you like to visit your local bar and enjoy a few pints of beer poured by your friendly bartender. But what about pouring your own? At T.J. Finley's Public House, a few tables on the side of the bar and near the door have their own tap lines, so you could pour your own.

A comfortable local bar with a steady stream of patrons, a wood interior, and sports on the several large-screen TVs, T.J. Finley's took home the Suffolk County Best Bar on Long Island Award at the annual Golden Tap Awards during Long Island Craft Beer Week in 2012 and also in 2013.

Long Island brewers including Montauk and Great South Bay take up the majority of the tap lines alongside some of New York City's most popular brewers like The Bronx Brewery and SingleCut Beersmiths. The staff is friendly, and behind the bar there is a helpful electronic draft list that offers suggestions for beers based on popular macro beers like Blue Moon and Coors Light.

The food is mostly classic pub fare with a menu full of sandwiches, burgers, and wings to feed the raucous crowds watching NFL games on Sunday. The bar's beer club recognizes patrons who have made it to 100 beers with an engraving on the wall and 50 percent off pints on Wednesday night.

Pub Crawl

Patchogue

Home to BrickHouse Brewery and Restaurant since 1996 and Blue Point Brewery since 1998, Patchogue has long been a craft beer destination. But in recent years a spate of new hot spots moved in; most are within a few blocks from each other. A pub crawl is a great way to see multiple places in one day and allows you to do so safely, as long as you walk, take a cab, or find someone willing to be your designated driver.

Blue Point Brewing Company, 161 River Ave., Patchogue, NY 11772; (631) 475-6944; BluePointBrewing.com

Blue Point Brewing Company is housed in an old ice factory and has been pumping out some of Long Island's most popular beer for over 15 years. Oddly the taproom doesn't get as crowded as you might expect, so it is a good spot to get started on a weekend beer excursion, with a pint of fresh Toasted Lager or White IPA.

Hoptron Brewtique, 22 West Main St., Patchogue, NY 11772; (631) 438-0296; HoptronBrewtique.com

A 2-minute drive or 15-minute walk from Blue Point Brewery is bottle shop/bar/home brew shop Hoptron Brewtique. If that special bottle you just have to have isn't here, you probably can't get it on Long Island. The awesome shop also has a bar with 16 taps, about half of which are from local brewers. The bartenders are happy to help with your selections, and you might even catch some live music. Snack on a cheese plate or a pretzel.

BrickHouse Brewery, 67 W. Main St., Patchogue, NY 11772; (631) 447-2337; BrickHouseBrewery.com

Walk across and down Main Street a bit to find BrickHouse, a brewery and restaurant that sits a cut above most of its kind from the 1990s, keeping a tap list of balanced but interesting house beers. Try to get a seat on the patio out back that is surrounded by hop plants in the summer. The snacks and foods are good here, but if you can hold out a little while longer, the mouthwatering smell that permeates the air outside is actually from your next stop.

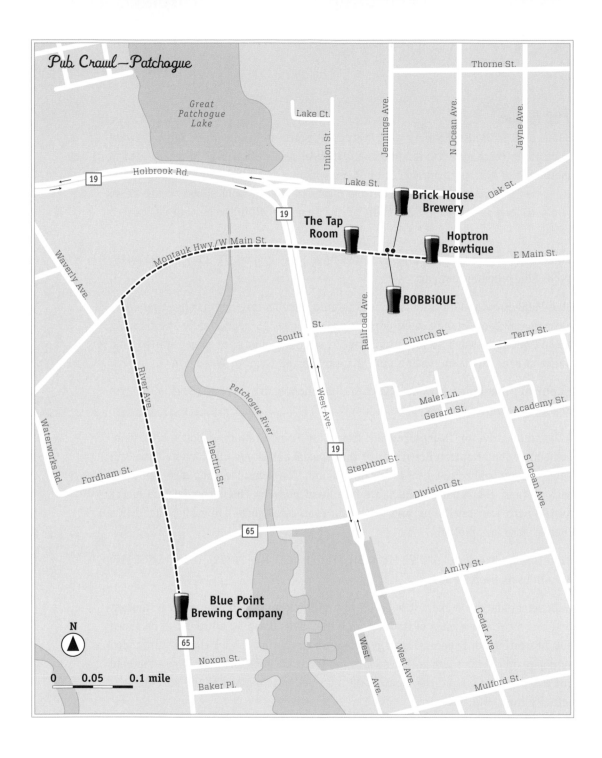

Pub Crawl—Patchogue

Great Patchogue Lake

Thorne St.

Lake Ct.

Union St.

Jennings Ave.

N Ocean Ave.

Jayne Ave.

19   Holbrook Rd.

Lake St.

Oak St.

19

Brick House Brewery

The Tap Room

Hoptron Brewtique

E Main St.

Montauk Hwy./W Main St.

BOBBiQUE

Waverly Ave.

Railroad Ave.

South   St.

Church St.

Terry St.

River Ave.

West Ave.

Maler Ln.

Gerard St.

Academy St.

Patchogue River

Electric St.

S Ocean Ave.

Waterworks Rd.

Fordham St.

19

Stephton St.

Division St.

65

Amity St.

Cedar Ave.

Blue Point Brewing Company

65

Noxon St.

West   Ave.

West Ave.

Mulford St.

Baker Pl.

N

0   0.05   0.1 mile

BOBBiQUE, 70 West Main St., Patchogue, NY 11772; (631) 447-7744; Bobbique.com

Across the street from BrickHouse, sit down and relax at BOBBiQUE for some barbeque from award-winner Chef Eric Rifkin and live music with your beers. If you're looking for something from one of the smaller local brewers, you'll find beers from Spider Bite or Rocky Point.

The Tap Room, 114 W. Main St., Patchogue, NY 11772; (631) 569-5577; TheTapRoomLI .com

The Tap Room, a minute's walk down Main Street from BOBBiQUE, keeps a great tap list with 28 beers, most of which are local. But the biggest reason to end here is the kitchen that stays open to 3 a.m. on Friday and Saturday nights. If you are a soccer fan, you can switch this stop to earlier in the day and take in a match.

Long Island

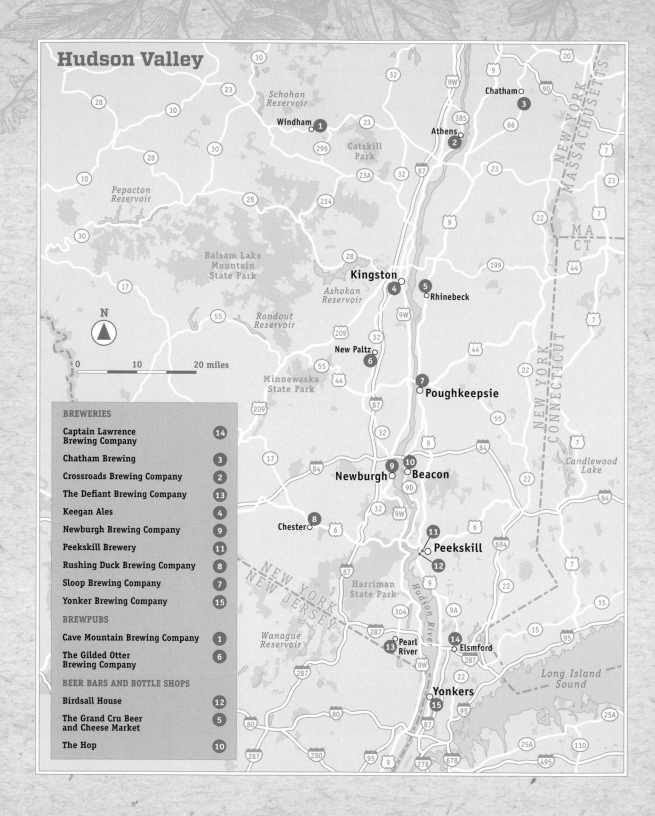

Hudson Valley

BREWERIES

Captain Lawrence Brewing Company	14
Chatham Brewing	3
Crossroads Brewing Company	2
The Defiant Brewing Company	13
Keegan Ales	4
Newburgh Brewing Company	9
Peekskill Brewery	11
Rushing Duck Brewing Company	8
Sloop Brewing Company	7
Yonker Brewing Company	15

BREWPUBS

Cave Mountain Brewing Company	1
The Gilded Otter Brewing Company	6

BEER BARS AND BOTTLE SHOPS

Birdsall House	12
The Grand Cru Beer and Cheese Market	5
The Hop	10

Hudson Valley

There's a sense of collaboration and pride among brewers in the Hudson Valley, perhaps more than any in other region of the state. Whether ordering supplies together for better rates or holding cross-promotional events, the Hudson Valley brewers seize opportunities to help each other and make the region's craft beer community stronger. With easy access to both New York City and locally produced agriculture, the region has enormous potential. The slow but steady resurgence of hop farming in the area can give breweries the opportunity to brew even more local character into their beers, and some brewers are already taking advantage.

The Hudson Valley also has some excellent and curated beer bottle shops with The Hop in Beacon and The Grand Cru Beer and Cheese Market in Rhinebeck.

Breweries

CAPTAIN LAWRENCE BREWING COMPANY

444 Saw Mill River Rd., Elmsford, NY 10523; (914) 741-2337; CaptainLawrenceBrewing
.com; @CptLawrenceBeer

Founded: 2006 **Founder:** Scott Vaccaro **Flagship:** Freshchester Pale Ale **Year-Round Beers:** Freshchester Pale Ale, Liquid Gold, Captain's Kolsch, Imperial India Pale Ale, Brown Bird Ale, Smoke Porter, IPA **Seasonals/Special Releases:** Sun Block, Pumpkin Ale, Winter Ale, Xtra Gold, St. Vincent's Dubbel, Nor' Easter, Golden Delicious, Smoke from the Oak Porter aged in Wine Barrels, Smoke from the Oak Porter aged in Apple Brandy Barrels, Barrel Select Series, Saison, Rosso e Marrone, Cuvee de Castleton, Espresso Stout, Hops N' Roses, Birra de Cicco, Little Linda's Liquid **Tours:** Yes; Saturday, 1 to 5 p.m. **Taproom:** Yes

Scott Vaccaro trained in fermentation science at UC Davis in California before working at Sierra Nevada and Colorado Brewing and making a trip to visit breweries in Europe. When Colorado Brewing closed (oddly enough it was in Connecticut), and he

Golden Delicious
Style: American Tripel
ABV: 10%
Availability: Limited

Golden Delicious has all the effervescence of a Tripel but with a softness that comes with being aged in apple brandy barrels. The beer is crystal golden colored with a brilliant white head. Apples are heavy in the aroma and come through with some honey sweetness in the beer. The addition of Amarillo hops for dry hopping adds extra fruitiness and dries out some of the sweetness. The barrel aging is noticeable but not overwhelming.

was faced with the decision of where to go next, Vaccaro decided to stay in the Hudson Valley, where he grew up, and contribute to the small craft beer community.

In 2006 Vaccaro opened Captain Lawrence, with its first years at a location in Pleasantville, New York, in a 20-barrel brewhouse. He slowly made a name for himself as one of the top brewers in the area. Since then the brewery has moved a short way to an industrial space in Elmsford, New York, now operating in a 40-barrel brewhouse.

Since its launch Captain Lawrence beers have become some of the most sought-after beers in the entire state. Beer geeks descend on the brewery in large crowds for special release brews and the chance to snatch up a few of the limited beers. Many of the limited beers are barrel aged, sour, or both. The **Smoke from the Oak** series featured the brewery's roasty and pitch-black Stout aged in a variety of different barrels. Sours like **Hops N' Roses,** brewed with flowers and fermented with wild yeast, is beautifully tart yet also posesses a noticeable delicate floral aroma. The Belgian-style Ale **Liquid Gold** might be the most well-known and popular in the area due to its clean flavors of citrus and moderate hop character.

Tokens are the currency at the tasting room, where visitors can enjoy beers on barrels that have been repurposed as tables or grab some bottles to take home. Growlers are available as well. Outside the tasting room, local Tarrytown restaurant Village Dog operates a cart, offering up gourmet hot dogs.

CHATHAM BREWING
30 Main St., Ste. 2, Chatham, NY 12307; (518) 697-0202; ChathamBrewing.com; @ChathamBrewing
Founded: 2007 **Founders:** Jake Cunningham, Tom Crowell **Brewer:** Matt Perry **Flagship Beer:** 8 Barrel Ale **Year-Round Beers:** O.C. Blonde Ale, Amber Ale, IPA, 8 Barrel Ale, Porter **Seasonals/Special Releases:** Brown Ale, Imperial IPA, Scotch Ale, Bourbon Barrel Aged 8 Barrel, Bourbon Barrel Brown, Maple Amber, Belgian Tripel, Summer Cream Ale, Raspberry Wheat, Winter Ale, Octoberfest, Dry Irish Stout, Red Ale, Blueberry Wheat, Pale Ale, Imperial Stout, 8 Barrel Super **Tours:** Yes **Taproom:** Yes

In the early 1990s Jake Cunningham studied brewing and worked at J.W. Lees family brewery in Manchester, England. When he came back to the States, he got a job at Brown's Brewing in Troy, New York, to help get it up and running, but he always wanted to start his own venture. Cunningham eventually convinced his friend Tom Crowell, who had spent time working at the now-closed Harbor Brewing in Brooklyn, to go into business with him, and they launched Chatham Brewing in 2007, bringing on Head Brewer Matt Perry in 2009.

From the beginning they intended to make drinkable and approachable beers, rather than specialty experimental ones that don't appeal to a wide variety of consumers. The fan favorite is Chatham's **8 Barrel Super IPA,** which is an American Double/Imperial IPA, a flavorful, malty brew with flavors of bitter hops and slight fruity overtones. Perry brews an Amber Ale and a Maple Amber Ale, made with maple syrup from local trees added after fermentation that contribute to a sweet and malty flavor with hints of maple. Chatham's **O.C. Blonde** is brewed with coriander and orange zest, producing a beer that has flavors of toast and citrus, finishing slightly sweet.

Since its launch Chatham Brewing has grown between 30 and 50 percent a year, and has been recognized with the 2012 Matthew Vassar Cup for Best Brewery in the Hudson Valley at TAP NY. In late 2013 Cunningham and Crowell completed an expansion and move down Main Street, from a 3.5- to 20-barrel brewhouse. Chatham beers are available at locations throughout the Hudson Valley and Capitol Region and at the Dive Bar chain in New York City.

Chatham Porter
Style: American Porter
ABV: 8%
Availability: Year-round on draft

Chatham Brewing's Porter pours a dark brown, black color, with almost no head retention. With malty aromas and flavors, this Porter has notes of chocolate and coffee. A smooth, medium-bodied beer, Chatham Porter would pair well with barbeque, soft cheeses, or dessert.

CROSSROADS BREWING COMPANY

21 Second St., Athens, NY 12015; (518) 945-BEER; CrossroadsBrewingCo.com; @Crossroads_Brew

Founded: 2010 **Founders:** Ken Landin, Janine Bennett **Brewer:** Hutch Kugeman
Flagship Beer: Outrage IPA **Year-Round Beers:** Outrage IPA, Black Rock Stout, Brick Row Red Ale, Bradys Bray Cream Ale and Lighthouse American Wheat **Seasonals/Special Releases:** White Dog Wit, Maggies Farmhouse Saison, Dr. Loomis Pumpkin Ale, First Pitch Pilsner, Block Head Bock **Tours:** Yes **Taproom:** Yes

Ken Landin and Janine Bennett were at a crossroads in their lives and were looking to start something new that would also combine their love of craft beer and music. They decided a brewery and restaurant would be a great way to do that, which would at the same time allow them to become a part of the community and use products from local farms. The pair purchased an old opera house in Athens in 2009, renovated it, and launched Crossroads Brewing Company in 2010 with a seven-barrel brewhouse and tasting room. The pub opened in June 2011, which expanded to a full restaurant in 2012.

Brewer Hutch Kugeman came to Crossroads after a tenure as brewer at Great Adirondack Brewing Company in Lake Placid, New York. Kugeman focuses on creating unique and high-quality beers. The **Brady's Bay Cream Ale** is a solid, refreshing

Outrage IPA
Style: American IPA
ABV: 7%
Availability: Year-round on draft
At 7 percent ABV, Outrage IPA from Crossroads isn't exactly sessionable, but it's a great IPA. A hop-forward beer, strong hops and citrus on the nose lead to a hoppy taste with notes of grapefruit and caramel malts. A balanced beer, Outrage finishes with lingering bitterness. It's an excellent brew to enjoy with a cheese plate at Crossroads.

offering, a clear golden color with piney, grassy, malty flavors. The **Black Rock Stout** is drinkable, smooth, and creamy, with plenty of coffee and chocolate aromas and flavors; it's a well-balanced roasted brew.

Crossroads beers can be found on tap throughout the Hudson Valley and Capital region, as well as at several locations in New York City. Of course the best place to enjoy these brews is at the large brewpub in Athens, where you can enjoy local eats such as cheese plates, barbeque wings, and burgers while sitting in the comfortable space looking out the walls of windows at the small town of Athens.

THE DEFIANT BREWING COMPANY

6 East Dexter Plaza, Pearl River, NY 10965; (845) 920-8602; DefiantBrewing.com; @DefiantBrewing
Founded: 2006 **Founder and Brewer:** Neill Acer **Flagship and Year-Round Beers:** Muddy Creek Lager, Medusa IPA, O'Defiant Stout, Porter **Seasonals/Special Releases:** Long Shadow Stout, Prohibition Lager, Lump of Coal Stout, Da Oaty, IPA, Hop Common, English Nut Brown, Headless Horseman Pumpkin Ale, Chocolate Porter, Porter, English Porter, Christmas Ale, Brooklyn Honey Porter, Raspberry Porter, Cabin Fever Stout, Baron Von Weizen, Belgian Tripel, Abominal Show Beer, Maibock, Oktoberfest, Single Finger IPA,

Summer Ale, The Horseman's Ale, Three Fingers IPA, Very Hoppy Pale Ale, Pale Ale, Golden Nugget **Tours:** No **Taproom:** Yes

A visit to The Defiant Brewing Company is unlike any other brewery experience. Walking into the brewery situated in a white warehouse at the Pearl River stop for New Jersey Transit, you'll find tables and chairs on your left and a bar on your right—with the entire 15-barrel brewing system behind it. In a long, slim space, the brew kettle and brite tanks stand against the wall behind the bar, with fermentation tanks taking up the space after the bar ends. If you so choose, you could sit at the bar next to a bottle labeler.

The taps are hooked up directly to the brite tanks, and you can easily observe the brewing process while enjoying your uber-fresh brew. Founded by Neill Acer in the fall of 2006, beers from Defiant take a decidedly Irish spin. **Little Thumper,** a single malt, single hop Pale Ale, is light bodied and low alcohol at 4.7 percent. A

O'Defiant Stout
Style: Dry Irish Stout
ABV: 5.5%
Availability: Year-round on draft

Poured on nitro at the brewery's bar, O'Defiant Stout is a creamy and smooth beer, an excellent example of the dry Irish Stout style. Clean on the palate, you'll taste notes of coffee and chocolate in this beer, which finishes with a subtle roasted bitterness. It's just like Guinness, only better, and a perfect compliment to slow-roasted barbeque.

flavorful brew, Little Thumper is grassy, floral, and easy drinking. The **Muddy Creek Lager** is an Amber Lager with notes of caramel and toffee, slightly sweet and also easy to drink at 5.6 percent ABV. Once a year on the winter solstice, Defiant brews the **Long Shadow Stout,** an Imperial Stout with 8 percent ABV.

Defiant beers are available on draft and some in 750-milliliter bottles. On Friday and Saturday at the brewery, authentic, slow-smoked barbecue is offered, along with a selection of meats and cheeses. There's also a flavorful and refreshing option for your designated driver: orange cream soda.

KEEGAN ALES
20 Saint James St., Kingston, NY 12401; (845) 331-BREW; KeeganAles.com; @KeeganAles
Founded: 2003 **Founder:** Tom Keegan **Brewer:** Tom Keegan **Flagship Beer:** Old Capital **Year-Round Beers:** Old Capital, Hurricane Kitty, Mother's Milk **Seasonals/Special Releases:** White Ale, Four Philosophers Belgian Tripple, Super Kitty, Longest Day IPA, Joe Mama's Milk, Helga, Black Eye, Octoberfest, Sarachi Slam, Swarmin' Hive **Tours:** Yes; Friday through Sunday, hourly from 1 to 6 p.m. **Taproom:** Yes; open Tuesday through Sunday

Tom Keegan comes from a brewing family. His great-grandfather brewed at Joseph Schiltz Brewing Company's Brooklyn location (long closed), and his father owns BrickHouse Brewery and Restaurant in Patchogue on Long Island. Keegan has a master's degree in brewing science from UC Davis and began his beer career working at Blue Point Brewing Company, also in Patchogue. In 2003 he opened Keegan Ales in the former home of Woodstock Brewery. The defunct brewery had been seized by the city of Kingston; Keegan purchased the brewery, complete with a bottling line in disrepair.

In August 2003, Keegan brewed his first batch of beer. That month **Old Capital** American Blonde Ale, **Hurricane Kitty IPA,** and **Mother's Milk** Milk Stout were all released, and they remain Keegan's core, year-round offerings. The name "Old Capital" is an homage to Kingston, the first capital of New York State. The beer is crisp and refreshing, with earthy and bready notes on the nose and palate. Mother's Milk is a creamy, malty Stout. To create another highly rated brew, **Joe Mama's Milk,** brown sugar is added to the Mother's Milk recipe. After primary fermentation, the beer is infused with cold coffee extract from the local Monkey Joe's Roasting Company. The resulting beer is thick, dark, and malty, with lots of coffee and chocolate.

Mother's Milk
Style: Milk Stout
ABV: 6%
Availability: Year-round, on draft and in bottles

Mother's Milk is probably Keegan Ales's most-loved offering. In 2003, the year it was first brewed, the beer received a gold medal at the Hudson Valley Microbrew Festival, and in 2010 the *New York Times* named it one of the top 10 Stouts in North America. Dark and creamy, Mother's Milk is easy drinking and slightly sweet. With a smooth and silky texture, this brew features flavors of oatmeal and chocolate.

Keegan Ales is open to the public every day but Monday. While the beers can be found throughout the state, the taproom frequently pours brews you won't find anywhere else. A small menu includes snacks, salads, and a variety of sandwiches. It's a shabby taproom, but a comfortable place to sit and enjoy a pint or a flight of fresh beers.

NEWBURGH BREWING COMPANY

88 South Colden St., Newburgh, NY 12550; (845) 569-BEER; NewburghBrewing.com; @NewburghBrewing
Founded: 2012 **Founders:** Chris Basso, Paul Halayko **Brewer:** Chris Basso **Flagship Beer:** Cream Ale **Year-Round Beers:** Cream Ale, Brown Ale, Peat-Smoked Stout, Saison **Seasonals/Special Releases:** Bitter English, C.A.F.E Sour, Chili Lime Stout, HoneyWeizen, Menditto-Madura Harvest Ale, NewBurton IPA, Old Tjikko Baltic Spruce Porter, Paper Box Pale Ale, Squashtober Ale, Sterk Aal Van Hoodie, Unkle Dunkel, RiverBREW Crown Maple Irish Red, The Newburgh Conspiracy, Von Steuben's Gose **Tours:** Yes; by request on Saturday before 5 p.m. **Taproom:** Yes; open Wednesday through Sunday

Newburgh's head brewer, Chris Basso, spent seven years at Brooklyn Brewery, working his way up the ranks and brewing alongside Garrett Oliver. He decided to strike out on his own and open a brewery in his hometown of Newburgh. Basso brought on his longtime friend Paul Halayko to run the business end, and the two enlisted Paul's Uncle Charlie Benedetti as their head of sales. They bought an old paper box factory to house the brewery and opened Newburgh Brewing Company in 2012.

Basso takes inspiration for his beers from not only his work at Brooklyn Brewery but also a background attending culinary school. He approaches new brews with food in mind, but also makes sure they're always sessionable, balanced, and drinkable. The flagship **Cream Ale** is clean, with bready, malty notes and a creamy taste, while the **Paper Box Pale Ale** (so named after the factory that used to reside in the building) is citrusy, toasty, and smooth, yet bitter. **C.A.F.E Sour,** one of Newburgh's most creative offerings, is a one-off sour beer made with 200 pounds of cold brew Ethiopian coffee. With a distinctive coffee aroma, C.A.F.E Sour tastes tart and refreshing, with the coffee carrying through to the palate.

Newburgh's brews are draft only and available at bars, restaurants, and for growler fills at stores throughout the Hudson Valley and occasionally in New York

Beer Lover's Pick

Brown Ale
Style: English Brown Ale
ABV: 4.2%
Availability: Year-round
Newburgh's Brown Ale pours a deep brown color. With a malty, smooth mouthfeel, the beer has low carbonation. This brew is nutty, with some hints of coffee, caramel and toffee. Not cloyingly sweet, the Brown Ale is well balanced. This beer would be great to enjoy anytime, but particularly on a rainy day alongside a soup or stew.

BREWED WITH HEART

NEWBURGH
BREWING COMPANY

City. The enormous taproom is on the top floor of the brewery's building, and copious windows overlook the Hudson River. Patrons can enjoy Newburgh beers alongside a full menu of locally inspired foods and play cornhole, Foosball, or one of a large selection of board games to wile away the day.

PEEKSKILL BREWERY

47-53 S Water St., Peekskill, NY 10566; (914) 734-2337; PeekskillBrewery.com; @PeekskillBrews

Founded: 2008 **Founders:** Keith Berardi, Morgan Berardi, Kara Berardi **Brewer:** Jeff O'Neill **Year-Round Beers:** Simple Sour, Eastern Standard, Hop Common **Seasonals/ Special Releases:** Amazeballs, Shotgun Willie IPA, Double Standard, Higher Standard, Dream of the 90s, C.R.E.A.M, Midnight Toker, Share the Rainbow, Zeitgeist Berlinerweisse, World's End, DRye Irish Stout, New Wagon Ale, Skills Pils, Lower Standard, The Liger, Vanilla Bourbon Stout, Double Feature IPA, Old Wagon, Saison de Chief, Wake Up Call, Night Walker, Irish Breakfast Stout, Chinookie, Sneak Peak IPA, Malibu, Shady Grove, DMango Unchained, Common Ground, Segal Standard, Brave Ulysses, Daywalker Wheat, Farmer John IPA, Ry Guy's Rye, Paramount Pale Ale **Tours:** Yes **Taproom:** Yes

In 2013 Peekskill Brewery, founded in 2008 by Keith Berardi, his wife Kara Berardi, and sister Morgan Berardi, moved operations from its original location directly across the street from the Peekskill Metro North Station to a large, four-floor brewery, brewpub, and restaurant a few blocks up the street. Outfitted with custom brewing equipment and a cool ship for sour beers, the move coincided with a complete rebranding of the brewery and hiring of Brewer Jeff "Chief" O'Neill, formerly of Ithaca Beer Company.

The change could not have been better. Peekskill always put out a solid lineup of beers, but when O'Neill took over he revamped almost the entire list. Brewing at Peekskill for less than two years, his **Higher Standard IPA** took home the TAP NY Governor's Cup for Best Beer in New York State. Higher Standard is an Imperial/ Double IPA and is full of citrus, piney flavors. **Amazeballs,** the tongue-in-cheek name for Peekskill's Pale Ale, has bold flavors of citrus and tropical fruit. **The Liger,** the brewery's Rye offering, has sweet pepper aromas with a biscuit, earthy taste complimented by hints of pepper.

Several Peekskill beers are available on draft in hot beer spots in New York City and Westchester: **Simple Sour, Eastern Standard, Amazeballs,** and **Hop Common.** The rest of the lineup can only be enjoyed at the brewery. Imbibe a flight of beers with snacks and pub food at the first-floor bar or enjoy them with brunch, lunch, or dinner on the second floor pub. The food is creative and delicious, utilizing many locally sourced ingredients.

Simple Sour

Style: Berliner Weissbier

ABV: 4.5%

Availability: Year-round on draft

Bright yellow in color with not much head retention, Peekskill's Simple Sour is a Berliner Weissbier that smells like tart berries and lemon zest. Puckering and refreshing, Simple Sour is balanced and sessionable. Easy drinking, with a light mouthfeel, this beer is thirst quenching, lemony, and grassy. You could drink this all day.

RUSHING DUCK BREWING COMPANY

1 Battiato Ln., Chester, NY 10918; (845) 610-5440; RushingDuck.com; @RushingDuck
Founded: 2012 **Founders:** Dan and Les Hitchcock **Brewer:** Dan Hitchcock **Flagship Beer:** Naysayer Pale Ale **Year-Round Beers:** Naysayer Pale Ale, Beanhead Coffee Porter, Nimptopsical, War Elephant, Bauli Saison, Ded Moroz, Kroovy **Seasonals/Special Releases:** Naysayer 05256 **Tours:** Yes **Taproom:** Yes; open Saturday 12 to 5 p.m.

While in college, New Jersey native Dan Hitchcock started homebrewing. It soon became a passion, and he decided to pursue brewing professionally. While taking the American Brewer's Guild's distant learning program for a degree in intensive brewing science and engineering, Hitchcock worked at Weyerbacher Brewing Company in Easton, Pennsylvania, getting promoted to head brewer after he completed his degree. Hitchcock and his father launched Rushing Duck Brewing Company in 2012, leasing space in a warehouse in Chester.

Beanhead Coffee Porter
Style: American Porter
ABV: 5.7%
Availability: Year-round on draft
Like the rest of Rushing Duck's beers, Bean-head Coffee Porter is balanced and delicious, an excellent example of the style. The beer pours deep brown and is balanced with roasty notes on the nose and palate. Strong coffee aromas and flavors abound in this brew, which finishes with a hint of vanilla.

Brewing on a seven-barrel system, Hitchcock produces a lineup of all the beers he likes to drink. Drawing from American and Belgian influences, his brews are great examples of their style. The **Naysayer Pale Ale,** Rushing Duck's flagship, is hoppy on the nose, while citrus, pine, and caramel flavors mingle on the palate. Hitchcock has brewed versions of the Naysayer with experimental hops. The **Bauli Saison** is a combination Saison and Farmhouse Ale, refreshing with lemongrass and peppercorn flavors. Rushing Duck beers are available on draft only throughout the Hudson Valley.

The Rushing Duck name is an homage to Hitchcock's grandfather, who, like many in post-Prohibition-era Hoboken, would carry beer home in any container they had. He carried beer in a metal pail dubbed "the duck." When the duck would get empty, someone would be enlisted to rush out for a refill, or "rush the duck." Today, amidst the craft beer resurgence in Hudson Valley, you don't have to rush, but you can get your growler filled at Rushing Duck Brewing Company.

SLOOP BREWING COMPANY
Poughkeepsie, NY 12603; SloopBrewing.com; @SloopBrewing
Founded: 2012 **Founders and Brewers:** Justin Taylor, Adam Watson **Flagship Beer:**
Sauer Peach **Year-Round Beers:** Red C, Black C, Sauer Peach **Seasonals/Special
Releases:** Olde World Pale Ale, Sloop Solstice **Tours:** No **Taproom:** No

Justin Taylor and Adam Watson met while they both were attending SUNY New Paltz and working at a local restaurant. They started homebrewing together and did so for years, but always wondered what it would be like to sell their brews. One day Watson ventured to the Beacon Farmers' Market to see what it would take to offer beers there. Turns out the licensing to sell at the market was basically the same as to start up a nanobrewery. So they did.

With Sloop Brewing Company, brewers Taylor and Watson make their beer in small batches on a three-barrel system in order to spend as much time as they can perfecting the recipes. First selling beers at several farmers' markets in the Hudson Valley region (including Beacon), Taylor and Watson expanded to craft beer bars and shops in the region in late 2012.

The duo brews only a handful of beers and offers them on tap and in bottles. **Sloop Solstice,** Sloop's summertime brew, is light bodied with hints of hops. Solstice is a wheat beer brewed with Belgian yeast and is complex and refreshing. Sloop offers two IPA variations, **The Red C,** an IPA made with three types of hops that all begin with the letter C, and **The Black C,** a Black IPA made with many different hops, most of which begin with the letter C. Both brews are bold and hop forward, with noticeable fruity flavors.

Beer Lover's Pick

The Sauer Peach
Style: Berliner Weiss
ABV: 4.3%
Availability: Year-round
Sloop's Sauer Peach beer is bottle conditioned and referred to by the brewery as their "artistic ale." Hints of peach and tartness in the aroma give way to full tart peach flavors. The beer is effervescent, crisp, and clear, and at 4.3 percent ABV, is refreshingly drinkable. Originally intended to be a limited release, Sauer Peach was so popular that Taylor and Watson decided to make it a year-round brew.

The brewery takes its name from the Sloop-style sailboat, which was used in the 18th and 19th centuries on the Hudson River as transportation and for commerce. Sloop Brewing's future is sure to include creative new brews, and hopefully one day, a taproom.

YONKERS BREWING COMPANY

31 Hilltop Acres, Yonkers, NY 10704; (914) 424-9918; YonkersBrewing.com; @YonkersBrewing
Founded: 2013 **Founders:** John Rubbo, Nick Califano **Brewer:** Sharif Taleb **Flagship and Year-Round Beer:** Yonkers Lager **Seasonals/Special Releases:** Honey Blonde Pale Ale, Pear Wit, IPA, Vanilla Bean Stout, Belgian Pale Ale, Irish Style Red Ale
Tours: No **Taproom:** No

John Rubbo and Nick Califano are childhood friends who used to make wine with their families, even though they preferred to drink beer. The pair wanted to give back to the community they grew up in, and when they began homebrewing together in 2009, decided starting a brewery was the answer. After coming up with a brand identity, they decided to start with a Lager and brought on Sharif Taleb, an attorney-turned-pro-brewmaster, to formulate the recipe.

Rubbo, Califano, and Taleb make beer at Thomas Hooker in Bloomfield, Connecticut, while they search for a permanent location in Yonkers. The flagship **Yonkers Lager** is an earthy, sweet, malty beer that is medium-bodied and clean. This beer was soon joined by a **Honey Blonde Pale Ale,** made with honey from the

Vanilla Bean Stout
Style: American Stout
ABV: 4.9%
Availability: Limited
This beer is poured on nitro and is almost black in color. Rich and creamy, Yonkers Vanilla Bean Stout has roasted aromas with notes of vanilla on the nose. On the palate, the vanilla bean taste is subtle at first but becomes more intense as the beer warms up. This brew is roasty and light bodied.

Hudson Valley. Honey aromas and flavors mingle with a slightly bitter but sweet taste. Yonkers also offers the **Pear Wit,** a Belgian-style Wheat Ale. While noticeable, the pear flavors are subtle and joined by a spiciness and wheaty flavor.

Yonkers beers can be found on tap at locations throughout the brewery's namesake city, elsewhere in Westchester, and also in the Bronx.

Brewpubs

CAVE MOUNTAIN BREWING COMPANY

5359 Main St. (Rt. 23), Windham, NY 12496; CaveMountainBrewing.com
Founded: 2008 **Founder:** Tim Adams **Brewer:** Jamie Caligure **Year-Round Beers:**
Hefeweizen, Belgian White, Sweet Oatmeal Stout, American IPA, West Coast Red,
Blueberry Wheat **Seasonals/Special Releases:** Blueberry Stout, Wedel Weiss, California
Common Lager, Peach Wheat, Chai Milk Stout, Guru Gluten-Free Pale Ale **Tours:** No
Taproom: Yes

The steep, winding drive to Cave Mountain Brewing Company can make you realize just how mountainous and picturesque New York State can be. Opened in 2008 in Windham, near Hunter Mountain, Cave Mountain Brewing is one of the smallest breweries or brewpubs in the state. Brewer Jamie Caligure brews 12 beers on the brewpub's one-barrel system located at the back of the bar area.

Six core beers make up the year-round offerings, while a rotating lineup of an additional six seasonals keeps the list changing. The smooth and roasty **Sweet Oatmeal Stout** is a great way to cap off a day of skiing at nearby Hunter Mountain. Hopheads will find comfort in the well-hopped bitterness of the hazy **American IPA** or the **West Coast Red.**

These beers are a great accompaniment to a food menu focused on sandwiches and

burgers. Cave Mountain's burger was even selected in 2011 as the Best Burger in the Hudson Valley by *Valley Magazine*. Other pub classics like fish-and-chips, ribs, and pulled pork round out the menu.

While sitting and enjoying a beer, be sure to look up and notice a collection of empty beer bottles on a shelf along the wall opposite the bar. Other beer decorations include a collection of vintage beer trays hanging on the walls and vintage beer cans on shelves in the bathrooms.

THE GILDED OTTER BREWING COMPANY

3 Main St., New Paltz, NY 12561; (845) 256-1700; GildedOtter.com
Founded: 1998 **Brewer:** Darren Currier **Year-Round Beers:** Huguenot St. American Lager, Three Pines IPA, New Paltz Crimson Lager, Stone House Irish Stout, Dusseldorf Altbier **Seasonals/Special Releases:** Belgian Spring Wit, Back Porch Summer Lager, Hefeweizen **Tours:** No **Taproom:** Yes

The Gilded Otter flies a bit under the radar in the busy town of New Paltz, but it still puts out a solid lineup of drinkable beers that go well with the pub-style eats. Brewmaster Darren Currier is a graduate of the Siebel Institute in Chicago.

The brewpub hits the popular styles with beers like the **Belgian Spring Wit**, **Three Pines India Pale Ale**, and **Stone House Irish Dry Stout.** The Belgian Spring Wit is a good example of the smoothness and citrus flavors that draw so many to the style. With a pale straw color and a frothy white head the fragrant and flavorful beer is great for taking in a summer evening in the Hudson Valley.

The interior of the brewpub is like a lodge. It's a two-floor dining room with pieces of the brewhouse scattered throughout (note the otter decal printed on the tanks). The second floor is open and feels like a loft. From your seat on that level you can look down at the fully stocked bar with brewing equipment behind it.

Beer Bars

BIRDSALL HOUSE
970 Main St., Peekskill, NY 10566; (914) 930-1880; BirdsallHouse.net; @Birdsall970
Draft Beers: 20 **Bottled/Canned Beers:** 25

Birdsall House has embraced a comprehensive approach to quality beer and farm-to-table food more than most restaurants in the state. With local brewers dominating the taps and much of the food sourced from local farms, or even the restaurant's backyard, freshness is clearly a priority for Owners Tim Reinke (also a co-owner of Blind Tiger) and John Sharp.

The taps showcase local brewers such as The Bronx Brewery, Port Jeff Brewing Company, and Brewery Ommegang, alongside West Coast brewers like Sierra Nevada and Firestone Walker. In addition to flights, beers are available in half pints for those who don't want to commit to a whole pint but also aren't in the mood for a full flight.

The food is high quality yet approachable, with dishes like Stout-glazed ribs and fried chicken sharing the menu with soft-shell crab tostada and house-made charcuterie. The restaurant is dimly lit and full of dark wood and has a spacious patio with bocce and live music in the summer. There are frequent events featuring breweries and even some beer-pairing dinners with brewers like Rushing Duck from just across the Hudson River.

THE GRAND CRU BEER AND CHEESE MARKET
6384 Mill St., Rhinebeck, NY 12572; GrandCruRhinebeck.com
Draft Beers: 10 **Bottled/Canned Beers:** 300

The Grand Cru sits among picturesque boutiques selling handmade and artisanal wares in the lovely hamlet of Rhinebeck. In a town that appreciates small and local businesses, The Grand Cru is just that.

The large selection of bottles and cans for purchase span the world of beer but have a particular focus on American craft and especially on local and regional brewers including Brewery Ommegang, Troegs Brewing, and Brooklyn Brewery. You often may be able to find limited-release beers at The Grand Cru that you wouldn't be able to find elsewhere in the region, such as the Kentucky Breakfast Stout from Founders Brewing Company.

The Grand Cru carries a good selection of cheeses that you can pair with your beer. The shop also makes sure to stock gluten-free brews for those with celiac disease. Monthly music events and regular brewery events from brewers like Victory Brewing Company and Long Ireland Beer Company help make The Grand Cru more than just a bottle shop.

THE HOP
458 Main St., Beacon, NY 12508; (845) 440-8676; TheHopBeacon.com; @TheHopBeacon
Draft Beers: 9 **Bottled/Canned Beers:** Over 150

Located in the quaint and artistic town of Beacon among the many art galleries and shops, The Hop takes an elevated but fun approach to beer and food. The combination bottle shop, bar, and eatery is full of brews from around the state and country. Bottles from Belgian and American brewers such as Westmalle and The Bruery are displayed horizontally, like wine, in dark wooden racks. Sitting on nearby shelves are bottles and cans from local breweries like Captain Lawrence Brewing Company, The Bronx Brewery, and Brooklyn Brewery.

The Hop also serves thoughtful and delicious food to pair with your brews. Try the polenta with kale and a fried egg paired with an effervescent Blonde Ale or Belgian Tripel. A rotating cheese plate is meticulously described by your server and comes with a delicious spicy mustard made with Porter. If you're not in a beer mood—or you're the designated driver—The Hop also offers a selection of house-made sodas.

Seating is a bit limited, with a handful of tables and chairs at the front of the shop. A rustic wooden interior contributes to a laid-back, comfortable atmosphere to enjoy fine beer and food.

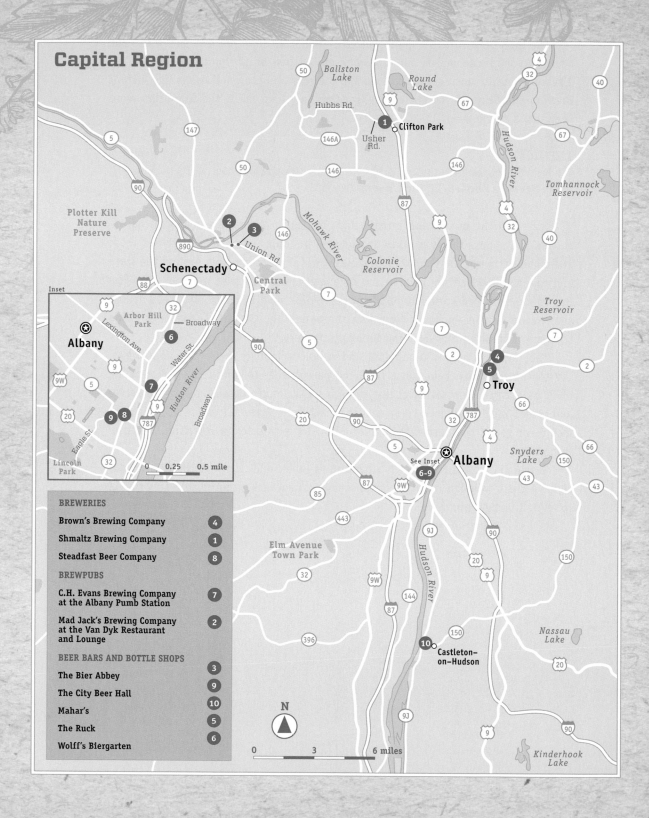

Capital Region

Ballston Lake

Round Lake

Hubbs Rd.

1 ● Clifton Park

Usher Rd.

Tomhannock Reservoir

Mohawk River

Colonie Reservoir

Hudson River

2
3
Union Rd

Schenectady ○

Central Park

Troy Reservoir

Plotter Kill Nature Preserve

Inset

9

Arbor Hill Park

— Broadway

6

Lexington Ave.

Albany ⊛

9

Water St.

Hudson River

7

Broadway

9W

5

9 **8**

Eagle St.

Lincoln Park

0   0.25   0.5 mile

4
5
Troy ○

Snyders Lake

6-9
See Inset   ⊛ **Albany**

Hudson River

BREWERIES

Brown's Brewing Company   **4**

Shmaltz Brewing Company   **1**

Steadfast Beer Company   **8**

BREWPUBS

**C.H. Evans Brewing Company
at the Albany Pumb Station**   **7**

**Mad Jack's Brewing Company
at the Van Dyk Restaurant
and Lounge**   **2**

BEER BARS AND BOTTLE SHOPS

The Bier Abbey   **3**

The City Beer Hall   **9**

Mahar's   **10**

The Ruck   **5**

Wolff's Biergarten   **6**

Elm Avenue Town Park

Nassau Lake

10
Castleton–on–Hudson

N

0   3   6 miles

Kinderhook Lake

Capital Region

New York's Capital Region, which centers around the cities of Albany, Troy, and Schenectady, has some pretty fantastic brewpubs and bars. At times the region seems isolated from the rest of the state, but one step into some of the bars in the area and you know that drinkers here are just as passionate about beer as elsewhere. Bars like The Ruck in Troy, The Bier Abbey in Schenectady, and The City Beer Hall in Albany are bringing enthusiasm to the community, while the brewpubs C.H. Evans Brewing Company at the Albany Pump Station and Brown's Brewing Company in Troy are becoming must stops on beer trips to the area.

The Capital Region lacks the number of breweries that other regions have, but there is clearly potential, with the Hudson Valley to the south and the Finger Lakes off to the west. The new location for Shmaltz Brewing Company that opened in 2013 in Clifton Park may help bring renewed interest to the area for brewers.

Breweries

BROWN'S BREWING COMPANY

417 River St., Troy, NY 12180; (518) 273-BEER; BrownsBrewing.com; @BrownsBrewing
Founded: 1993 **Founders:** Garry and Kelly Brown **Brewer:** Peter Martin **Flagship Beer:** Pale Ale **Year-Round Beers:** Brown Ale, Cherry Raspberry Ale, Dry Irish Stout, Hefeweizen, Imperial Stout, IPA, Oatmeal Stout, Pale Ale, Porter, Tomhannock Pilsner **Seasonals/Special Releases:** American Wheat Ale, Bat Shea Red, Belgian Blonde Ale, Best Bitter Ale, Dunkel Weizen, Irish Amber Ale, Maibock, NY Harvest IPA, Oktoberfest, Pumpkin Ale, Raspberry Lambic, Rauch, Bourbon Barrel Aged Imperial Stout, Whiskey Porter, Hoodoo Voodoo Ale, Maple Nut Brown Ale **Tours:** Yes; call ahead for appointments **Taproom:** Yes

Garry and Kelly Brown opened Brown's Brewing Company as a brewpub in Troy in 1993 after three years of rehabilitating their location, which originally housed a printing company and was gutted by a fire. In 2013 the Browns completed a $3 million brewery on the Walloomsac River in North Hoosick, New York, financed in part

Beer Lover's Pick

Oatmeal Stout
Style: Oatmeal Stout
ABV: 5.25%
Availability: Year-round
Brown's Oatmeal Stout begins with aromas of toast and chocolate. A smooth beer, flavors of chocolate, coffee, sweet caramel, and more toast mix on the palate. This Oatmeal Stout has a silky texture and goes down easy.

by selling the Troy buildings to an investor. The new facility will increase production from 2,400 barrels a year to more than 20,000.

Brown's brews a consistently delicious lineup of beers, including a **Hefeweizen, Porter,** and a **Best Bitter.** The Hefeweizen is an excellent example of the style, with banana flavors that mingle with pepper, orange, and wheat on the palate. With orange aromas, this beer is effervescent and finishes with hints of spice. Brown's Porter smells strongly of chocolate and has a roasted bitterness on the palate, with sweet caramel and toffee flavors. Sweet aromas in the Best Bitter lead to a chewy mouthfeel, with notes of orange zest and toast and a slight bitterness.

The atmosphere at Brown's Brewery is that of bustling pub: It's a full working brewery and restaurant. On the menu you'll find standard pub fare, including chicken wings, burgers, and sandwiches. In 2013 Brown's Brewing became a licensed Farm Brewery and also opened its new facility, the Walloomsac Brewery on the Walloomsac River in North Hoosick. A 50-barrel brewhouse, the facility will produce all of Brown's bottles and kegs for wholesale distribution throughout the state and New England. Located on over 20 acres, barley and hops will eventually be grown there.

SHMALTZ BREWING COMPANY

6 Fairchild Sq., Clifton Park, NY 12065; (518) 406-5430; ShmaltzBrewing.com; @ShmaltzNYC

Founded: 1996 **Founder:** Jeremy Cowan **Brewer:** Paul McErlean **Flagship Beer:** HE'BREW Genesis Ale **Year-Round Beers:** HE'BREW Series: Genesis Ale, Messiah Bold, Bittersweet Lenny's R.I.P.A., Origin **Seasonals/Special Releases:** Rejewvenator, Jewbelation, Genesis 10:10, Hop Manna, R.I.P.A on Rye, Vertical Jewbelation, Genesis 15:15 **Tours:** Yes **Taproom:** Yes

In his late teens in the San Francisco Bay Area, Jeremy Cowan and some friends were playing volleyball and had the idea for a Jewish beer; they'd call it He'Brew. The idea resurfaced years later, and a now–ex-girlfriend's father told Cowan to go for it. He found a brew-on-premises operation and formulated the recipe for **HE'BREW Genesis Ale** with brewer Simon Pesch, now the head brewer at Pyramid Breweries in California. Cowan's intention was to reach "non-affiliated" Jews, Jews who felt Jewish, were proud to be Jewish, but didn't do much about it. The Shmaltz experience combines beer and Jewish tradition with just the right amount of shtick. HE'BREW beers have whimsical names like **Rejewvenator** and **Jewbelation,** labels with graffiti-like cartoonish characters and quotes from the Torah. In 1997 Shmaltz was contracted out to Anderson Valley Brewing Company, and in 2003 Cowan moved production of his beers to Olde Saratoga Brewing Company.

In the summer of 2008 Shmaltz partnered with nonprofit Coney Island USA to launch a new brand: **Coney Island Craft Lagers.** Using the same type of whimsical packaging, Coney Island beers took inspiration from sideshow freaks ubiquitous on Coney Island. In 2010 Cowan opened the Coney Island Brewing Company, "The World's Smallest Brewery," in its namesake Brooklyn neighborhood, producing one-gallon test batches at a time.

Shmaltz Brewing Company's beers are available in six-packs of 12-ounce bottles, large-format bottles, or on draft across the country. In the HE'BREW series, **Bittersweet Lenny's R.I.P.A,** a Double IPA with rye malt, is highly rated. Clocking in at 10 percent ABV, the beer is a tribute to Lenny Bruce and has an American hop bitterness and a full mouthfeel and is slightly sweet.

In 2013 Shmaltz Brewing opened a new 50-barrel brewing facility in Clifton Park, marking its departure from contract brewing. Shortly following the launch of the new brewery, Cowan finalized the sale of his Coney Island Craft Lager brand to the craft beer incubator Alchemy & Science, a subsidiary of The Boston Beer Company. Cowan stayed on with the brand in an advisory capacity, while still maintaining leadership and control of the HE'BREW beers.

Hop Manna IPA
Style: IPA
ABV: 6.8%
Availability: Year-round
Named for the nourishing food found by
the Israelites while wandering the desert,
Hop Manna is aggressively dry hopped. The
Centennial, Cascade, and Citra hops give
the beer a bright floral aroma with a hint of
citrus. The hops' bright citrus and earthy fla-
vors remain snappy over the light malt body.
The beer is available in 22-ounce bottles
and on draft.

STEADFAST BEER COMPANY

90 State St., Floor 7, Ste. 9, Albany, NY 12207; (518) 928-1435; SteadfastBeer.com;
@steadfastbeerco
Founded: 2012 **Founders:** Jeremy Hosier, Mark Crisafulli **Brewer:** Jeremy Hosier
Flagship Beer: Sorghum Pale Ale **Year-Round Beers:** Sorghum Pale Ale, Golden Blonde
Ale **Seasonals/Special Releases:** Pumpkin Spice Ale **Tours:** No **Taproom:** No

When Jeremy Hosier worked in the beer retail business, he noticed that gluten-
free beers were popular and often sold well, so he tried some. To his dismay,
many of them didn't taste very good and they weren't hoppy, a curious choice
since hops don't have gluten. So Hosier decided to homebrew his own gluten-free
beer, one that had hop characters and was made from sorghum extract, which can
be swapped out for the same amount of malt extract in beer. When Hosier decided
to mass-produce the beer, he turned to Paper City Brewing Company in Holyoke,
Massachusetts, brewing on its 20-barrel system.

His flagship **Sorghum Pale Ale** has a spicy, hoppy aroma. Big and bold, this Pale Ale has hints of citrusy flavors and a good amount of bitterness. Hosier followed up with a **Golden Blonde Ale,** meant to mimic a Belgian-style White Ale, brewed with sorghum, honey, coriander, orange peel, and a Belgian yeast strain. This beer has soft citrus aromas and is refreshing with a hint of tartness and spice on the palate. With a light mouthfeel, Steadfast's Golden Blonde Ale is a drinkable offering.

Hosier and Crisafulli aim to create the most flavorful gluten-free beers on the market. Their brews are available in bottles and distributed throughout Upstate New York, the Hudson Valley, and the New York City metro area, as well as Colorado, New Jersey, and Chicago.

Sorghum Pale Ale
Style: American Pale Ale
ABV: 6.8%
Availability: Year-round
Sorghum Pale Ale is a well-rounded brew that pours an amber color. Aromas of pine, citrus, and hops lead to a medium-bodied beer that has sweet and spicy flavors with a lingering bitter finish. To make this gluten-free beer, sorghum extract is used in place of barley and wheat, while still maintaining big flavors present in Pale Ales that do have gluten. Clocking in at 6.8 percent ABV, Sorghum Pale Ale was meant to be modeled after West Coast IPAs.

Brewpubs

C.H. EVANS BREWING COMPANY AT THE ALBANY PUMP STATION

19 Quackenbush Sq., Albany, NY 12207; (518) 447-9000; EvansAle.com;
@ALBPumpStation

Founded: 1999 **Founder:** Neil Evans **Brewer:** Ryan Demler **Year-Round Beers:** BdG,
ESB, Breakfast Stout, Czech Yourself Pils, Kickerbocker Lager, Imperial American IPA,
Bourbon Barrel Aged Porter, Kick Ass Brown, Old Musty Barleywine, Pumpstation Pale
Ale, Evans Extra Stout **Seasonals/Special Releases:** Autumn Apple Ale, Bavarian
Hefeweizen, Belgian Pale Ale, Belgian Style Strong Ale, Biere de Garde, Blueberry Tripel,
Bock, Capitol Light, Cherry Dubbel, Ginger Wit, Halfmoon IPA, Honey Wheat Saison,
Irish Potato Red Ale, Maerzenbier, Maibock, Munich Dunkel, Oatmeal Stout, Poor Soldier
Porter, Smoked Hefeweizen, Smoked Weizen Bock, Raspberry Hefe, Winter Warmer, XXX IPA
Tours: No **Taproom:** Yes

C.H. Evans Brewing Company at the Albany Pump Station embodies much of what
we all love about brewpubs. At its heart the Pump Station is a neighborhood
place that serves fresh beer alongside solid pub-style food. The brewpub makes a

wide range of American, British, and Belgian styles. Drinkers who like beers that pack a punch will enjoy the **Belgian Strong** at 9 percent ABV and the **Imperial IPA** at 9.2 percent ABV. Those looking to imbibe more than one beer can try the **Simple Belgian** at 4.8 percent ABV or the **Breakfast Stout** at 4.7 percent ABV. The mahogany-colored **Kick Ass Brown Ale** has won three Gold Medals at the Great American Beer Festival in Denver with a strong American-style hop character balancing the British-style malt backbone.

The brewery has a rich history. C.H. Evans Brewing Company originally opened in 1786 out of Hudson, New York, but did not survive Prohibition. The founder was Cornelius H. Evans; the operation was resurrected and revitalized by Cornelius H. Evans's descendant C. H. "Neil" Evans IV in 1999, and built in the Albany Pump Station building. This reclaimed industrial building used to pump water from the Hudson River into a reservoir and still has two of the giant cranes in place for patrons to marvel at while they drink.

MAD JACK'S BREWING COMPANY
AT THE VAN DYCK RESTAURANT AND LOUNGE

237 Union St., Schenectady, NY 12305; (518) 348-7999; VanDyckLounge.com/MadJack; @MadJackBrewing
Founded: 2011 **Founders:** The McDonald Family **Brewer:** Drew Schmidt **Year-Round Beers:** Brodey'o Blonde Ale, 2025 Heffeweizen, Dutchmen Lager, Pinhead Pale Ale, Fightin Irwin IPA, Billy's Bock, Tubs Stout **Seasonals/Special Releases:** Bierre de Fleur, McToberfest, Liberty Lager, Mad Jack Frost, Kwik Krek, Struffolino Italian Lager, Jack Hammer Scotch, Jack the Ryepper **Tours:** No **Tap Room:** Yes

The Van Dyck is one of Schenectady's best-known spots for food, drinks, and jazz, and with a lack of brewing in the city, it was a natural spot for a brewpub. The McDonald family, led by Jeff and his father John (Jack), who owns several other restaurants and bars in the Schenectady area, bought the Van Dyck in 2008 and added brewing to the operation in 2011 under Drew Schmidt, formerly of Olde Saratoga Brewing Company.

The brewery cranks out standard styles like **Brodey'O Blonde, Pinhead Pale Ale,** and **Fightin Irwin IPA.** Their **Struffolino Italian Lager** is a fun take on what most people would associate with mass-produced Lagers, with more body and a nice bitterness from Noble hops. The most interesting beer, however, is the **Biere de Fleur,** a Belgian-style Pale Ale that uses lavender and hop flowers. The aroma of the lavender is unmistakable, and the flavor delicately remains on the palate after

finishing the sip. Weighing in at 4.5 percent ABV, the beer is also very drinkable and especially good for warm-weather days.

The traditional pub food you might expect like wings, salads, and pizzas are on the menu, but they are joined by some more interesting dishes like lobster quesadillas, prosciutto tortellini, and grilled salmon with spinach risotto. Paired with the solid beers, the food makes Mad Jack's at the Van Dyck an excellent example of a brewpub.

Beer Bars

THE BIER ABBEY

613 Union St., Schenectady, NY 12305; (518) 388-8597; TheBierAbbey.com;
@TheBierAbbey
Draft Beers: 29 on tap, 1 on cask **Bottled/Canned Beers:** 10

Many may be surprised to hear that one of the best beer bars in the Capital Region is in Schenectady. The Bier Abbey, located on Union Street, serves up an eclectic beer list from local newcomers like Rushing Duck and Belgian classics like St. Bernardus. Beers are not only served in their proper glassware but also at their proper temperatures, which are indicated next to each beer on the menu. The large wood bar is a good place for grabbing a quick pint, or you can head outside in the warm months to sit on the front patio. Owner George Collentine drove home the abbey theme by purchasing old pews from a church in New Jersey and repurposing them as bar booths.

The Bier Abbey is also a restaurant, and one that can have a significant wait of 45 minutes or more on a busy night. The menu features Belgian-style mussels, cooked in a variety of Wit beer sauces, and frites. Several other items also use beer in cooking, like the beer-battered chicken fingers and the onion soup.

THE CITY BEER HALL

42 Howard St., Albany, NY 12207; (518) 449-2337; TheCityBeerHall.com;
@TheCityBeerHall
Draft Beers: 15 **Bottled/Canned Beers:** 30

The City Beer Hall is an expansive, roomy beer hall with long communal tables, fireplaces, and chandeliers; an outdoor beer garden; a speakeasy-style down-stairs lounge; and an upstairs "rodeo," featuring a mechanical bull (reportedly the only one in Albany). Oh, and it also offers free nine-inch personal pizzas with every beer you purchase. Hard to believe you can find all of this in one place. But it's true: The City Beer Hall in Albany has it all.

Located on a small side street near the Times Union Center, The City Beer Hall was opened in 2011 by Kaelin Ballinger and Kenny Schacter and is a great place to grab a tasty brew. The bar is often the setting for special events that feature local breweries, hosts a hookah night every Tuesday on its patio, and puts out a raw bar every Friday evening. Breweries on tap range from small local ones like Adirondack and Crossroads, to larger craft favorites, including Sierra Nevada and Green Flash.

There's a full food menu with upscale pub fare like truffled mac and cheese, foie gras mousse on toast, steak, burgers, and salads. Visit on Saturday or Sunday and enjoy brunch from an extensive menu featuring eggs, omelets, French toast, and waffles. But, remember, there's free pizza with your beer. How can you top that?

MAHAR'S
14 S. Main St., Castleton-on-Hudson, NY 12033; (518) 336-4013; ItsOnlyBeer.com
Draft Beers: 11 **Bottled/Canned Beers:** 100 to 150

In 1989 Jim Mahar opened a neighborhood pub in Albany, and carried almost no beer. By the time the bar was shuttered in 2013, it had served over 10,000 different beers and counted 35,000 members in its beer tour, a club for frequent drinkers who would receive awards for drinking a certain amount of beers.

While the infamous Albany location no longer exists, the spirit of Mahar's lives on in its second location in Castleton-on-Hudson, opened in 2010. With 11 tap lines and between 100 and 150 bottles and cans, this location of Mahar's also runs a beer tour with Castleton-on-Hudson members, and continues to honor members of the Albany tour.

Mahar doesn't think about style or region when sourcing beers for the bar, but instead tries to serve as many different beers as possible—every beer he can lay his hands on, so customers will definitely find something they like. With a neighborhood pub atmosphere, Mahar's serves pub food such as bangers and mash, paninis, cheese plates, and shepherd's pie. The bar is the scene for frequent beer-pairing dinners, a monthly potluck, and live music.

THE RUCK
104 3rd St., Troy, NY 12108; (518) 273-1872; GetRucked.com; @GetRuckedTroy
Draft Beers: 26 on tap, 1 on cask **Bottled/Canned Beers:** 29

The Ruck has led the charge for the craft beer bar resurgence in Troy, which is also home to Brown's Brewing. The bar has 27 taps, including a cask offering, a solid selection of bottles and cans, and brewery nights that showcase some of the nation's best breweries like Dogfish Head and also New York State's rising stars, including Rushing Duck and The Bronx Brewery. Beers are from a wide range of regions in a variety of styles. Abita, Ommegang, Stone, Firestone Walker, and Butternuts are several breweries on tap. The less-discerning drinker can also choose a Budweiser, Coors Light, or Blue Moon.

Friendly bartenders chat with patrons to help them find beers that match well with their tastes, or share unexpected finds with the more adventurous drinker. On the divey side—the bar is described on its own website as a hole-in-the-wall—The Ruck has minimal decor. As you walk in, the bar is on your right, tables are on your left, with plenty of open space in between to accommodate a crowd. The Ruck has a full menu, with ever-popular wings, sandwiches, burgers, salads, and fried snacks.

WOLFF'S BIERGARTEN
895 Broadway, Albany, NY 12207; (518) 427-2461; WolffsBiergarten.com; @WolffsBiergartn
Draft Beers: 14 **Bottled/Canned Beers:** 23

When you walk into Wolff's Biergarten, the crunch of peanut shells under your feet and the full liters of beer that most of the patrons are holding immediately signal that you are in for a good time. Wolff's was opened in 2009 by the

owners of the well-known Bomber's Burrito Bars, and is a welcome addition to the area just north of Downtown Albany.

The sprawling space of Wolff's is more an updated version of a bier hall than anything else, covered in wood and with high ceilings. Traditional German beers and food are offered and enjoyed on long wooden tables. While not technically a beer garden (true beer gardens are outside), Wolff's maintains a beer garden feel with an indoor tree. Even though it's artificial, it's still a nice touch.

You can dive right into a liter of Hofbrau Original or Paulaner Dunkelwiezen. The beers are of course served in the proper glassware and, as is to be expected, pair perfectly with the German dishes available at the food counter. If you aren't into bratwurst or spaetzle, you can certainly get behind the free peanuts, even if the shells are all over the floor. Wolff's is also a great place to catch a soccer match, especially a German one, and the bar keeps a schedule of matches on their website. A large number of dartboards are on the back wall of the bar, in case you'd like to start a tournament.

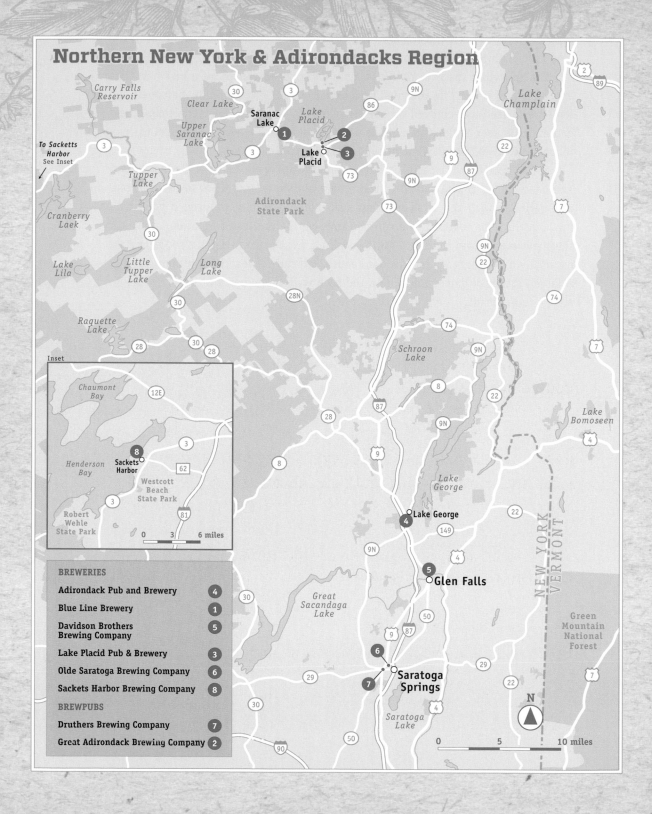

Northern New York & Adirondacks Region

Carry Falls Reservoir

Clear Lake

Saranac Lake

Upper Saranac Lake

Lake Placid

1 Saranac Lake

2

Lake Placid **3**

To Sacketts Harbor See Inset

Tupper Lake

Cranberry Laek

Adirondack State Park

Lake Lila

Little Tupper Lake

Long Lake

Raquette Lake

Lake Champlain

Inset

Chaumont Bay

Henderson Bay

Sackets Harbor **8**

Westcott Beach State Park

Robert Wehle State Park

0   3   6 miles

Schroon Lake

Lake Bomoseen

Lake George

4 Lake George

5 Glen Falls

Great Sacandaga Lake

6

7 Saratoga Springs

Saratoga Lake

NEW YORK | VERMONT

Green Mountain National Forest

N

0   5   10 miles

BREWERIES

Adirondack Pub and Brewery	**4**
Blue Line Brewery	**1**
Davidson Brothers Brewing Company	**5**
Lake Placid Pub & Brewery	**3**
Olde Saratoga Brewing Company	**6**
Sackets Harbor Brewing Company	**8**

BREWPUBS

Druthers Brewing Company	**7**
Great Adirondack Brewing Company	**2**

Northern New York & Adirondack Region

The Adirondacks' brewers have flown under the radar in recent years. With explosive growth in areas like New York City, Long Island, and the Finger Lakes, the Adirondacks quietly continued doing what they have been doing for years. That the region has become an enclave for brewers focused on classic malt-forward styles, especially British styles, has gone largely unnoticed. While breweries like Lake Placid Pub & Brewery and Druther's Brewing Company branch out to many different styles, they still feature ESBs, Oatmeal Stouts, and Brown Ales. Meanwhile breweries like Great Adirondack Brewing Company and Davidson Brothers Brewing Company openly state their love for malty styles and have chosen not to enter the fashionable fray of hop-obsessed drinkers and brewers.

The breweries themselves fit snugly into their towns or landscapes and eschew the industrial aesthetic of many breweries and brewpubs. The bar scene may be rather sparse, but the region begs more for visitors to stop into breweries for a fresh beer after a day skiing, hiking, or boating on a lake.

ADIRONDACK PUB AND BREWERY

33 Canada St., Lake George, NY 12845; (518) 668-0002; ADKPub.com; @ADKBrewery
Founded: 1999 **Founder and Brewer:** John Carr **Flagship Beer:** Bear Naked Ale
Year-Round Beers: Bear Naked Ale, Dirty Blonde Ale, Iroquois Pale Ale, Fat Scotsman
Ale, Bobcat Blonde Lager, Beaver Tail Brown Ale, Cafe Vero Stout **Seasonals/Special
Releases:** Black Watch IPA, French Louie's Ale, Headwater Hefe, Chiatiemac Black Lager,
2010 Vintage Bourbon Barrel Aged Fat Scotsman Ale, Snow Trout Stout, Belgium Amber
Ale, Belgium White Peach, British Red, Oktoberfest, Maple Porter, Double Mocha Stout,
Czech Pilsner, Wheat-er-Melon **Tours:** Yes; Friday at 4 p.m., Saturday at 11:30 a.m.,
Tuesday at 4 p.m. (Memorial Day through Labor Day only) **Taproom:** Yes

Vermont native John Carr went on a backpacking trip to Europe, where he tried lots of delicious European beers. Upon returning to the States, Carr searched for but couldn't find the beers he craved. So he turned to homebrewing. After 10 years

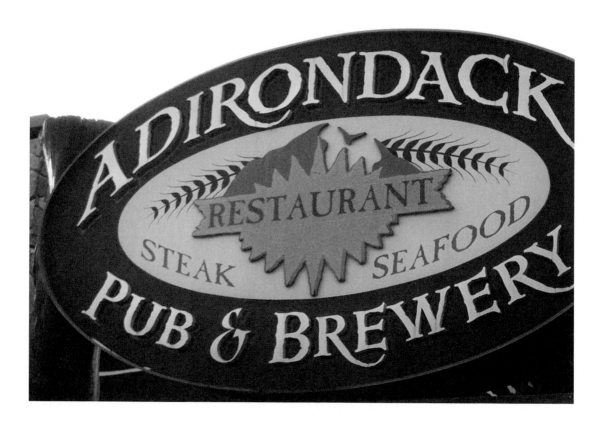

making his own beer, Carr decided to open a brewpub in tourist-destination Lake George. In 2011 Adirondack Pub and Brewery increased production to a 15-barrel brewhouse and added a bottling line.

The majority of Carr's brews are sessionable, and many of them are tributes to local Adirondack legends. **Bear Naked Ale,** for example, an American Amber/Red Ale with caramel and biscuity flavors, is named for the Adirondack black bear that forages and indulges in a lot of fermented fruit in the fall season. The fruit causes the bear to do wild things, such as run around the woods "bear naked." The **Iroquois Pale Ale,** a grassy American Pale Ale with citrus, piney notes, is brewed in honor of the Iroquois Native American tribes, who once made the Adirondack's their home. The **Dirty Blonde Ale,** an American Pale Wheat Ale with a balanced interplay of malt and citrus, recalls the flappers of the 1920s who flocked to private estates in the Adirondacks.

Adirondack beers are available on draft at the brewpub and in bottle form throughout Upstate New York.

Beer Lover's Pick

Cafe Vero Stout
Style: Dry Stout
ABV: 3.7%
Availability: Year-round
The Adirondack Pub and Brewery is committed to bettering its local community, and this philosophy carries over to its beer, most notably the Cafe Vero Stout. The beer is brewed in collaboration with Lake George's Cafe Vero, made with its fresh, locally roasted coffee. Bold flavors of coffee and chocolate mingle on the palate of this extremely sessionable Stout.

BLUE LINE BREWERY

555 Lake Flower Ave., Saranac Lake, NY 12983; (518) 354-8114; BlueLineBrew.com
Founded: 2012 **Founder and Brewer:** Mark Gillis **Beers:** Red Skin Red, Saranac Lake
6'er, Black Fly IPA, Maple Porter, Lake Flower Ale, Blue Line Brown Ale, Forest Home Black
Lager, APA **Tours:** Yes **Taproom:** Yes; open Thursday through Sunday

When Mark Gillis moved to Saranac Lake in the Adirondacks, he discovered that Saranac beer wasn't brewed in Saranac (it's made at Matt Brewing Company in Utica), and he decided to be the person to serve beer that was truly made in Saranac Lake. Gillis had previously lived in Westchester, where he saw Captain Lawrence Brewery start from the ground up, using an old warehouse. Gillis wanted to do the same and found adequate space in a defunct car wash, enough to build a small brewery with room for expansion in the future. Blue Line Brewery opened for business right before the holidays in 2012.

A Massachusetts native, Gillis decorated his tasting room with Red Sox and Celtics paraphernalia, alongside photos of his two children. His beers are unique and experimental interpretations of classic styles, such as a **Red Ale** with ginger. Gillis' **Pisgah #7** is a fun twist on the iconic Pale Ale style. The malt base is featured prominently in this beer instead of the hops, giving the brew a deep amber color, sweet notes of toffee, and a medium body. Blue Line's **Forest Home Black Lager** is made with honey and rosemary, is smooth yet earthy, and is nicely carbonated.

Beer Lover's Pick

Maple Porter
Style: American Porter
Availability: Limited
ABV: 6.5%
With a nice roasted bite, the Maple Porter is characterized by a noticeable but not overpowering maple character. The beer pours dark brown with a light tan head and has mocha aromas. Slightly sweet, Blue Line's Porter has flavors of chocolate and nuts.

Blue Line beer is on tap at local restaurants and is available for tastings and growler fills at the brewery. The name "Blue Line" is the term used for the boundaries of the Adirondack and Catskill Parks, so called because blue ink was used when they were first drawn on New York State maps.

DAVIDSON BROTHERS BREWING COMPANY

184 Glen St., Glens Falls, NY 12801; (518) 743-9026; DavidsonBrothers.com
Founded: 1996 **Founders:** Rick and John Davidson **Brewer:** Jason Kissinger **Flagship Beer:** IPA **Year-Round Beers:** IPA, Irish Red Ale, Brown, Oatmeal Stout, Scotch Ale **Seasonals/Special Releases:** Sagamore Ale, Dacker Scotch Ale, Swimmin' Cow British Rye Cream, Strong Ale, Ctrl-Alt-Del Altbier, Golden Ale, Belgian Trippel, Danish Continental Lager, Wheat Ale, Farmhouse Ale, ESB, Double Hop IPA, Mega Hop IPA, Smoked Porter, Magnum IPA, Cohan's Porter, Ryely **Tours:** No **Taproom:** Yes

The story behind Davidson Brothers Brewing Company is one you don't hear very often. When Rick and John Davidson started the process to open their brewery in 1996, neither of them had ever brewed before. They decided that they wanted to use an authentic Peter Austin brewing system. They went to Shipyard Brewing Company in Portland, Maine, to train under Alan Pugsley, who brought this type of brewing to the States. An Austin system is a traditional English brewing system

rarely found in the United States. It is notable because the brew kettle is surrounded by bricks and the fermenters are all open-top and surrounded by wood. Every brewer who works with one has trained at Shipyard, since it's a more labor-intensive process than a regular brewing system.

Since training at Shipyard, Rick hasn't changed anything about the way he brews. British brewing was the first type of brewing to come to this area of New York, and it's important to Rick to keep this style of brewing alive. His beers, brewed by Jason Kissinger, who took over from Rick's son AJ, who followed Rick as head brewer, are remarkably consistent, excellent examples of traditional styles. Davidson's **IPA,** the flagship brew, has been made with the same recipe since 1996 and is a bitter, dry, medium-bodied beer. The **Oatmeal Stout** is smooth, rich, and creamy, with roasty, chocolately flavors.

Currently Davidson Brothers Beers are produced on the seven-barrel system at its brewpub in Glens Falls, with bottled beers contracted at Shipyard. The brews are distributed at locations in the Capitol Region and Northern New York. 2014 will see an expanded Davidson Brothers, with a new, 50-barrel brewery in the nearby town of Queensbury. That location will be a teaching brewery for future Austin brewers and will bring much-needed economic growth to the area and allow Davidson Brothers to bring all beer production to New York.

Ryley
Style: Warm-weather seasonal made with rye
ABV: 4.8%
Availability: Seasonal
Nice and refreshing, the Ryley pours a clear pale color. Light on the palate, this beer is dry and herbal. With a hint of sweetness, Ryley is a unique beer because it features regular seasonal beer flavors like citrus fruits playing off the peppery notes of the rye. Low enough in alcohol to enjoy for a whole afternoon.

LAKE PLACID PUB & BREWERY

813 Mirror Lake Dr., Lake Placid, NY 12946; UbuAle.com; @UbuMan
Founded: 1996 **Founder and Brewer:** Chris Ericson **Flagship Beer:** Ubu Ale **Year-Round Beers:** Ubu Ale, Lake Placid IPA, Bruce's Brown Bag Ale, 46'er Pale Ale, Moose Island Ale **Seasonals/Special Releases:** Imperial Pumpkin, Shot in the Dark IPA, Nippletop Milk Stout, French-Style Biere De Garde, Threesome American-Style Tripel, Wolf Jaw Wit, Twice Bitten Barleywine, Grace's Summer Ale, Adirondack Gold, Smokin' Blonde Ale, Summer Wheat, Colonel's Kolsch, Cascade Pale Ale, Patriot Pale Ale, CJ's Honey Rye, Autumn Rye, Imperial IPA, Backfence IPA, Barkeater Amber Ale, Leaping Cow ESB, Bruce's Brown Bag Ale, Dr. Fogg's Oatmeal Stout, Sunrise Stout, Vanilla Porter, Chocolate Porter, Monster Fogg's Imperial Stout, High Peaks Hefeweizen, Alpine Ace Double Wit, Maibock, Ectoberfest Lager, KB's Wee Heavy, Belgian-Style Pale Ale, Belgian-Style Saison, Belgian-Style Flanders Brown Ale, Maple Sap Ale **Tours:** Yes; Saturday at 4:30 p.m. and upon request **Taproom:** Yes

Lake Placid Pub & Brewery has a reputation for consistently brewing some of the best beer in the Adirondacks. Christopher Ericson, who started his brewing career at Kennebunkport Brewing and Shed Brewing, opened Lake Placid Pub in 1996. He has since expanded the operation to include contract brewing at Matt

Brewing in Utica for kegs and bottles distributed off-site, and the original brewpub has been expanded to allow for additional dining space, and more space for brewing and fermentation has been added. The brewpub, which functions on a seven-barrel brewhouse, usually turns out eight batches a week.

The brewery keeps a small selection of beers available year-round but brews a wide range of English, Belgian, and German beer styles. The brewery also makes sure to have low-alcohol beers in rotation with beers like **Adirondack Gold, Colonel's Kolsch,** and **Grace's Summer Ale,** all coming in under the 5% ABV mark. Lake Placid's **Wolf Jaw Wit,** a Belgian-style wheat beer is lightly hopped, made with dried curacao, orange peel, and coriander. A subtle beer with complex flavors, Wolf Jaw Wit is refreshing and light bodied.

Located at the tip of Mirror Lake, Lake Placid Pub & Brewery is in one of the most picturesque beer locations in the state. If the weather is clear, try to get a table on the "Hop Loft" patio for a wrap and a sampler. If you end up inside, you can scan the walls of the second-floor bar area, which are covered in college pennants. The food is mostly pub style, with dishes such as burgers and shepherd's pie, but also features chili made with **Ubu Ale,** and ale and onion soup made with Moose Island Pale Ale.

Beer Lover's Pick

Ubu Ale
Style: English Strong Ale
ABV: 7%
Availability: Year-Round
The dark flagship Ubu Ale is famously named after a patron's chocolate lab. A malty English-style strong ale, Ubu has notes of toffee and caramel and weighs in at 7 percent ABV. Flavors of dark fruits and nuts play off of each other in this smooth, medium-bodied brew.

OLDE SARATOGA BREWING COMPANY

131 Excelsior Ave., Saratoga Springs, NY 12866; (518) 581-0492; OldeSaratogaBrew.com
Founded: 1997 **Founder:** Mendocino Brewing Company **Brewer:** Luke Erdody **Flagship
Beer:** Olde Saratoga Lager **Year-Round Beers:** Olde Saratoga Lager, Saratoga IPA
Tours: Yes **Taproom:** Yes

Olde Saratoga Brewing Company is a subsidiary of Mendocino Brewing Company, based out of California. Opened in 1997, six full-time brewers at Olde Saratoga brew Mendocino's line of brews for the East Coast. In 2001 Olde Saratoga became the only brewery in the Northeast that makes and distributes Kingfisher Premium Lager, an Indian beer. Olde Saratoga is also a contract brewer, making beers for other breweries, many of them in New York, including Fire Island Beer Company and the Harlem Brewing Company.

But the team at Saratoga also makes its own beer, starting with the flagship **Olde Saratoga Lager** and also the **Saratoga IPA,** both recipes envisioned by former brewer Paul McErlean. The Lager is a German/Austrian-style Marzenbier that pours a coppery reddish color. Medium bodied with a full hop aroma, Saratoga Lager has sweet malty characters.

Beer Lover's Pick

Saratoga IPA
Style: IPA
ABV: 7%
Availability: Year-round
Saratoga IPA is made in the West Coast IPA style, brewed with Cascade and Fuggles hops. This beer pours an amber/copper color and has good head retention. Malty, earthy notes balance out the strong citrusy flavors of this full-bodied brew.

Saratoga's tasting room is open every day but Sunday, and brewery tours are available by appointment on Saturday. Beer is offered on tap and in bottles available at local bars, restaurants, and beer stores.

SACKETS HARBOR BREWING COMPANY

212 W. Main St., Sackets Harbor, NY 13685; (315) 646-2739; SacketsHarborBrewpub.com
Founded: 1995 **Founders:** Stephen and Errol Flynn **Current Owners:** Tom and Pearl Scozzafava **Brewer:** Andy Gersten **Flagship Beer:** War of 1812 Amber Ale **Year-Round Beers:** War of 1812 Amber Ale, Thousand Island Pale Ale, Malicious Intent Double IPA, 1812 Light, St Stephen's Stout, Pillar Point Porter **Seasonals/Special Releases:** Lake Effect Lager, ApriCats-Meow, Oktoberfest, Railroad Red, Brown, Russian Roulette Vanilla Stout, Sacketts Vienna, German Alt **Tours:** Yes **Taproom:** Yes

Situated on the shore of Lake Ontario, Sackets Harbor Brewing Company in Sackets Harbor was founded in 1995 by Stephen and Errol Flynn in an old New York Central railroad depot. Sackets started out as a brewpub and started distribution several years later. In the 2009 Tom Scozzafava and his wife Pearl took over ownership of the brewery and brought back Andy Gersten, a former brewmaster.

The Scozzafavas had been living in New York City for over a decade, and they decided it was time for a change. They heard the brewpub in Tom's hometown was up for sale, so they took the opportunity to move to the quaint, lakefront spot and operate the facility. All beers served at the pub location are made on premises, but several beers distributed throughout the area are made at Sly Fox Brewery in Pottstown, Pennsylvania.

Many names of Sackets beers are inspired by the town, such as **Lake Effect Lager** and **Railroad Red.** The Lager is a German-style Pilsner, easy drinking with malty flavors and slight spicy hop aromas. The Red was a silver medalist in the 1998 World Beer Championships and is made with a blend of four hops varietals. Well-balanced, this Irish-style ale pours a deep red color and has notes of roast chocolate in the flavor. The **ApriCats-Meow** is a summer seasonal, a Wheat beer made with 180 pounds of apricot. **Russian Roulette Vanilla Stout** is a winter seasonal from Sackets, smooth and silky with vanilla notes on the aroma and finish.

The dining room at Sackets Harbor Brewing Company has panoramic views of beautiful Lake Ontario, and a large outdoor patio that seats 100 is a fine place to enjoy a few brews during warm weather. A full menu features standard pub fare, with sandwiches, burgers, salads, and several seafood options.

Beer Lover's Pick

War of 1812 Ale
Style: Amber
ABV: 5.2%
Availability: Year-round, at the pub and also at places throughout Northern New York

Sackets' flagship beer was awarded a silver medal in its category in the 1998 World Beer Championships. The palate is dominated by malty and nutty flavors, with notes of citrus from the hops. The 1812 Ale is well balanced and medium bodied.

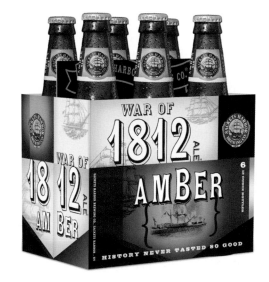

Brewpubs

DRUTHERS BREWING COMPANY

381 Broadway, Saratoga Springs, NY 12866; (518) 306-5275; DruthersBrewing.com; @DruthersBrewing

Founded: 2012 **Founders:** Chris Martell, Brian Martell, George de Piro **Brewer:** George de Piro **Year-round Beers:** Golden Rule, Brevity Wit, Simple Truth Barley Wine, Druthers Porter, Fist of Karma Brown Ale, All in IPA **Seasonals/Special Releases:** Vienna Style Lager, ESB, Oatmeal Stout, Weizen Doppel Bock, Oktoberfest, Smokey Bacon Ale, Pilsner, Autumn Amber **Tours:** No **Taproom:** Yes

Saratoga is a bustling upstate town full of restaurants and shops, but Druthers, founded in 2012 by Chris Martell, Brian Martell, and George de Piro, is the only brewpub located in the downtown area. De Piro is the brewer and helped to start Druthers after working at C.H. Evans Brewing Company at the Albany Pump Station. Set back behind a gate and patio on Broadway, Druthers pours a wide variety of beers across many styles: German, Belgian, English, and American.

The servers are friendly and helpful when going over the beer list. The inky black **Oatmeal Stout** has great roasted coffee flavors and keeps the silkiness from the oats to a perfect level. The **Blonde Ale** is clear and golden with a nice crispness followed by some fruity sweetness. The food is high-quality pub style, with burgers, pasta, and fish-and-chips. Pairing the pulled pork sandwich with the ESB, which has a great caramel flavor and is balanced out by a distinct hop bitterness, works very well.

The brewery itself is on the second floor and visible from the bar area, where you can enjoy a beer and a televised sporting event. Restaurant seating is available behind the bar underneath the brewing equipment. Additional seating is available in the front patio area during the summer months along with an outside bar.

GREAT ADIRONDACK BREWING COMPANY

2442 Main St., Lake Placid, NY 12946; (518) 523-1629; AdSteakAndSeafood.com/Brewery; @GreatAdirondack

Founded: 1996 **Founders:** The Kane Family **Brewer:** Frank Koester **Year-Round Beers:** White Face Black Diamond Stout, Ausable Wulff Red Ale, Haystack Blonde, John Brown Pale Ale, Smoked Porter **Seasonals/Special Releases:** Adirondack Abbey Ale, American Wheat, Avalanche IPA, Belgian Gold, Belgian Saision, Belgian Summer, Black and White Porter, Giant, Snail Trail Pale Ale, Pumpkin Spice, Tripel Diamond, Wheat Wine, Sean's Super Nugget IPA, Lil John Session IPA, Farmhouse Pale Ale **Tours:** By request **Taproom:** Yes

Great Adirondack Brewing Company has been located in the back of Great Adirondack Steak and Seafood on Main Street in the town of Lake Placid since 1997. The brewery's focus is crafting accessible beers that pair well with the restaurant's food. Brewer Frank Koester, a photographer and former New York City policeman turned brewer, brews on the seven-barrel brewhouse and always tries to emphasize drinkability with malt-forward beers that don't overwhelm the palate with hops.

Koester's **Whiteface Black Diamond Stout,** a nod to the popular skiing site nearby, is a full-bodied Stout that brings out roasted flavors of coffee and chocolate. The **Haystack Blonde Ale** is light bodied and easy drinking with a slight sweetness that's balanced out with a bit of grassy hop character. Great Adirondack's **Ausable Wulff Red Ale** is one of the best Red Ales in a region of brewers who all seem to brew one. The beer pours a deep amber color with a white head. The nose has some sweetness with a bit of floral hop aromas. Toffee and caramel flavors are dominant but not overwhelming, and the carbonation lifts the sweetness off the palate well.

The bar at Great Adirondack is full of details that make it a fun place to spend an afternoon. Walls are covered with different service badges from the police, fire, and military sent in by patrons from around the world. Koester carved the wooden tap handles, and the wooden coasters are branded with Lake Placid images.

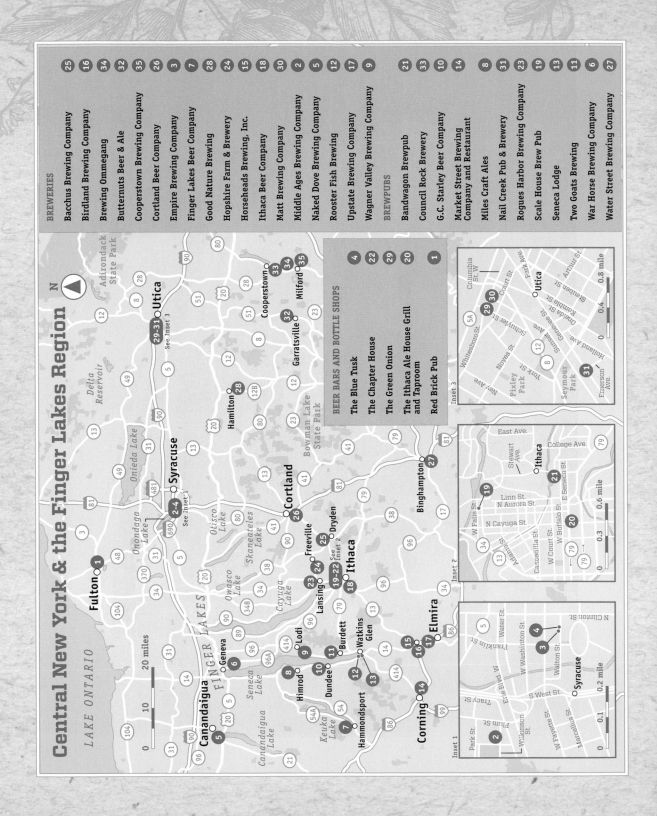

Central New York & the Finger Lakes Region

LAKE ONTARIO

FINGER LAKES

BREWERIES

Bacchus Brewing Company 25
Birdland Brewing Company 16
Brewing Ommegang 34
Butternuts Beer & Ale 32
Cooperstown Brewing Company 35
Cortland Beer Company 26
Empire Brewing Company 3
Finger Lakes Beer Company 7
Good Nature Brewing 28
Hopshire Farm & Brewery 24
Horseheads Brewing, Inc. 15
Ithaca Beer Company 18
Matt Brewing Company 30
Middle Ages Brewing Company 2
Naked Dove Brewing Company 5
Rooster Fish Brewing 12
Upstate Brewing Company 17
Wagner Valley Brewing Company 9

BREWPUBS

Bandwagon Brewpub 21
Council Rock Brewery 33
G.C. Starley Beer Company 10
Market Street Brewing Company and Restaurant 14
Miles Craft Ales 8
Nail Creek Pub & Brewery 31
Rogues Harbor Brewing Company 23
Scale House Brew Pub 19
Seneca Lodge 13
Two Goats Brewing 11
War Horse Brewing Company 6
Water Street Brewing Company 27

BEER BARS AND BOTTLE SHOPS

The Blue Tusk 4
The Chapter House 22
The Green Onion 29
The Ithaca Ale House Grill and Taproom 20
Red Brick Pub 1

Central New York & the Finger Lakes Region

While historically known for its wineries, Central New York and the Finger Lakes Region are home to the largest concentration of breweries in the state. And the diversity is astounding. You'll find a hot and spicy chili beer from Horseheads Brewing Inc., made with Anaheim and jalapeño peppers, or a classic Belgian Saison from Brewery Ommegang, or even a Riesling Ale—made using the juice of Riesling grapes—from War Horse Brewing Company.

The region doesn't have one central hub that acts as a centerpiece for the beer trend. Instead clusters of small breweries have popped up in both rural and urban areas, almost all with a focus on their communities. In the Finger Lakes, sandwiched between I-90 in the north and Route 17 (also known as the Southern Tier Expressway) to the south, breweries are catching up with the already popular vineyards in the area, and the region is leading the way in use of the new farm brewery license available in the state. In Utica you'll find the venerable brewing giant Matt Brewing Company, one of the oldest in the state and the first to officially serve beer after Prohibition, and Syracuse has a vibrant and tight-knit group of breweries and bars.

Breweries

BACCHUS BREWING COMPANY

15 Ellis Dr., Dryden, NY 13053; (607) 844-8474; BacchusBrewing.com; @BacchusBrewCo
Founded: 2012 **Founder:** David McCune **Brewer:** Christina Poulos **Year-round Beers:**
IPA, Blonde Ale, Irish Red Rye Ale, Pale Ale **Seasonals/Special Releases:** Oatmeal
Stout **Tours:** Yes **Taproom:** Yes

When David McCune opened his physical therapy practice in 2005, he purchased a large building that would also house a planned fitness center. But when the local community college began building a public fitness center as well, McCune knew the small town of Dryden couldn't support both. Within a 15-mile radius of his building are four colleges and universities, and knowing how much beer college students consume, McCune had a perfect solution for the empty space.

Irish Red Rye Ale
Style: Red Rye
ABV: 5.5%
Availability: Year-round on draft

Brewed with a two-row base malt and a blend of Munich and Victory malts, the Irish Red Rye Ale from Bacchus is full bodied and slightly sweet at the start. Columbus and East Kent Golding hops add a good bitterness. Many Rye beers are overly hopped, but this one is well balanced. A slight spice of rye carries throughout, with an overarching taste of toast. At a manageable 5.5 percent ABV, the Irish Red Rye Ale isn't quite sessionable, but it's easy drinking and refreshing.

The only problem was that McCune didn't know how to brew beer on a large scale. He was introduced to local homebrewer Christina Poulos, and they began working together. In 2007 Poulos started refining and perfecting the first recipes for Bacchus Brewing Company, named for the god of libations. The brewery officially launched and offered up its first beers in 2012.

Poulos grew up in Michigan and takes inspiration from Bell's Brewery, Founders Brewing Company, and New Holland, acclaimed breweries in her home state. She aims to create flavorful beers that are a bit different. Bacchus beers are only distributed locally; the brewery's mission is to bring fresh beer to the neighborhood.

At Bacchus's taproom you can taste beers and get growler fills, while taking a peek at the brewing operation through large windows. The **IPA** is a great version of the style: bitter but well balanced, with not many floral qualities. Brewed with Nugget and Centennial hops, this beer has a hint of citrus and is an easy-drinking 6.5 ABV. The **Blonde Ale** is a Belgian-style Blonde Ale and is crisp and refreshing. Dry but not too sweet, the Blonde Ale comes in at 5.5 percent ABV and finishes cleanly.

BIRDLAND BREWING COMPANY

1015 Kendall St., Horseheads, NY 14845; (607) 769-2337; BirdlandBrewingCo.com
Founded: 2012 **Founders:** Dennis Edwards, Susan Edwards, Michael Hess **Brewer:**
Dennis Edwards **Year-round Beers:** Mountie Brees, Kewlerskald, Red Wing, Blue Jay
Seasonals/Special Releases: Sap Sucker, Blue Bird, Falcon, Phoenix, Peacock, Wild
Canary, Flabingo **Tours:** No **Taproom:** Yes

For two decades Dennis Edwards was a fervent homebrewer learning the ins and
outs of the brewing process while staying flexible and allowing his ingredients
and conditions to help him develop new recipes. After years of encouragement from
friends and family, Dennis and his wife Susan decided to team up with their friend
Mike Hess to open a brewery in Horseheads, New York. Visit the taproom where the
team serves four year-round beers and several seasonal and specialty beers, and you
can experience firsthand how they exude excitement for their beers.

Peacock
Style: Golden Ale
ABV: 5%
Availability: Spring and summer
Most Golden Ales are light bodied and crisp with muted flavors
balancing each other out for
an easy-drinking experience.
So it comes as quite a surprise
when you take your first sip of
Peacock and are greeted by the
smooth mouthfeel and body
usually reserved for Oatmeal Stouts. The roundness from the oats acts to further level
the playing field between the malty sweetness and the slight grassiness of the hops.

Dennis looks to brew approachable yet interesting beers that new beer drinkers
can get excited about and experienced drinkers can be surprised by. The seasonal
Sap Sucker features a full body backed by malt flavors of molasses that is given
a boost from the addition of local maple sap. To satisfy hopheads, the brewery
crafted **Blue Jay** with a blend of the American hop varieties Cascade, Simcoe, and
Centennial for a strong bitterness and slight citrus aroma. For a bit of fun, Dennis
also brews **Flabingo,** a tart and fruity blend of berries and cranberry. The team refers
to this beer as a "malternative."

With a small three-barrel system, demand is quickly pushing the limits of what
Dennis can brew; he plans to eventually expand to a 10-barrel system. The larger system will allow the brewery, which currently self-distributes to a handful of accounts,
to deliver to more local bars and restaurants.

BREWERY OMMEGANG

656 County Hwy. 33, Cooperstown, NY 13326; (607) 544-1800; Ommegang.com;
@BreweryOmmegang
Founded: 1997 **Founders:** Don Feinberg and Wendy Littlefield **Brewer:** Phil Leinhart
Flagship Beer: Abbey Ale **Year-round Beers:** Abbey Ale, Rare Vos, Witte, Hennepin,
BPA (Belgian Pale Ale), Three Philosophers **Seasonals/Special Releases:** Scythe and
Sickle, Art of Darkness, Aphrodite, Cup O Kyndnes, Zuur, Chocolate Indulgence, Biere de
Mars, Ommegeddon, Fleur de Houblon, Seduction, Biere d'Hougoumont, Duvel Rustica,
Gnomegang, Adoration, Game of Thrones Series **Tours:** Yes; 7 days a week on the hour
Taproom: Yes

Driving on the sleepy county roads around Cooperstown, home to the Baseball Hall of Fame, it might be difficult to believe that there are no less than four breweries in the area. Still more difficult that one is Brewery Ommegang, one of the most recognizable brewers of Belgian beer styles in the United States. Brewery Ommegang was originally launched by Don Feinberg and Wendy Littlefield, owners of the importing business Vanberg and Dewulf, as a way to get Belgian styles of beer into the glasses of American drinkers at a time when importing was difficult. After making a name for the brewery and building a successful importing business, Feinberg and Littlefield sold the company to Duvel Moortgat Inc., well-known as one of the largest breweries in Belgium. Under the agreement Ommegang serves as

an entry point for importing Duvel and other Belgian beers into the United States, and the brewery has autonomy over the beers they brew, with access to its parent company's resources, especially equipment.

The brewery started out with only one beer, then called **Ommegang Ale,** now named **Abbey Ale,** a deep brown Belgian-style Dubbel with notes of dark fruit like plum and raisin. Now the brewery offers a long lineup of Saisons, Wits, and Stouts as well as numerous seasonals and special releases. Among the most popular is **Rare Vos,** an Amber Ale brewed with sweet orange peel, grains of paradise, and coriander for a full-bodied ale with notes of spice and pepper. The brewery has also experimented with funky and sour beers like **Ommegeddon** and **Biere de Mars,** both of which were fermented with Brettanomyces.

The brewery runs tours that are very informative and fill up quickly, so make sure to arrive early to get a spot. Even if you can't make it onto a tour, the cafe is a great way to spend an afternoon either inside or out on the patio looking out on the brewery's property. The Belgian-inspired food menu features some of the best mussels you are likely to have, along with crepes, sandwiches, and waffles. The brewery also hosts Belgium Comes to Cooperstown (p. 272), one of the most popular festivals in the state.

Witte

Style: Belgian-style Wheat Ale

ABV: 5.2%

Availability: Year-round, in large bottles and on draft

A glass of fresh Ommegang Witte is a wonderful thing on a warm day. The hazy beer has a rocky white head with a sweet bready aroma that has a touch of lemon. The use of malted and unmalted wheat lends a creamy body to the beer that the effervescence from the Ommegang's house yeast balances out well. The beer makes a great pairing for summer salads.

BUTTERNUTS BEER & ALE

4021 New York 51, Garrattsville, NY 13342; (607) 263-5070; ButternutsBeerAndAle.com;
@ButternutsBeer
Founded: 2005 **Founder and Brewer:** Chuck Williamson **Flagship Beer:** PorkSlap
Pale Ale **Year-round Beers:** Snapperhead IPA, Moo Thunder Stout, PorkSlap Pale Ale,
Heinnieweisse Weissebier **Seasonals/Special Releases:** Brown Ale, Brutus Imperial
IPA, E.S.P (Extra Special PorkSlap), Trappist Ale, Country Gold Saison, Landis Harvest Ale
Tours: Yes **Taproom:** Yes

Just off route 51 in the town of Garrattsville in the Butternut Mountains in Upstate New York sits an old white dairy barn. Driving up to it you wouldn't think there was much going on; you may even pass right by. But inside is booming Butternuts Beer & Ale, founded by Chuck Williamson in 2005. Williamson started brewing professionally in his 20s, when he had an apprenticeship at the now-defunct Long Island Brewing Company, then brewed in Manhattan and Brooklyn before thinking about opening his own operation. Williamson was working in Red Hook on September 11, and after witnessing the World Trade Center attacks decided

to find property Upstate for his venture. He brews Butternuts beer on a Peter Austin brew kettle, characterized by the bricks that line the outside.

Butternuts has always canned its beer, due to cans' portability and ability to shield the beer from light. The brewery is known for its whimsy, whether in beer names or can artwork. **PorkSlap Pale Ale** (the moniker is a play on Brooklyn's Park Slope neighborhood) is Butternuts's flagship offering. A drinkable, sessionable beer at 4.3 percent ABV, PorkSlap is medium to light bodied, with notes of ginger, a slight sweetness, and low bitterness. **Snapperhead IPA** is also a light bodied but bitter IPA, crisp and tasty out of the can, a drinkable 6.8 percent ABV. The **Heinnieweisse Weissebier** is a sweet Wheat beer, citrusy on the nose and palate, with hints of clove and spice. Low in alcohol, Heinnieweisse comes in at 4.9 percent ABV, a crisp beer great for warm-weather drinking.

Since opening Butternuts, Williamson has expanded, purchasing Butternut Valley Golf and Recreation—whose Clubhouse & Brewery serves his beers—and Cooperstown Brewing Company. Williamson contracts for many other breweries at his two facilities, such as Spider Bite Beer Company, Evil Genius Beer Company, and

Beer Lover's Pick

Moo Thunder Stout
Style: Milk Stout
ABV: 4.9%
Availability: Year-round, in cans and on draft

Sometimes it's nice to drink a Stout that you don't have to worry about creeping up on you as the day or night goes on. Moo Thunder, at 4.9 percent ABV, is smooth and drinkable and not overly roasted. A Milk Stout, you'll definitely taste the lactose, which also contributes to a milky, creamy texture and smooth mouthfeel.

Ruckus Brewing Company. Butternuts' beers are widely distributed, and the canned offerings are available year-round. For $2 during a visit to the brewery's taproom, you can taste the canned lineup as well as any special or contract brews they may have on tap.

COOPERSTOWN BREWING COMPANY

110 River St., Milford, NY 13807; (607) 286-9330; CooperstownBrewing.com; @CoopBrewCo
Founded: 1995 **Founders:** Stan and Brian Hall **Brewer:** Chuck Williamson **Flagship Beer:** Old Slugger **Year-round Beers:** Old Slugger, Nine Man Ale, Benchwarmer, Strike Out Stout, Back Yard IPA, Pride of Milford, Striker **Tours:** Yes **Taproom:** Yes; open daily

During a baseball game, it's practically obligatory to enjoy a hot dog and a beer. Cooperstown, with the Baseball Hall of Fame and yearly youth ball tournaments, is the ultimate baseball city. It's only fitting that the city has a brewery to its name: Cooperstown Brewing Company, which is actually in Milford, the town next door. Father/son team Stan and Brian Hall started the Cooperstown Brewing Company in 1995. The pair owned and operated the facility until 2011, when they sold it to

Old Slugger
Style: American Pale Ale
ABV: 5.5%
Availability: Year-round, in bottles or on draft
Cooperstown Old Slugger is a Pale Ale, and the brewery's flagship offering. Brewed with Fuggles, Cascade, and Mount Hood hops, Old Slugger pours an amber color with a foamy white head. Slightly bitter, malt and caramel flavors come through in the taste.

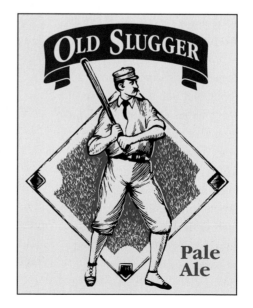

Chuck Williamson, founder and brewer of Butternuts Beer and Ale. Williamson kept the original recipes and continued brewing the Cooperstown lineup. The beers are produced on an authentic Peter Austin brewing system, All the beers are brewed and bottled on premises.

All of Cooperstown's beers are British-style Ales made with Ringwood yeast. The **Pride of Milford Special Ale** (a shout-out to the town that the brewery calls home) is an English Strong Ale with malt, caramel, and toffee aromas. Not exactly easy drinking at 7.7 percent ABV, this brew is medium bodied with a malt-forward taste and notes of caramel, dark fruit, nuts, and toffee on the palate. Cooperstown's English Porter brew, the **Benchwarmer,** has coffee and chocolate aromas that carry over to the taste, which finishes with a mild roastiness. The **Nine Man Golden Ale** is a sessionable Blonde Ale at 4.3 percent ABV. Floral and grassy, a slight hop character lends this light-bodied brew a piney quality.

When you stop by Cooperstown Brewing Company you can go on a tour of the facility and enjoy a tasting of whatever's on tap. It's a shabby building, adorned with a decal of a baseball player wielding a bat on the outside; vintage beer trays line one of the walls inside. You can fill up a growler or purchase bottles of beer to go. Make sure to take a peek at the hop bines growing outside.

CORTLAND BEER COMPANY

16 Court Street, Cortland, New York 13045; (607) 662-4389; CortlandBeer.com; @CortlandBeerCo
Founded: 2007 **Founders:** Tom Scheffler, Terry Vestal, Dan Cleary **Brewer:** Tom Scheffler
Year-round Beers: Naked Lap Lager, Firehouse Pale Ale, Sunrise Coffee Stout, Industrial IPA, Red Dragon Ale, Seven Valley Stout **Seasonals/Special Releases:** Heifer Weizen, Flight Level 410, Pumpkin Ale, Black Widow Stout, Bourbon Barrel Flight Level 410 **Tours:** No **Taproom:** Yes

Cortland Beer Company's 900-square-foot taproom bustles on Friday afternoon with a variety of age groups visiting the brewery. The tasting room's involvement in Cortland's regular art walks keeps the crowd and decor interesting. Cortland started as a small contract brewing operation in 2007 out of Butternuts Beer & Ale in Garrettsville with their Crown City Kolsch, which the brewery has since replaced in the lineup. In 2010 the brewery finished an expansion to a 20-barrel brew system that helps them supply the surrounding areas with kegs and 22-ounce bottles. Since moving into its own facility, Cortland added seasonal and special-release beers. The brewery received media attention in 2011 when senator Charles Schumer visited as part of his "I Love NY Brew" campaign to raise public awareness of the state's craft brewing industry.

The brewers brew to their own tastes but manage to keep a wide variety of beers on tap in the tasting room. The recipes are predominantly malt forward with only the **Industrial IPA** showing strong American-style hop character with citrus aromas and aggressive bitterness. Among the bestsellers is the clear golden **Naked Lap Lager,** which adds some more depth to the traditional pale Lagers. As many other Upstate brewers do, Cortland Beer Company produces a Red Ale, in this case the **Red Dragon Ale** with a caramel sweetness and surprisingly strong bitterness at 47 IBUs. The brewery's Stouts seem to be where its strength lies with **Seven Valley Stout, Sunrise Coffee Stout,** and **Black Widow Stout.** Sunrise Coffee Stout screams dark-roasted coffee in the aroma and smoothes things out with sweet, almost cookie-like malt character. The popular **Flight Level 410,** a big English-style Barleywine that packs a punch at 10% ABV, took home the 2011 Silver Medal for Best Individual Beer in the state at TAP NY.

Beer Lover's Pick

Bourbon Barrel Flight Level 410
Style: Bourbon Barrel-aged English Barleywine
ABV: 10%
Availability: Limited
Big bold flavors you might expect from aging an English Barleywine in bourbon barrels are all there in the Bourbon Barrel Flight Level 410. The deep ruby color produces a tan head and some impressive lacing on the glass. Intense toffee and caramel sweetness mixes with the toasted oak and finishes with vanilla from the bourbon.

EMPIRE BREWING COMPANY

120 Walton St., Syracuse, NY 13202; (315) 475-BEER; EmpireBrew.com; @EmpireBrew
Founded: 1994 **Founder:** David Katleski **Brewer:** Tim Butler **Flagship Beer:** Amber
Ale **Year-round Beers:** Cream Ale, Amber Ale, IPA, Black Magic Stout, Empire State Pale
Ale (ESPA), White Aphro **Seasonals/Special Releases:** Empire Strikes Back Maibock,
Roasted Pumpkin Ale, Summer Ale, Winter Warmer, Hefe-Weizen, American Strong Ale,
Critz Apple Ale, Deep Purple, Barley Wine, Downtown Brown, Maple Porter, Wheat Wine,
Golden Dragon, Hop Harvest, Liv and Let Rye, Local Grind, Smoked Porter, Purple Dragon,
Skinny Atlas Kolsch, Empire Saison, Blueberry Wheat, Cherry Stout, Chocolate Mint
Stout, Critz' Hard Raspberry Cider, Instigator Doppelbock, Scotch Ale, Sub-Terranian Ale
Tours: No **Taproom:** Yes

David Katleski opened Empire Brewing Company as a brewpub in 1994 with
Michael Hodgdon. Over the next several of years, they opened additional loca-
tions in Rochester and Buffalo, then had closed all three by 2003. The original
Syracuse brewpub remained empty, but exactly as Katleski and Hodgdon had left it.
In 2007, Katleski decided to pick up where he left off, and opened Empire again,
with Brewmaster Tim Butler making all the beer at the Syracuse brewpub until 2010.
That year, Katleski expanded brewing operations through Greenpoint Beer Works in
Brooklyn, where brewer Kelly Taylor began making some of Empire's beers for wider
distribution.

Empire Brewing Company's brewpub is basement level, and when you walk down
the stairs from Walton Street, you'll find a brick-lined restaurant, with shiny copper
brewing equipment visible through glass windows behind the bar. The menu reflects
a sustainable mind-set important to Katleski. Locally grown and raised ingredients
dot the menu, with offerings such as a farmstead chili with local elk and other
free-range, grass-fed, locally sourced meats. The spent grain from Empire beers is
donated to a nearby farm, and Butler uses many regional ingredients in his beers,
like fresh, farm-grown pumpkin for the fall seasonal **Critz's Pumpkin Ale. White
Aphro** is a Witbier brewed using ginger and lavender, a refreshing, crisp citrusy beer,
with notes of coriander, pepper, and honey.

Katleski is the founder and president of the New York State Brewers Association,
where he was instrumental in obtaining new legislation for New York brewers, like
the Farm Brewery Law, which went into effect in January 2013. Katleski lives in
Cazenovia, where he plans a farmstead brewery for Empire that will take advantage
of the new law. Ground was broken on the facility in 2013.

Cream Ale
Style: Cream Ale
ABV: 5.2%
Availability: Year-round on draft
Empire's Cream Ale has been
brewed at Greenpoint Beer
Works in Brooklyn since 2010.
An incredibly drinkable beer, at
5.2 percent ABV, the Cream Ale
is smooth and of course creamy. There's a light bitterness and bready, malty flavors,
with a subtle sweetness. It's a refreshing beer, and if you can find it poured on nitro,
try a pint.

FINGER LAKES BEER COMPANY

8462 SR 54, P.O. Box 356, Hammondsport, NY 14840; (607) 569-3311;
FingerLakesBeerCompany.com; @FLXBeer
Founded: 2009 **Founders and Brewers:** Wayne Peworchik, Mark Goodwin **Flagship
Beer:** Vanilla Porter **Year-round Beers:** Aviator, Newton's Pale Ale, 11/11 IPA,
Copperline Ale, Ring of Fire, Nut Brown, Hammonds Porter **Seasonals/Special Releases:**
Mr. Melon, Indian Summer Ale, Whiteout Wassail **Tours:** Yes **Taproom:** Yes

After homebrewing for years, Wayne Peworchik and Mark Goodwin (formerly of
Keuka Brewing) decided to take the leap to start their own brewery in 2009.
After attending the Concise Course in Brewing Technology from the Siebel Institute,
the pair bought a seven-barrel brewing system and opened their doors to the public
on November 11, 2010. The pair purchased a building in Hammondsport, at the
southern tip of the scenic Keuka Lake, for Finger Lakes Beer Company, just outside
the main clusters of breweries around Seneca and Cayuga Lakes. Peworchik and
Goodwin picked a building with enough space to expand capacity in the future to
keep up with demand and maintain a taproom. At the taproom, beers are served
directly from tanks for tastings and growler fills. You can also purchase some beer
soaps, shampoo, and lip balm made from the brewery's beers by local producer For
Claudia's Sayke.

Hammonds Porter
Style: Vanilla Porter
ABV: 5.6%
Availability: Year-round
Instead of using extract, Peworchik and Goodwin opted to use real vanilla beans in their Vanilla Porter, giving the beer a rich aroma. Dark and sweet, the Vanilla Porter keeps the roasted qualities of Porters in check, allowing the vanilla flavors to come through while staying in balance. This is a great dessert beer to pair with cookies or cake.

The beers span from hoppy to malty and make good food pairings. The **11/11 IPA,** the largest beer of the year-round offerings at 7% ABV, has an amber hue and is dry hopped for a full week for some significant floral hop notes. The **Ring of Fire,** a ruby-colored Scotch Ale, has a touch of smoke from the use of smoked malt. The brewery also brews three seasonals, including the **Whiteout Wassail** for winter, which has nutmeg and cinnamon flavors. For some added oak character, Finger Lakes Beer started experimenting with aging the Whiteout Wassail in Jack Daniels barrels. As a brewery that requires you to drive for a visit, the root beer is a much-appreciated option for designated drivers.

Finger Lakes beers are available at a handful of restaurants and bars in the area. In 2013 the brewery added bottling to the operation for the Aviator Wheat, Newton's Pale Ale, Copperline Ale, and Hammonds Porter.

GOOD NATURE BREWING

37 Milford St., Hamilton, NY 13346; (315) 824-BEER; GoodNatureBrewing.com;
@GoodNatureBeer

Founded: 2012 **Founders:** Carrie Blackmore, Matt Whalen **Brewer:** Matt Whalen
Year-round Beers: Good Natured Blonde, American Pale Ale, IPA, American Brown Ale,
Chicory Mocha Porter, The Nor'easter **Seasonals/Special Releases:** Hypocrite Witte,
Belgian IPA, Solstice Oat Stout, CNY Harvest, The Great Chocolate Wreck, The Warm N'
Toasty, Anniversary Ale, Rabbit in the RyePA, Solera Bourbon-Aged Porter **Tours:** Yes; by
appointment **Taproom:** Yes; located at 8 Broad Street in Hamilton

Husband-and-wife team Carrie Blackmore and Matt Whalen is committed to sustainability. Blackmore has a farm-to-table background, and Whalen is a trained chef and homebrewer. Together they opened Good Nature Brewing in 2012, first on a two-barrel system then soon expanding to seven barrels. From the beginning, the pair sourced all their hops from local New York State growers and also began using barley from local farmers. Since they are so committed to using ingredients from New York State, the duo were able to take advantage of the Farm Brewery Law in the state to be licensed as a farm brewery.

Rabbit in the RyePA
Style: Session Rye IPA
ABV: 5.0%
Availability: Limited

The second offering in Good Nature Brewing's Artist Series, Rabbit in the Rye is a collaboration beer with a Hamilton-based folk rock trio of the same name. Joseph Mettler, who plays guitar and harmonica in the group, designed this beer's label. Dubbed a "Session Rye IPA," Rabbit in the RyePA comes in at 5 percent ABV, slightly higher than session beers usually are, and is a great brew to enjoy more than one pint of during a drinking session. With the New York State hops lending this beer floral and spicy notes, it is nicely dry with a pronounced rye flavor.

When the law went into effect in January 2013, to qualify as a farm brewery, 20 percent of the beer's hops and 20 percent of other ingredients by volume (not including water) must be from New York. The percentage will increase to 60 after seven years, and to 90 five years after that. In Good Nature's case, the law allows them to sell beers by the pint. Taking advantage of their license (which they applied for the month it went into effect), Blackmore and Whalen opened a tasting room at 8 Broad Street in Hamilton, a few blocks from their original location. At the spacious and welcoming tasting room, patrons can order beers by the pint or flight, and occasionally be treated to live music from local acts.

Whalen is the head brewer and creates all of Good Nature's recipes. He strives to make beers that have complex flavors but are also clean and crisp. Shying away from hop bombs, Whalen draws much of his inspiration from his culinary background, striving to make his brews approachable, where each flavor stands out in the taste. His **Good Natured Blonde** is refreshingly sessionable at 4.5 percent ABV, slightly sweet but clean. Good Nature's brews are mostly available on draft, with its **Artist Series** line of specialty beers bottled in 750-milliliter large-format bottles, with labels designed by local artists. You can find these beers in Hamilton and its surrounding areas, the Capital Region, the Finger Lakes, Utica, and Rochester.

HOPSHIRE FARM & BREWERY

1771 Dryden Rd., Freeville, NY 13068; (607) 279-1243; Hopshire.com; @HopshireBrews
Founded: 2013 **Founders:** Diane Gerhart, Randy Lacey **Brewer:** Randy Lacey **Flagship Beers:** Shire Ale Scottish Ale, Near Varna IPA **Year-round Beers:** Beehave Honey Blonde, Shire Ale, Near Varna **Seasonals/Special Releases:** Blossom Cherry Wheat, Brambles Raspberry Wheat, Bog Cranberry Wheat; Zingabeer Pale Ale with Ginger, Abbey Normal dark Belgian, Sympathy Strong Golden; Daddy-O English Pale Ale, Acers Wild Imperial Maple Nut Brown **Tours:** Yes; except during brew days (usually Sunday) **Taproom:** Yes

When the Farm Brewery Law was passed in New York and went into effect in January 2013, it was a return to form. In the 19th century the state was the primary hop producer in America. While many factors contributed to the industry's demise (not the least of which were Prohibition and a mold outbreak), the Farm Brewery Law is helping put it back together. To be considered a farm brewery, the beers must be made with 20 percent New York ingredients. Hopshire Farm & Brewery, founded by Randy Lacey and his wife Diane Gerhart, is the fifth brewery to receive the Farm Brewery license.

Hopshire uses as many New York ingredients as possible to create local brews with the highest-quality ingredients, and grows a lot of its own hops. In addition to grains and hops, Lacey (also the head brewer) has incorporated local honey, cherries, and maple syrup in his beers. A main feature of his brewery is a re-creation of a New York hop kiln, used to dry the hops grown at Hopshire. Lacey's beers have whimsical names such as **Zingabeer,** a Belgian Pale Ale with the addition of ginger, which has clove, banana, and dark fruit flavors enhanced by the distinct notes of ginger. The ginger also contributes a subtle sweetness to the brew, which comes in at a drinkable 5.5 percent ABV. **Beehave,** a Honey Blonde Ale, is made using 100 percent New York–grown ingredients: barley from Omara Farm in Canastota, 65 pounds of basswood honey from Morse Mills in Moravia, and hops grown by Clair Haus in Lansing. With sessionable 4.2 percent ABV, the honey lends this brew a subtle sweetness.

In addition to ingredients that are as local as possible, Hopshire incorporates other sustainable elements into its facility. A sand bed under the tasting room stores waste heat from the brewing process and uses it to heat the building. Tubing

Near Varna
Style: IPA
ABV: 7.5%
Availability: Year-round on draft
Clocking in at 7.5 percent ABV,
Near Varna IPA is Hopshire's big-
gest offering, followed closely
by the 7.0 percent Hop Onyx.
This IPA is made with a base of pale and caramel malts, with hops added five times
during the boil, and then again while the beer is in the serving tank. With lots of
citrus and pine on the nose, Near Varna is a hop-forward brew that's balanced by a
noticeable malt quality.

submerged in a spring behind the building circulates water for cooling fermenters
and keeping the aging room at right temperature. Lacey and Gerhart plan to add
more eco-friendly elements in the future, including a biomass boiler and a solar
water heater.

HORSEHEADS BREWING, INC.

250 Old Ithaca Rd., Horseheads, NY 14845; (607) 739-8468; HorseheadsBrewing.com
Founded: 2007 **Founders:** Ed and Brenda Samchisen **Brewer:** Ed Samchisen **Year-round Beers:** Brickyard Red Ale, Chemung Canal Towpath Ale, Horseheads IPA, Hol-Jale Heim Beer With Bite, Newtown Brown Ale, Pale Expedition Ale **Seasonals/Special Releases:** Horseheads Orion, Chocolate Porter, Black Horse Ale, Maple Amber Ale, Blueberry Ale, Christmas Ale, Domination Ale, Horseheads Hefe, Iroquois Wheat Beer, Peach Wheat Beer, Lackawanna Steam Lager, Pumpkin Ale, Rye P.A., Sullivan's Stout
Tours: No **Taproom:** Yes; open Tuesday through Sunday at noon

Before starting Horseheads Brewing with his wife Brenda in 2007, Ed Samchisen
homebrewed for eight years and studied at the Siebel Institute in Chicago,
receiving his certificate of concise brewing technology. Since opening his brewery,
Samchisen and his beers have been widely acclaimed. In 2010 he was awarded the
F.X. Matt Memorial Cup for Best Craft Beer Brewery in New York State, and in 2012
and 2013 he received the Bronze and Silver Medals (respectively) for Best Craft Beer
in New York State.

Samchisen doesn't brew session beers, instead leaning toward bigger beers with bold flavors. His **IPA,** which comes in at 8.8 percent ABV, is full bodied with strong hop notes that contribute to a good citrus and floral quality. The **Chemung Canal Towpath Ale** is a Cream Ale, but while many Cream Ales tend to be subtle or mild, this one is bold and forward. With 7.2 percent ABV, the Towpath Ale has strong sweet flavors, but with just enough hop character to balance them out. Samchisen's spring offering, **Horseheads Hefe,** is a great beer for warm weather. Lower alcohol content than his other brews, the Hefe is a drinkable 5.6 percent ABV with banana and clove aromas distinctive of the style, a pleasant mouthfeel, and a subtly sweet palate. You can sample Horseheads beer and fill up growlers at its taproom, or find it on tap and in large-format bottles in Central and Eastern New York, as far down as New York City.

Hot-Jala-Heim Beer with Bite
Style: Fruit/Vegetable Beer
ABV: 7.2%
Availability: Year-round, on draft
and in large-format bottles

The Hot-Jala-Heim Beer with Bite is brewed with a mix of hot peppers, including jalapeños and Anaheims. A strong peppery aroma leads to a spicy palate in this brew, but the real showstopper here is the finish. A pleasant sensation of heat and spiciness lingers in the back of your mouth and throat. This beer is the perfect accompaniment to a salty bag of chips.

ITHACA BEER COMPANY

122 Ithaca Beer Dr., Ithaca, NY, 14850; (607) 273-0766; IthacaBeer.com; @IthacaBeer
Founded: 1998 **Founders:** Dan and Mari Mitchell **Brewers:** Bill, Mike, and Andrew Schwartz **Flagship Beer:** Flower Power **Year-round Beers:** Apricot Wheat Ale, Cascazilla, Flower Power IPA, Nut Brown, Pale Ale **Seasonals/Special Releases:** Cold Front, Country Pumpkin, Gorges Smoked Porter, Ground Break, Partly Sunny, Excelsior! White Gold, Excelsior! Anniversary Series, Excelsior! Le Bleu, Excelsior! Old Habit, Excelsior! AlpHalpHa **Tours:** Yes; Saturday and Sunday hourly between 12 and 4 p.m.
Taproom: Yes

From small beginnings in 1998, Ithaca Beer Company has become a central figure in the brewing community of the Finger Lakes and greater New York. Its tap handles are visible at bars and restaurants throughout the state. Beers like **Flower Power, Apricot Wheat,** and **Nut Brown** are well-known standbys, but the brewery also makes a wide variety of seasonal and special-release beers. The late-winter seasonal **Ground Break** is a popular Saison with some American twists, brewed with flaked rye and Amarillo hops. The beer is a dry and crisp way to end a season dominated by Stouts and Porters. The acclaimed **Excelsior!** series features the brewery's anniversary beers as well as annual limited beers like the **Excelsior! Le Bleu** brewed with New York State blueberries and Brettanomyces yeast. **Excelsior! AlpHalpHa** combines organic Pilsner malt, New York State–grown Cascade hops, and local alfalfa honey for a floral aroma and crisp bite to the end. When visiting the brewery, those not partaking of the brews can enjoy some top-notch root beer and ginger beer.

The experience at the new brewery, which opened in October 2012 with double the capacity of the old location, is about more than just the beer. Hop-lined paths greet visitors and lead them to the brewery's tasting room. Once inside you can view a spotless brewhouse through floor-to-ceiling windows before sidling up to the bar, grabbing a table, or heading out to the patio for a game of bocce. The fields that stretch out beyond the patio windows belong to the brewery, where future plans include growing hops and grain for brewing and produce for the taproom's kitchen.

Beer Lover's Pick

Flower Power IPA
Style: American IPA
ABV: 7.5%
Availability: Year-round

Ithaca Beer Company's Flower Power IPA might fly a bit under the radar, but it can stack up next to the best IPAs in the country. The golden-colored beer is capped by a fluffy white head that emits great floral and grapefruit aromas. The hops are aggressive, with strong citrus notes and a piney resinous character that is balanced with slight toasted bread flavors. A fresh pint at the brewery is especially aromatic.

Flights are offered by category: Excelsior!, Hop, Year-round, and Seasonal. Recently Ithaca started serving some interesting cask ales like a dark mild aged on cherry wood or their Apricot Wheat with whole apricots in the cask. The kitchen puts out tasty sandwiches, cheese plates, and pizzas.

MATT BREWING COMPANY

811 Edward St., Utica, NY 13502; (800) 765-6288; Saranac.com; @SaranacBrewery
Founded: 1888 **Founder:** Francis Xavier Matt I **Product Development Manager:** Rich Michaels **Flagship Beers:** Saranac Pale Ale, Utica Club **Year-round Beers:** Utica Club, Pale Ale, Adirondack Lager, Black Forest, Black & Tan, Black Forest, Belgian White, Pomegranate Wheat, Brown Ale, Irish Red Ale, Kölsch, Traditional Lager **Seasonals/ Special Releases:** Big Moose Ale, Chocolate Lager, Roggen Bock, Belgian Ale, Black Diamond, Bock, Caramel Porter, Chocolate Amber, Extra Special Bitter, Golden Pilsner, Hefeweizen, Imperial IPA, Imperial Stout, Marzenbier, Mocha Stout, Mountain Ale, Oatmeal Stout, Nut Brown Ale, Octoberfest, Pumpkin Ale, Rauchbier, Scotch Ale, Season's Best, Single Malt, Summer Ale, White IPA, Winter Wassail **Tours:** Yes; June through August: Monday through Saturday at 2 and 3 p.m.; September through May: Friday and Saturday at 1 and 3 p.m. **Taproom:** Yes; only for those who have just completed a tour

Matt Brewing Company is the oldest continually operating brewery in New York State. Its namesake, Francis Xavier Matt I, immigrated to the United States after working at the Duke of Baden Brewery in Germany. He found work at the

Charles Bierbauer Brewery in Utica (in operation since 1853), and in 1888 Matt reorganized the brewery into The West End Brewing Company. When Prohibition hit, the company was able to survive by producing sodas under the label Utica Club. When Prohibition ended, **Utica Club** became the flagship beer. Matt was at the helm of the brewery until 1951, when his son Walter Matt took over as president, modernizing brewery equipment. In 1980, F. X. Matt II took over the business and renamed it F.X. Matt Brewing Company after his grandfather; it goes by Matt Brewing Company. In 1985 he introduced the Saranac brand, and in 1986 started making beer as a contract brewery. In 2010 the business purchased Flying Bison Brewing Company in Buffalo as a subsidiary. And in 2013 a two-barrel pilot brewery was installed for testing new flavors.

Currently Matt Brewing Company is led by a fourth generation of family owners: Nick Matt as chairman and CEO, and his nephew Fred Matt as president. It has built up its Saranac lineup of beers, which are not only distributed across the country but also to Japan, Canada, and Australia. Under the Saranac name the brewery makes a handful of sodas, including root beer, flavors of cream soda, and ginger beer. And of course it has kept on producing the iconic **Utica Club.**

Utica Club
Style: American Adjunct Lager
ABV: 5%
Availability: Year-round, on draft and in cans

Matt Brewing Company's Utica Club was the first official beer sold in the United States after Prohibition. An American adjunct Lager, you're going to taste the hallmark nonflavors of that style. Sure, it's not the best beer, but it's one of the most historic and iconic brands you'll find in New York State. It's a must-try for any beer enthusiast.

A major facet of Matt Brewing Company's business is contracting for other breweries. One of the most notable examples is Brooklyn Brewery, which was able to get off the ground with its flagship Brooklyn Lager by having it brewed by Matt. Today most of Brooklyn's core selection of beers is still made at the facility, as well as its lineup of cans. Make sure to visit the Matt Brewing Company when you can go on a tour, because beer tastings are only available to those who have just completed one. Otherwise you can always stop by to browse the extensive gift shop for glassware, knickknacks, and of course bottled brews.

MIDDLE AGES BREWING COMPANY

120 Wilkinson St., Syracuse, NY 13204; (315) 476-4250; MiddleAgesBrewing.com; @MiddleAgesBeer

Founded: 1995 **Founders:** Marc and Mary Rubenstein **Brewer:** Marc Rubenstein **Flagship Beer:** Grail Ale **Year-round Beers:** Beast Bitter, Black Heart Stout, Double Wench, Double Wit, Dragon Slayer, Druid Fluid, Duke of Winship, Grail Ale, ImPaled Ale, Kilt Tilter, Middle Ages Pale Ale, Old Marcus, Swallow Wit, Syracuse Pale Ale, Tripel Crown, Wailing Wench, X Double India Pale Ale **Seasonals/Special Releases:** Apocalypse Ale, Apricot Ale, Boxing Day Bitter, Highlander Scotch Ale, Imperial ESB, Imperial Pale Ale, Raspberry Ale, Session Pale Ale, Winter Wheat, Wizard's Winter Ale **Tours:** Yes **Taproom:** Yes

Middle Ages Brewing Company has focused on brewing English styles since Marc and Mary Rubenstein opened the brewery in 1995. The Rubensteins still run the brewery out of the old Sealcrest Ice Cream Factory that they founded the brewery in, and Marc Rubenstein is still the brewmaster 18 years later. To create traditional English ales, the Rubensteins purchased one of the country's few Peter Austin systems, a brick-covered brew kettle heated with an open flame. The large open-top fermenters give off a powerful yeasty and bready aroma that fills the fermentation room. The system helps to lend distinct notes of caramelization that are not present in most modern brew systems. The brewery uses a majority of English malts and its house yeast strain, originated in Yorkshire, England.

The beer names and labels have fun with the medieval theme, but the beers themselves are serious renditions of classic styles. Middle Ages Brewing's focus on British styles doesn't mean they don't branch out. The **ImPaled Ale** uses Cascade hops to bring a bit of American punch but keeps the beer firmly based in the bready malt character that British IPAs are known for.

Several beers have been around since the beginning or just shortly after, such as the **Grail Ale,** which debuted in 1995, and the **Beast Bitter,** which was first brewed in 1996. Other beers, like the **Wizard Winter,** originally brewed in 1995, are

Beer Lover's Pick

Old Marcus
Style: ESB
ABV: 6.6%
Availability: Year-round

The ESB is a traditional English brew that doesn't receive a lot of attention in the American craft beer community, but Middle Ages Brewing gives the style a faithful rendition with Old Marcus. Old Marcus is well balanced and has a nice interplay between earthiness from the use of East Kent Golding hops and the full chewy malt character. The house Yorkshire yeast adds to the bready flavors that help round out the beer.

continuously tinkered with to keep them interesting. The anniversary beers, which the brewery started producing after 10 years, are usually Imperial styles or amped up versions of other beers like the 12% ABV–strong Ale **Double Wench.** Middle Ages beers are widely available in Central New York and other regions of Upstate New York. Six-packs and 22-ounce bottles occasionally make it as far as New York City.

NAKED DOVE BREWING COMPANY

4048 US 20, Canandaigua, NY 14424; (585) 396-ALES; NakedDoveBrewing.com; @NakedDove

Founded: 2010 **Founders:** David Schlosser, Donald Cotter, Ken Higgins **Brewer:** David Schlosser **Year-round Beers:** Windblown Amber Ale, 45 Fathoms Porter, Starkers IPA, Berry Naked Black Raspberry Ale **Seasonals/Special Releases:** Roll in the Hay Farmhouse Ale, Hopulus Localus Harvest Ale, Oktoberfest, Young Red Tart Flemish Red Ale, Scotch Ale, Hop Cone-a-Copia 2XIPA, Bare Bock, Exposinaor Doppelbock, Anniversary Roggen Beer, Maibock, Mcbane's Tall Blonde and Naked, Munich Helles Lager, Nice and Naughty Christmas Ale **Tours:** Yes **Taproom:** Yes

Dave Schlosser has been working in the brewing industry his whole professional life. After college he brewed at Rohrbach Brewing Company in Rochester, left to attend Siebel to get his degree, after which he returned to Upstate New York to

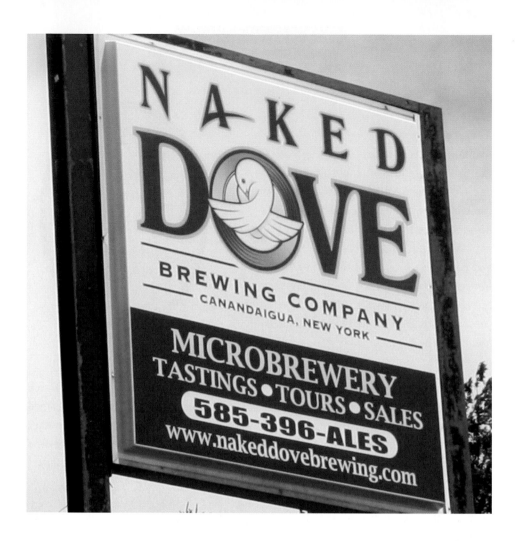

work at Custom BrewCrafters (now called CB Craft Brewers) then High Falls Brewing Company (now Genesee). In 2010 he opened Naked Dove Brewing Company, along with his friends Donald Cotter and Ken Higgins. The three guys got the idea for the name "Naked Dove" because it's an anagram of their names: Dave, Don. and Ken.

Schlosser is the brewer, and he produces all his beer in the 15-barrel brewhouse. His beers are classic styles that have fun, whimsical names. **Roll in the Hay** is Schlosser's seasonal Farmhouse-Style Ale, and at 4.5 percent ABV is an excellent, light-bodied warm-weather brew. The **45 Fathoms Porter** pours a deep dark brown and has a restrained quality in the roasted flavors. Rich malted tastes have notes of sweet milk chocolate and coffee, with a smooth milky texture. **Berry Naked**

Young Red Tart
Style: Flemish Red Ale
ABV: 5.0%
Availability: Limited
The ability to make good, flavorful, and drinkable sour beers is an indication that a brewer knows what it's doing. Naked Dove's Young Red Tart is a delicious version of the style. Perfectly tart, but not too much, this bright red colored Ale has overtones of cherries. Possessing a clean palate, Young Red Tart is a sweet beer that you'll want to return to again and again.

Raspberry Ale is a great version of a fruit beer, with not too much sticky sweetness from the raspberries but distinct raspberry aromas and tastes. There's an earthy quality to the malt in this beer and a dry finish.

Naked Dove Brewing Company is equipped with a bottling line, but its first focus is on its draft offerings, available in the Finger Lakes and surrounding areas. When you take a trip to the taproom, you can try a sampling of Naked Dove's beers for $2 and fill a growler to take home.

ROOSTER FISH BREWING
223-301 N. Franklin St., Watkins Glen, NY 14891; (607) 535-9797; RoosterFishBrewing
.com
Founded: 2004 **Founder and Brewer:** Doug Thayer **Flagship Beer:** Hop Warrior IPA
Year-round Beers: Aspen Wit Ale, Firehouse Blonde, Summer Sky Hefeweizen, Wee
Heavy Scotch Ale, Mysterious Amber, Tripel Witch Ale, Dog Tooth Pale Ale, Hop Warrior
Imperial IPA, Original Nut Brown, Raven Black IPA **Seasonals/Special Releases:** Cocoa
Porter, Golden Belgian, Coffee Porter, Gray Weasel ESB, Hop Harvest IPA, Imperial Coffee
Stout, New York Fresh Hop Octoberfest Ale, Old Cascade Amber Ale, Salvador Dali Oatmeal-

Coffee Stout, Scotch Ale, Summer IPA, Summer Sky Hefeweizen **Tours:** By request on slow days **Taproom:** Yes

In 1990 Doug Thayer opened The Wildflower Cafe, always intending to create a microbrewery in the space but unable to afford it at the time. The cafe is in the town of Watkins Glen, walking distance from the edge of Seneca Lake. In 1998 he opened another location, The Crooked Rooster Brewpub, down the street. In 2002 Thayer started homebrewing and in 2004 launched his first beer under the Rooster Fish label, the **Original Nut Brown Ale,** and in 2006 Rooster Fish began distributing. Beers are produced on a 10-barrel system and can be found in good craft beer bars throughout the Finger Lakes and as far west as Buffalo.

The **Raven Black IPA** pours inky black with a tan head. The black IPA has a bitterness from the hops but also from the roasted character, leaving you with a taste of dark-roasted coffee. The **Triple Witch Ale** is effervescent, fruity, and light bodied. At 9.6 percent it's a pretty big beer, but nice to sip alongside some of the pub eats.

Beer Lover's Pick

Hop Warrior IPA
Style: American Double/Imperial IPA
ABV: 8.0%
Availability: Year-round, on tap and in bottles

Rooster Fish Brewing's Hop Warrior IPA is its flagship brew. With bready malt, pine, lime zest, and grapefruit aromas on the nose, Hop Warrior is a medium-bodied beer with a slight bitterness at the front of the palate and a citrus quality throughout, with notes of caramel.

Food at the brewpub is tasty, more elevated than a regular pub. Fried mozzarella doesn't taste frozen, cheese plates are comprised of aged and fresh offerings, all sourced from New York State. There's a selection of pizzas, salads, and sandwiches, and all of the seafood items on the menu are sustainable and eco-friendly. There aren't official tours, but on a slow day you might be able to get one by request. If not, you can check out some brewing equipment in the back of The Crooked Rooster Brewpub.

UPSTATE BREWING COMPANY

3028 Lake Rd., Elmira, NY 14903; (607) 742-2750; UpstateBrewing.com; @UpstateBrewing
Founded: 2012 **Founders and Brewers:** Mark Neumann, Ken Mortensen **Flagship Beer:** Common Sense Ale **Year-round Beers:** Common Sense Ale, IPW (India Pale Wheat) **Seasonals/Special Releases:** Irish Blonde, Summer Haze, Oktoberfest **Tours:** No **Taproom:** Yes

Mark Neumann and Ken Mortensen grew up and went to Horseheads High School together. Having been homebrewing partners, the friends dreamed of opening their own brewery as adults, but they lived on opposite ends of the country. When they moved back home, they decided that given the influx of breweries in Upstate New York, it was the right time to do it. The duo strives to make unique beers that

satisfy many different tastes—beers that would appeal to craft beer lovers as well as those who prefer macro beers like Budweiser and Blue Moon.

Upstate's flagship beer, the **Common Sense Ale,** is a Kentucky Common Ale, a pre-Prohibition style of beer. Neumann and Mortensen decided to revive this style, which, along with the California Common Beer and Pumpkin Beer, is one of two beer styles known to have originated in the United States. While many are of the opinion that the Kentucky Common Ale—which originated in Louisville, Kentucky—is tart with the use of a sour mash, Neumann and Mortensen found reference to the style in a 100-year-old homebrewing reference text that showed no mention of a sour taste. A key characteristic of the style is its dark color but light, easy-drinking taste. Upstate's Common Sense Ale has a caramel character and is light bodied and a manageable 5.3 percent ABV. Neumann and Mortensen brew three different seasonal beers: an **Irish Blonde** in the spring, a **Summer Haze** Wheat beer in the summer, and an **Oktoberfest** Dunkelweizen in the fall. Unlike many blonde beers, Upstate's Irish Blonde is full bodied with a strong malt character. A floral aroma leads to a crisp palate and a dry finish.

I.P.W.

Style: India Pale Wheat

ABV: 6.5%

Availability: Year-round

Neumann and Mortensen both love the IPA and American Wheat beer styles. They thought it would be a great experiment to make a hybrid of the two. They brewed a 30 percent wheat pilot batch and liked how it tasted so much that they kept it on. Brewed with Magnum, Zythos, and Nugget hops, the Upstate I.P.W. has floral, citrusy notes. This beer has the smooth, creamy mouthfeel of a Wheat beer and the bitterness and aroma of an IPA.

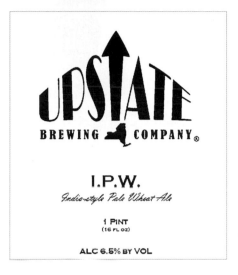

Upstate Brewing Company beers are available on draft in the Finger Lakes and Catskills Region as well as in New York City. In mid-2013 the team brought in the We Can mobile canning company to put its beers in four-packs of 16-ounce cans.

WAGNER VALLEY BREWING COMPANY

9322 SR 414, Lodi, NY 14860; (607) 582-6450; WagnerBrewing.com; @WagnerVineyards
Founded: 1997 **Founder:** John Wagner **Brewer:** Brent Wojnowski **Flagship Beer:** Dockside Amber Lager **Year-round Beers:** Mill Street Pilsner, Dockside Amber Lager, Wagner IPA, Sled Dog Doppelbock, Sled Dog Trippelbock, Caywood Station Oatmeal Stout **Seasonals/Special Releases:** Grace House Honey Wheat, Sugar House Maple Porter, Summer Sail Hefeweizen, Sled Dog Trippelbock Reserve **Tours:** Yes **Taproom:** Yes

In the Finger Lakes region, it's become increasingly common for an established winery to start a brewery on its premises. A fourth-generation family business, Wagner Vineyards was opened by Bill Wagner in 1979. The cafe Ginny Lee was added in 1983 as a place to enjoy fresh foods while sipping Wagner wines, and in 1997 Wagner Valley Brewing Company was launched by John Wagner. You don't often hear

that a non-German brewery follows the *Reinheitsgebot*, or the German Purity Law. But Wagner Valley Brewing Company does. According to the law, only malt, hops, yeast, and water can be used to make beer. Brewmaster Dean Jones (now brewer at Genesee) was at the helm from 2004 to 2012, when his assistant Brent Wojnowski took over.

The brewery is fully committed to its German inspiration, being modeled after a German-style brewhouse. Wojnowski brews on a 20-barrel system and produces beer on draft and in bottles that are distributed throughout New York State. The **Sled Dog Doppelbock,** a complex beer at a hefty 8.5 percent ABV, pours a dark, reddish-brown color with a large head and good lacing. Caramel malt on the nose carries over to the palate and is slightly syrupy, with dark fruit notes and a sweet finish. Wagner's **Mill Street Pilsner** is a light copper color with lightly hopped aromas. There are strong malty flavors with hints of spice and citrus in this light-bodied Pilsner, an easy-drinking beer at 4.2 percent ABV. Wojnowski brews a medium-bodied **IPA,** a crisp offering that finishes dry. Citrus and biscuit flavors provide a refreshing, hop-forward beer.

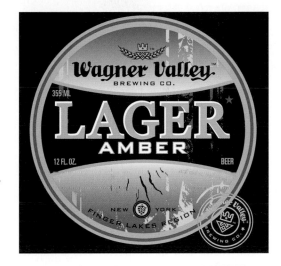

Beer Lover's Pick

Dockside Amber Lager
Style: Vienna Lager
ABV: 5.1%
Availability: Year-round, on draft
and in bottles

Dockside Amber Lager is Wagner Valley Brewing Company's flagship offering, available year-round. It pours a clear amber color and has malty, caramel flavors and a slightly sweet aftertaste. This Vienna-style Lager is light bodied and has subtle bitter flavors from the hops.

On a visit to Wagner Valley Brewing Company, you have the opportunity to taste all the beers on tap and check out the brewing operation through windows across from the bar. The brewhouse and bar are located inside a dark wood building that has a distinct cabinlike feel. The best feature of Wagner Valley Brewing Company is the large deck that lines the back of the building. You can take your brew outdoors, sit on the patio, and enjoy a gorgeous view of Seneca Lake.

Brewpubs

BANDWAGON BREWPUB

114 N. Cayuga St., Ithaca, New York 14850; (607) 319-0699; BandwagonBeer.com; @BandwagonBeer

Founded: 2009 **Founders:** Nick Antczack, John Hughes, Alex and Mike Johnson, Will Olson **Brewer:** Lars Mudrack **Year-round Beers:** Hidden Rabbit Hefeweizen, Pedro's Pale Ale, Erza Red Ale, Pirate Eye I.P.A., Honey Brunette, Tartan 80/ Scottish Ale, High Step Weizenbock, Sully's Irish Stout **Seasonals/Special Releases:** Humulus Hefeweizen, Strawberry Cream, Watermelon Wheat, Loc-ale, Pop's Session Ale, Raspberry Jalapeno, Pumpkin Ale, Frosty's Winter Ale, Scotch Ale, Peanut Butter Chocolate Stout

From the giant hop on the bright yellow door that leads to the subterranean Bandwagon Brewpub you might think that big hop-dominated IPAs fill the beer list, but the small brewpub actually hits a wide variety of styles, emphasizing balance and experimentation. The enthusiastic staff will help guide you through the house brews and guest beers. The dark mahogany **Tartan 80/** is sweet but not cloyingly so, and the **Erza Red Ale** is a great accompaniment to items on the food menu. Experimental beers like the **Peanut Butter Chocolate Stout** and **Raspberry Jalapeño Ale** keep drinkers on their toes. The **Loc-ale** uses 90 percent locally grown New York State malt, a rare thing and only possible for small brewers like Bandwagon. The beers are available for growler fills, and some are offered in bottles. Bandwagon started bottling Peanut Butter Chocolate Stout, **Hidden Rabbit Hefeweizen,** and the **High Step Weizenbock** in 2013.

If you are looking for flights, you can get a Bandwagon Brewery Flight or one of the New York State, First Class, or Full Spectrum flights that mix in beers from other breweries. American craft beer classics like Oscar Blues Dale's Pale Ale and fresh local brews like Bacchus Brewing IPA keep things rotating in the flights. The beef, eggs, bacon, and many other ingredients on the food menu are locally sourced for dishes like the grilled NY strip steak or the burgers.

COUNCIL ROCK BREWERY

4861 NY 28, Cooperstown, NY 13326; (607) 643-3016; CouncilRockBrewery.com; @CouncilRockBrew

Founded: 2012 **Founder and Brewer:** Roger Davidson **Year-round Beers:** Goldenrod Ale, Full Nelson, Sleeping Lion Red Ale, Leatherstocking Brown Ale, Sunken Island Scotch Ale, Heffeweizen **Seasonal/Specialty Releases:** Imperial Stout, Honey Hefe, Vienna Lager, Pumpkin Ale, Belgian Blonde, Belgian Lager

Roger Davidson didn't much care for beer until his son came home from college and suggested a good father/son activity would be to make it. So they went out, bought a kit, and made some beer. After tasting the brew, Davidson liked it so much he was hooked. He brewed more and more, increasing from 5-gallon batches to 10-gallon batches, and eventually decided to pursue opening a brewpub. He found a small space in Cooperstown, started as a tiny bar and dining room, took over the chocolate shop next door for more dining space, and expanded to an outdoor patio.

Davidson keeps a regular lineup of six beers on tap—the six local favorites—and rotates others in and out of the lineup. His **Goldenrod Ale**, a light Blonde Ale–style brew that is refreshing and clean with a creamy mouthfeel and notes of citrus, is a good gateway beer, the beer he suggests whenever someone comes in asking for a Bud Light. Many of Davidson's beers are inspired by memories he has, or flavors he craves. When his daughter went to Belgium for a year after high school, he visited her and tasted Scotch Ales and Belgian Blondes, beers he's since re-created at Council Rock. For his **Pumpkin Ale** he went pumpkin picking at a local patch and brewed a beer with those roasted pumpkins.

G.C. STARKEY BEER COMPANY

5428 NY 14, Dundee, NY 14837; (607) 678-4043; StarkeysLookout.com;
@StarkeysLookout
Founded: 2012 **Founders:** Dave Bunnell and Olaf Leiberg **Brewer:** Dean Jones
Flagship Beer: Scotch Ale **Year-round Beers:** Scotch Ale, Czech Pilsner, Tangerine Wit,
Belgian Amber, IPA **Seasonals/Special Releases:** English-Style Brown Al, Margarita Wit,
Pumpkin Ale, Belgian White

A white mansion on top of a hill facing Seneca Lake houses Seneca Hayes Wine Cellars and G.C. Starkey Beer Company, known as Starkey's Lookout. Dave Bunnell and Olaf Leiberg are the owners and founders of BWF Holdings, the company that operates the winery and brewery. They brought on Brewmaster Dean Jones to create the recipes for the Starkey beers, which are then brewed at Rohrbach's in

Rochester. Jones has over 20 years of brewing experience, and has worked in the Finger Lakes before at Wagner Valley Brewing Company. He's also the brewmaster at the Genesee Brew House.

Jones's most intriguing beer is the **Margarita Wit.** A summer seasonal, this beer is made using the Belgian White as a base and adds in Key West lime juice. Really crisp and bright, this beer has bold and distinct flavors of lime, with almost no sweetness. The lime character, while intense, doesn't detract from the Wheat Beer qualities, and at 4.8 percent ABV is light and refreshing, perfect for summer. Starkey's **Scotch Ale** has the characteristic sweetness of the style, a deep ruby color with molasses and caramel tastes. The **Czech Pilsner** is a great Pilsner, light bodied, dry, grassy, and incredibly drinkable at 4.3 percent ABV.

Beers at Starkey's Lookout are available in sets of two flights, a light and a dark flight. Each includes a house-made nonalcoholic beverage, either an orange cream soda or a root beer. Sit and enjoy your brews looking out at a beautiful view of Seneca Lake, while choosing from an array of tapas and small plates on the menu, or more substantial options like pasta or flatbread pizza.

MARKET STREET BREWING COMPANY AND RESTAURANT

63 W. Market St., Corning, NY 14830; (607) 936-BEER; 936-Beer.com; @MarketstBrewing
Founded: 1997 **Founders:** Theresa and Pelham McClellan **Brewer:** Pelham McClellan
Year-round Beers: Mad Bug Lager, Blackberry Lager, Wrought Iron Red Ale, Wheelhouse IPA, D'Artagnan Dark Ale **Seasonals/Special Releases:** Hefeweizen, Baltic Porter, Oktoberfest, Pale Ale, The Hibernator

Historic Market Street in Corning, New York, is a quaint, bustling main street complete with ice cream parlors, art galleries, cafes, and gift boutiques. The Market Street Brewing Company and Restaurant is centrally located in this cute town, founded in 1997 by husband-and-wife team Pelham and Theresa McClellan. Pelham is a former homebrewer.

Topping the beer list is the **D'Artagnan Dark Ale,** an English Dark Mild Ale. At 6.5 percent ABV, it's a sweet brew with dark fruit flavors like cherries and figs. D'Artagnan has a nice effervescence that balances out the sweetness, since there isn't a strong presence of hops, and contributes to a clean finish. Other tasty libations

include the **IPA,** which is not overly hoppy, with malty and piney flavors; **The Hibernator** Imperial Stout; and the **Mad Bug Lager.** The Hibernator, at 7.5 percent ABV, is a rich, full-bodied brew with caramel, dark malt, and toffee flavors. Market Street's Mad Bug Lager is an American adjunct Lager, but a good and drinkable version of the style. Crisp and clean, the Lager is light bodied and has a dry finish.

You can sit and enjoy your beer and food inside the brewpub or outside on the patio, looking at a nearby fountain and watching the passersby. Just a short drive from the brewpub is the tourist destination Corning Museum of Glass, where you can wander through galleries of glass art, watch a glass-blowing demonstration, or even make you own glass.

MILES CRAFT ALES

168 Randall Rd., Himrod, New York 14842; (608) 243-7742; MilesWineCellars.com
Founded: 2010 **Founder and Brewer:** Evan Miles **Year-round Beers:** Callisto Pale Ale and Scottish Lure Ale **Seasonals/Special Releases:** Bonfire Brew

Miles Wine Cellars is a hub for everything that draws visitors to the Finger Lakes: wine, cafes, inns, boating, events, lake views, and now beer. Entering the tasting room through the columns outside the impressive farmhouse on the lake, you will most likely be greeted by a member of the Miles family. The atmosphere is welcoming and their enthusiasm for their products is charming. Evan Miles, the brewer at Miles Craft Ales, has seemingly boundless energy, and he channels it into his love of fermentation and his family's business. His involvement in the family's wine making led him to a degree in fermentation science, a decade of homebrewing, and then seasonal work at Custom BrewCrafters outside Rochester in Honeoye Falls (now known as CB Craft Brewers). With his additional experience, Miles brought brewing back with him to the family business, where he started brewing before moving the operation to CB Craft Brewers, where he has more flexibility and capacity.

With plenty of space and the resources of the family farm at his disposal, Miles plans to build an on-site brewery along with a tasting room. The separate brewing operation will eventually allow him to experiment with Farmhouse Ales that utilize brettanomyces and wild yeast strains that are popular with beer drinkers but can ruin wine. Next to the brewing operation, Miles plans to apply his experience in what he calls "low-impact precision farming" to create what would be one of the largest hop fields in the state.

Currently Miles brews three beers, **Callisto Pale Ale, Scottish Lure Ale,** and **Bonfire Brew.** The Callisto Pale Ale uses all American hops and focuses on subtle citrus flavors layered over Pilsner base malt and a touch of Cara Amber malt. In 2013 the Miles family also added a cafe to the Inn, where visitors can stop for a sandwich or some fruit and cheese with their wine or beer.

NAIL CREEK PUB & BREWERY

720 Varick St., Utica, NY 13502; (315) 793-7593; NailCreekPub.com; @NailCreek
Founded: 2008 **Founders:** Chris and Tracy Talgo **Brewer:** Chris Kogut **Beers:** Belgian Double, Belgian Strong, Breakfast Stout, Saison, Saint Patrick's Nitro Stout

Nail Creek Pub & Brewery takes its name from Utica's Nail Creek, which once ran through the city where Matt Brewing Company is now. In the beginning of the 20th century, with Utica's growing population, it made sense for the creek to be diverted underground. It now runs underneath Matt Brewing Company and its parking lot, just down the street from its namesake brewpub. Owners Chris and Tracy

Talgo purchased the building that now houses their brewery from the city of Utica in 2003. With the building in great disrepair, it took the couple several years to renovate and rehabilitate it, leaving exposed brick walls as the only vestige of its former self.

Designed to resemble pubs Chris visited while studying abroad in Europe, Nail Creek Pub opened in 2008, and the brewing operation started up three years later in 2011, with Brewer Chris Kogut starting with the **Belgian Double** and **Breakfast Stout** on the three-barrel system. The Belgian Double is 7 percent ABV and pours a hazy amber color. Strong banana, coriander, and clove notes are on the nose and palate of this beer.

Depending on when you visit the Nail Creek Pub & Brewery, you may or not be able to sample their house beers. If none of them are on tap or they've all kicked, you have an extensive draft and bottle list to choose from. Saranac and Utica Club are main fixtures of the menu, which also features regional breweries like Good Nature Brewing, Adirondack, and Middle Ages. Frequent visitors to Nail Creek can participate in the World Beer Tour rewards program for people who imbibe 100, 200, 500, or 1,000 unique beers at the bar. Nail Creek keeps track of the World Beer Tour records in a huge binder bursting at the seams.

ROGUES HARBOR BREWING COMPANY

2079 E. Shore Dr., Lansing, NY 14882; (607) 533-3535; RoguesHarbor.com; @RoguesHarborInn

Founded: 2011 **Founder:** Eileen Stout **Brewer:** Chris Williams **Flagship Beer:** Cayuga Cream Ale **Year-round Beers:** Route 34 Red Ale, East Shore Pale Ale **Seasonals/ Special Releases:** American Wheat, Oktoberfest, Rye IPA, Spiced Winter Ale, Summer Saison, Underground Black IPA

There aren't too many breweries attached to inns, but Rogues Harbor, just north of Ithaca in Lansing, New York, combines the two with a large dose of history. Historical legends include tales of money counterfeiting and murderers, but the inn was also known as a stop on the Underground Railroad. Built in 1830 and originally named the Central Exchange Hotel, Rogues Harbor can claim some 19th-century heavyweights like Secretary of State William Seward and Harriet Tubman as visitors. Entering the brick building with green trim, you feel transported in time, and thankfully that feeling involves beer, which was added to the operation in 2011 by owner Eileen Stout.

Brewer Chris Williams started out the brewery with just the **Cayuga Cream Ale** as an easy-drinking beer that is especially popular in the region. He has since added two year-round beers, a rotating Belgian Ale and a rotating "Brewer's Choice" beer. Recent beers have included a **Summer Saison,** with the style's classic effervescence and light body, and the popular **Underground Black IPA.**

The restaurant and bar at the inn of course serves the beer in flights and pints as well as growlers to go. The fresh beer pairs well with the restaurant menu, much of which is local with local Wagyu beef, Berkshire pork, vegetables, and pasta throughout.

SCALE HOUSE BREW PUB

23 Cinema Dr., Ithaca, NY 14850; (607) 257-0107; ScaleHouseBrewpub.com
Founded: 2006 **Founder and Brewer:** Steve Fazzary **Year-round Beers:** Red Ale,
Pilsner Dark Bock **Seasonal/Specialty Releases:** Winter Wheat

Pizza and beer. It's a tried-and-true combination. And pretty surprising that
places like Scale House Brew Pub aren't everywhere. Owner Steve Fazzary bought
a stretch of business spaces in an Ithaca strip mall in 2006. One of the spaces was
a pizzeria, which he turned into Northeast Pizza and Beer Company, and two doors
down he opened a Laundromat. But in the middle, he imagined a brewpub. In 2008
all the licensing came through and he was able to start. You can enter through
the pizza place door or the one to the brewpub, since the wall has been taken out
between them. Fazzary built up the brewpub himself, with help from some friends.
Order food at the pizza counter, drinks at the bar. And you'll be able to check out
the brewing equipment: it lines the wall behind the bar.

Fazzary brews three main beers—a **Red Ale, Pilsner,** and **Dark Bock—**as well
as a **Winter Wheat** seasonal. The Red Ale is well balanced and a little sweet with a
moderate back-end bitterness that balances it out. Slightly biscuity, this beer is easy
drinking and makes a great accompaniment to pizza. Fazzary's Pilsner pours hazy
golden, with slight flavors of toast and lemon zest. There's not only pizza on the
menu, but also pasta, calzones, salads and subs. The food is good and so is the beer.

Decorations on the walls of the pub are newspaper and magazine clippings.
You'll spot a picture near the bar of Fazzary standing in front of New York City's historic McSorely's Old Ale House. Every Sunday is jazz night at Scale House, featuring
local band The Neal Massa Trio. And on Thursday, treat everyone to your own voice
during karaoke night.

SENECA LODGE

3600 Walnut Rd., Watkins Glen, NY 14891; (607) 535-2014; SenecaLodge.com
Founded: 2009 **Founder and Brewer:** Brett Brubaker **Year-round Beers:** Amber
Ale, Blonde Ale, IPA, Porter, Harvest Ale, Pale Ale, American Wheat, Belgian Abbey Ale
Seasonals/Special Releases: Pumpkin Ale, Harvest Ale

Seneca Lodge might feel like a place where your grandparents may have vaca-
tioned, but that all adds to the charm. You can stay in cabins, A-frame houses,
or the motel on the property and participate in activities like tennis and archery.
The brewpub, bar, and hotel are tucked away just outside the town of Watkins Glen
near Seneca Lake and have been run by the Brubaker family since Don Brubaker
opened the lodge in 1948. In 2009 Brett Brubaker started brewing for the lodge, and

his beers are served in the Tavern Room along with popular beers from some other brewers. The wood-covered bar has a unique combination of archery and car-racing decorations that you aren't likely to find anywhere else. While laurels from 1970s Formula 1 races are stuck on the wall behind the bar by arrows that have been shot into the wall, tires from championship NASCAR cars hang from the ceiling.

Seneca Lodge started its brewing operation with an **Amber Ale** that has restrained caramel and toffee notes with a light body. The **Blonde Ale,** with a slight hop bitterness that keeps the beer dry, has a manageable 4.8% ABV. The food menu is full of classic dishes like shrimp scampi, chicken Parmesan, and New York strip steak. If you're looking for the classic lodge dinner feel, there's a salad bar.

TWO GOATS BREWING

5027 SR 414, Hector, NY 14818; (607) 546-2337; TwoGoatsBrewing.com
Founded: 2010 **Founders:** Jon and Jessica Rodgers **Brewer:** Jon Rodgers **Beers:** IPA, Redbeard Red Ale, Cream Ale, Amber Logger, Oatmeal Stout, Hefeweizen, Dirty Shepherd Brown Ale, Goat Master Ultra Pale Ale, WYCK'D Nuggets IPA, Danger Goat! Blonde Doppelbock, Whiskey Richard Stout

Two Goats Brewing is exactly what beer lovers will want out of a brewpub in the Finger Lakes. Located in a 19th-century barn right smack on Seneca Lake, a spacious deck offers some of the most spectacular views of the lake you can find. The brewpub also hosts frequent live music performances, listed on its website. The drama of the location can hide the fact that Two Goats has a neighborhood feel, with

a steady stream of locals filling growlers and playing darts on the wall seemingly as though there was no lake out the back door.

The beers themselves are about freshness and mostly traditional styles. Classic English styles like the hazy and slightly bitter **ESB** and the familiar roast and silky texture of the **Oatmeal Stout** sit alongside the drinkable **Hefeweizen** and the sweet **Danger Goat! Blonde Doppelbock.** A full-bodied brown ale, the **Dirty Shephard Brown Ale** is well balanced with nice toasted caramel flavors and a touch of hop bitterness. You can also ask for a **Headbutt,** a popular mix of the brewery's Cream Ale and Stout for a smooth crowd pleaser. The bar also serves two draft beers from other craft brewers like Ommegang, Dogfish Head, and Southern Tier. Flights are not available, so choose wisely, as you are committing to an entire pint. If you are looking for a wide selection of food to match the beers, you are out of luck; the only item on the food menu is a roast beef sandwich au jus with horseradish.

WAR HORSE BREWING COMPANY
623 Lerch Rd., Geneva, NY 14456; (315) 585-4432; 3BrothersWinery.com/War-Horse.html; @3BrosWine
Founded: 2008 **Founder:** Dave Mansfield **Brewer:** CB Craft Brewers **Flagship Beer:** Riesling Ale **Year-round Beers:** Riesling Ale, East Coast Amber, Gunny Mac Black Lager,

India Pale Ale, Royal Kilt Inspector Scotch Ale **Seasonals/Special Releases:** Raspberry Wheat Ale

Three Brothers Wineries & Estates is a veritable Disneyland of libations. Driving onto the property, you'll pass a field of grape vines. The estate is home to three wineries (inspired by owner Dave Mansfield and his brothers Mark and Mike) and one brewery, a tribute to the Mansfield brothers' father. The tasting room of War Horse Brewing Company is constructed in an old barn, its interior renovated to resemble a World War II airplane hangar. Just outside the tasting room is a small prop plane.

War Horse's beers are brewed at CB Craft Brewers (formerly Custom BrewCrafters), a contract brewing operation in Honeoye Falls, though the concepts come from Mansfield. The best beer from this brewery is its **Riesling Ale,** a blend of Wheat Beer Wort with New York Riesling juice—the first of its kind in the United States. Slightly fruity, the Riesling Ale is effervescent with a subtle sweetness. A little tart, this is a light-bodied beer with a low bitterness and a clean finish. The **Gunny Mac Black Lager** has a little bit of roasted flavors and a smooth texture. This almost sessionable Schwarzbier has notes of chocolate and coffee, contributing to a malty character and a medium-bodied mouthfeel. Designated drivers or nondrinkers have an option as well: War Horse makes a root beer.

During a visit to Three Brothers Wineries & Estates, you can purchase a tasting passport for wine at all the wineries and beer at the brewery, or visit just the brewery. Definitely make your way to Bagg Dare Winery (it's pirate themed), where you'll find a snack shack serving burritos, pulled pork sandwiches, and fried snacks.

WATER STREET BREWING COMPANY

168 Water St., Binghamton, NY 13901; (607) 217-4546; WaterStreetBrewingCo.com; @WSBCBinghamton

Founded: 2012 **Founders:** John and Michele Bleichert **Brewer:** John Bleichert **Year-round Beers:** Southern English Mild, Munich Helles, Thousand Year Porter, IPA, Porter, Head First Pale Ale, Cream Ale **Seasonals/Special Releases:** Weizenbock, Hefeweizen, Belgian Dubbel, American Bitter

John and Michele Bleichert founded Water Street Brewing Company in Binghamton to bring straightforward and fresh beers to the city. The Bleicherts started homebrewing in 2000, and John took on industrial-size brewing in Chicago and Germany. As the first brewing operation in the city in years, the brewpub didn't have much in the way of competition, but their beers are still brewed with care, attention, and consistency.

To focus on balance, the Bleicherts have chosen classic styles that don't encourage over-hopping. The Lagers they brew, like the **Munich Helles,** a crisp and refreshing style that beer geeks and novices alike can appreciate, are crafted according to the German Purity Law, the *Reinheitsgebot*. The **Southern English Mild** has the roasted malt flavors so many love at only 4.1% ABV, so you can relax and have a couple. Those looking for something a little different will enjoy the **Sweet Summer Rye** that keeps things interesting by allowing the slight spice of the rye malt to come through the light hop character. To make sure the beers are fresh, they are served directly into your glass from the tanks through the taps.

The beers pair well with dishes like the *Scheinefleishaft mit Biersenf* (pork shank served with house beer mustard) or the black bean burger. The dimly lit brewpub—in a historic building that once housed a burlesque theater—is spacious and has plenty of room for large groups. Try to grab a table by the brewing equipment that sits opposite the bar.

Beer Bars

THE BLUE TUSK

165 Walton St., Syracuse, NY 13202; (315) 472-1934; BlueTusk.com; @TheBlueTusk
Draft Beers: 69 **Bottled/Canned Beers:** Under 10

The Blue Tusk has been a fixture in the Syracuse beer scene since opening in 1995. The bar has expanded several times over the years and currently has 69 beers on tap. Located in Armory Square in downtown Syracuse, near some of the best beer and food spots in the city, The Blue Tusk is highly recommended by locals. Compared to other Syracuse beer spots, The Blue Tusk has more of an upscale decor and expensive beer list. The large tap list has beers for almost every taste but tends to focus on American craft beer and Belgian imports. Local breweries like Empire Brewing, just across the street, and Middle Ages from just a few minutes away are mainstays on the list. St. Bernardus, Petrus, Duvel, and other Belgian brewers are regularly featured. With outdoor seating, The Blue Tusk is a great place to watch the passing scene and snack on a meat or cheese plate. The rest of the food menu focuses on sandwiches, quesadillas, and salads.

THE CHAPTER HOUSE

400 Stewart Ave., Ithaca, NY 14850; (607) 277-9782; ChapterHouseIthaca.com
Draft Beers: 49

The Chapter House in Ithaca may feel ancient to most visitors, because by beer bar standards it is. A bar and restaurant called Jim's Place changed its name to The Chapter House in the mid-1960s, a time when the bar served as a watering hole for Cornell's Greek organizations. After a brief stint as an ice cream parlor in the 1980s, the bar was resurrected as The Chapter House and even brewed its own beer, called Clement's, on-site in the late 1980s and 1990s. The brewing operation has since closed, replaced with brews from the exploding American craft-brewing community. Now the bar has more of a reputation for serving Cornell's graduate students than the undergraduate Greeks who helped name the bar.

The beer menu at The Chapter House is stacked with some of New York's best beers. Breweries such as Middle Ages, Lake Placid, and Southern Tier are regulars, while the hometown Ithaca Beer Company maintains several draft lines. The 49 taps

also feature beer fan favorites including Left Hand Nitro Milk Stout, Great Lakes Edmund Fitzgerald, and Stone's Arrogant Bastard. The bar itself is covered in wood, and while the beer is the star here, the bar also has regular live music, pool tables, and free popcorn—pretty much whatever you want for a relaxing pub experience. Even in a town full of college students, The Chapter House is a welcome dark corner where you can relax with a pint of local craft beer.

THE GREEN ONION
2018 Genesee St., Utica NY, 13502; (315) 507-2895; GreenOnionPub.com
Draft Beers: 12 **Bottled/Canned Beers:** 10 to 20

The city of Utica may have fallen on hard times, but that doesn't mean you can't get great beer. Located between the lively Uptown Theater and a muffler shop, The Green Onion can naturally be identified by the large green onion that hangs in the front window. The bartenders are knowledgeable and handle the selection of draft and bottle beers well. Many of the draft beers are from local breweries like Good Nature Brewing; Ithaca Beer Company; and the super-local Saranac and Utica Club, both brewed at Utica's own Matt Brewing. Nationally popular breweries such as Founders Brewing, Dogfish Head Brewing, and Stillwater Artisanal Ales are also represented. The bottle list is small but solid, with large bottles like the sour Cascade Kreik Flanders Red Ale and Brooklyn Brewery's popular saison Sorachi Ace.

The bar itself is a great place to chat with locals and find out what is going on in Utica. If you want something more private, you can grab one of the booths against the wall. The bar is decorated with historical beer-related photos and ads.

THE ITHACA ALE HOUSE GRILL AND TAPROOM
11 North Aurora St., Ithaca, NY 14850; (607) 256-7977; IthacaAleHouse.com; @IthacaAleHouse
Draft Beers: 20 **Bottled/Canned Beers:** 20

Right in the center of downtown Ithaca near the Commons, The Ithaca Ale House strikes the balance between local beer bar and hub for visitors to the city's colleges. Most of the 20 beers on tap are from local brewers like Ithaca Beer Company, Horseheads Brewing, and Ellicottville Brewing. The bar also provides a beginner's flight that takes new craft drinkers from light Lagers through Wheats, IPAs, and Stouts. The bartenders are helpful and knowledgeable of what beers on tap are fresh or pouring well. If you aren't sure what to order, it's a good bet they can help you out.

On a sunny day head outside for one of the few spots on the sidewalk, or if you prefer to stay indoors, sit at a high-top table in the back or one of the booths that run along the side of the bar. The food menu spans a wide range of dishes from standard sandwiches and salads to blackened tuna and spicy Thai and lemongrass chicken. Each menu item is listed with suggested beer styles for pairings. Local consensus is to save room for the fried Oreos served with melted chocolate. The place can get busy, so try to get there early if you are looking for a table.

RED BRICK PUB
224 W. 1st St. S., Fulton, NY 13069; (315) 592-9797; RedBrickPub.com
Draft Beers: 40 **Bottled/Canned Beers:** 17

John Bertrand and his wife Judy founded Red Brick Pub in 2009, renovating the space that formerly house the Chubby's Bar and Grill sports bar. Since its opening with 12 taps, Red Brick Pub has increased that number to 26, then again to 40. The Bertrands make sure to emphasize New York breweries on their list, including the local Middle Ages Brewing Company and Empire Brewing Company, and the farther away Southern Tier, Cortland Brewing Company, and Adirondack. You can purchase regular pints of beer or beer flights of four five-ounce pours. The exterior of the bar is whimsically painted and styled to look like a circus wagon, and the Bertrands restored the hardwood floors and installed hardwood booths in the dining and taprooms.

Red Brick Pub has a cozy, neighborhood pub feel. During Friday happy hour from 4 to 6 p.m., the pub offers complimentary food and half-priced drinks in the taproom. On the menu are hearty options like strip steak and barbeque pig wings and ribs, as well as bar snacks, salads, wraps, and sandwiches. For Sunday brunch, from 11:30 a.m. to 2 p.m., Red Brick Pub offers a menu with pancakes, waffles, and eggs several ways.

Pub Crawl

A pub crawl is a great way to see multiple places in one day and allows you to do so safely, as long as you walk, take a cab, or find someone willing to be your designated driver.

Syracuse

The city of Syracuse is home to two great breweries: Middle Ages and Empire, within a few minutes of each other. Those two spots plus a handful of high-quality bars make Syracuse a craft beer lover's dream.

Middle Ages Brewing Company, 120 Wilkinson St., Syracuse, NY 13204; (315) 476-4250; MiddleAgesBrewing.com

Start out at Middle Ages Brewing Company, open daily. You'll be able to spot the brick-lined brew kettle of the Peter Austin brewing system through windows in the taproom and try a sampling of British-inspired beers. Say hello to the suit of armor standing near the door on your way out.

The Blue Tusk, 165 Walton St., Syracuse, NY 13202; (315) 472-1934; BlueTusk.com

A 5-minute drive or 15-minute walk away from Middle Ages Brewing Company is The Blue Tusk (not open on Sunday). With almost 70 beers on tap, you're guaranteed to find a brew that suits your tastes. Grab a bite to eat here; choose from sandwiches, paninis, and meat and cheese boards, or hold out for the farm-to-table eats at your next spot.

Empire Brewing Company, 120 Walton St., Syracuse, NY 13202; (315) 475-2337; EmpireBrew.com

Empire Brewing Company is practically right across the street from The Blue Tusk, a basement-level, brick-lined brewpub. Behind the bar you can spy shiny copper brewing equipment while tasting an array of seasonal or year-round brews and ordering from a locally focused menu.

J.Ryans Pub, 253 E. Water St., Syracuse, NY 13202; (315) 399-5533; JRyansPub.com

Six blocks away from Empire Brewing Company is local favorite J.Ryans Pub, a great place to end your beer-filled afternoon or evening. Take your pick of almost 40 beers on draft and imbibe alongside some solid pub-style grub like sandwiches, salads, and burgers.

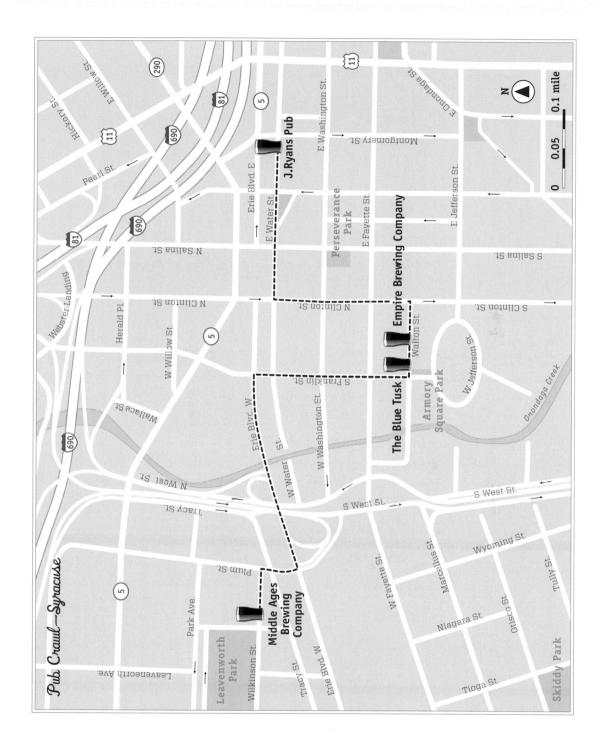

Pub Crawl—Syracuse

J.Ryans Pub

Empire Brewing Company

The Blue Tusk

Middle Ages Brewing Company

Perseverance Park

Armory Square Park

Leavenworth Park

Skiddy Park

N

0   0.05   0.1 mile

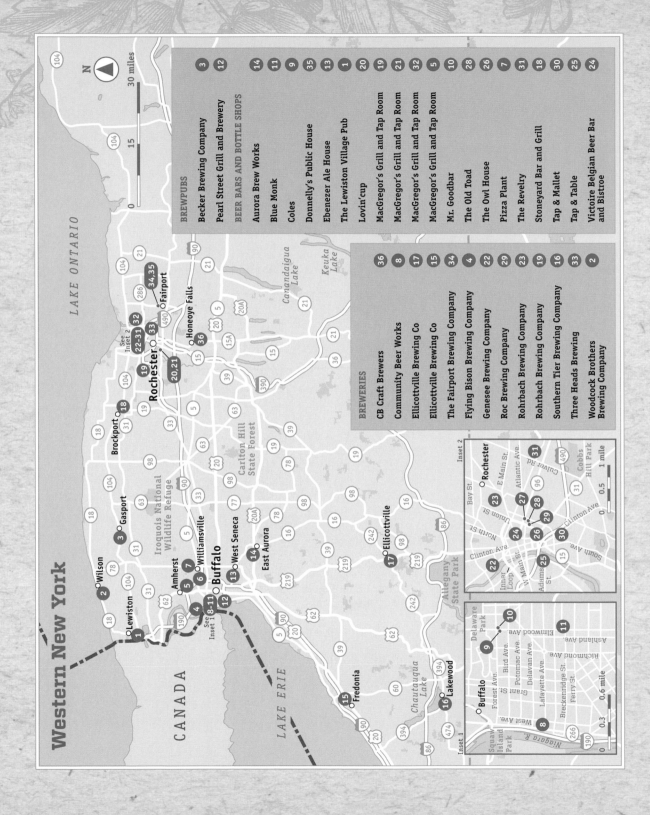

Western New York

LAKE ONTARIO

CANADA

LAKE ERIE

N

30 miles

15

0

BREWPUBS

Becker Brewing Company	3
Pearl Street Grill and Brewery	12

BEER BARS AND BOTTLE SHOPS

Aurora Brew Works	14
Blue Monk	11
Coles	9
Donnelly's Public House	35
Ebenezer Ale House	13
The Lewiston Village Pub	1
Lovin'cup	20
MacGregor's Grill and Tap Room	19
MacGregor's Grill and Tap Room	21
MacGregor's Grill and Tap Room	32
MacGregor's Grill and Tap Room	5
Mr. Goodbar	10
The Old Toad	28
The Owl House	26
Pizza Plant	7
The Revelry	31
Stoneyard Bar and Grill	18
Tap & Mallet	30
Tap & Table	25
Victoire Belgian Beer Bar and Bistroe	24

BREWERIES

CB Craft Brewers	36
Community Beer Works	8
Ellicottville Brewing Co	17
Ellicottville Brewing Co	15
The Fairport Brewing Company	34
Flying Bison Brewing Company	4
Genesee Brewing Company	22
Roc Brewing Company	29
Rohrbach Brewing Company	23
Rohrbach Brewing Company	19
Southern Tier Brewing Company	16
Three Heads Brewing	33
Woodcock Brothers Brewing Company	2

Inset 2

Rochester

1 mile

0.5

0

Inset 1

Buffalo

0.6 mile

0.3

0

Western New York

Western New York doesn't get a lot of national attention for its beer, located between Midwestern states and eastern hubs like New York City and Boston, cities like Buffalo and Rochester are sometimes overlooked. But there is a serious beer culture in this area, one that's older and more developed than most realize. Rochester is home to one of the oldest breweries in the country, Genesee Brewing Company, which was founded in 1878. New upstarts like Roc Brewing Company in Rochester and Community Beer Works in Buffalo demonstrate that local pride and attention to detail can yield delicious results. In the remote town of Lakewood, Southern Tier Brewing Company has in recent years been a permanent fixture in the top 50 craft breweries in the country in terms of production.

Communities are getting excited as well: Both Buffalo and Rochester have thriving beer weeks with bars and restaurants showcasing the wide range of beers available. You can get traditional cask ale at the famous The Old Toad, sample Belgian beer and food at Blue Monk, experience an old-time bar that opened a year after the end of Prohibition at Coles, and be doted on at The Revelry.

Breweries

CB CRAFT BREWERS

300 Village Square Blvd., Honeoeye Falls, NY 14472; (585) 624-4386; cbcraftbrewers.com; @CustomBrewCrfts

Founded: 1997 **Founders:** Mike and Luanne Alcorn **Brewer:** Bruce Lish **Flagship Beer:** Caged Alpha Monkey **Year-round Beers:** Caged Alpha Monkey, Canadaigua Lake Ale, EPA, MacBubba Scotch Ale, Double Dark Cream Porter, Red Rhino Imperial Red Lager, Black Jack Licorice Stout, Black IPA, Blonde Lager, Brown Ale, Saison **Seasonals/Special Releases:** Cassie Belgian-Style Black Currant Ale, Krysztoff, Mannix, Christmas Ale, Finger Lakes Summer Wheat, White Hop Belgian IPA, Margaux, Xinnam, St, Patrick's Irish Ale, Experiment X, Borislav, Oktoberfest, Spring Fever, Fresh Hop Harvest Ale, Coffee Stout, Tripel, George, Mabel **Tours:** Yes; Saturday 11 a.m. to 5 p.m., Sunday 1 to 5 p.m. **Taproom:** Yes

Contract brewing is one of the most controversial issues in craft beer. Whatever your take on the subject, it's universally acknowledged that the practice allows for more breweries to open and supply beer to drinkers. CB Craft Brewers, originally known as Custom BrewCrafters, began in 1997 as a result of owners Mike and Luanne Alcorn comparing beer in Western New York to states like Colorado and California

White Hop Belgian IPA
Style: Belgian IPA
ABV: 4.3%
Availability: Limited

Large additions of Amarillo, Centennial, and Simcoe hops amp up the floral and bright citrus notes in White Hop Belgian IPA. The combination of wheat sweetness and fruity esters from the Belgian yeast strain balances out the intensity of the hops. At 4.3% ABV, you can have a few on a summer day without worrying.

and seeing brews in New York to be lacking. To rectify this, the couple started the brewery to help bars and restaurants in the area get their hands on fresh local beer made just for them. In addition to their own line of CB brand beers, the brewery began brewing exclusive beers for local bars and taking contracts from regional brewers who didn't yet have the space and resources to brew themselves.

The original brewery was a small operation on Papermill Street that quickly outgrew itself, and despite an expansion in 2002 that doubled the brewery's space, Custom BrewCrafters was looking to expand again by 2006. In 2008 the brewery moved to its current location just outside the town of Honeoeye Falls. With the expansion, the brewery's offerings exploded from 6 beers in the CB brand to 23. In 2013 Custom BrewCrafters changed its name to CB Craft Brewers and completed another expansion that increased capacity by 115%.

The beers brewed under the CB brand hit traditional styles that are accessible and easy to have with a meal. The dark, sweet **Double Cream Porter** makes a great pairing with ice cream or cake for dessert. The brewery is well-known for its **Caged Alpha Monkey IPA** and indulges hop heads with four different hop varieties in both pellet and whole-leaf forms for intense citrus qualities. Visiting the brewery, you can taste CB's own beers as well as those brewed for other breweries, bars, and restaurants. The brewery was especially proud to have brewed the official beer, the **White Hop Ale,** for 2013's Rochester Real Beer Week.

COMMUNITY BEER WORKS

15 Lafayette Ave., Buffalo, NY 14213; (716) 759-4677; CommunityBeerWorks.com; @CommunityBeer

Founded: 2012 **Founders:** Ethan Cox, Rudy Watkins, Dan Conley, Gregory Patterson-Tanski, David Foster, Matt Daumen, Chris Smith **Brewer:** Rudy Watkins **Flagship Beer:** Frank **Year-Round Beers:** Frank, The Whale, De Maas, The IPA **Seasonals/Special Releases:** Rutherford B. Haze, The Soft Bulletin, The Jam series, Funkrays, Buffalo Beer Week special brews, First Anniversary special beers **Tours:** Yes; if it's not too crowded **Taproom:** Yes

Tucked in the back of an industrial building that used to house the defunct Meyer Malting Company, a block and a half away from the Niagara River, sits Community Beer Works (CBW). Founded by a group of homebrewing friends who all have roots in Buffalo, they aim to foster the growth of craft beer in the city and give back to the community; the spent grain from CBW's beers is donated to the Massachusetts Avenue Project. To start operations, the group of friends raised money through crowd-funding website Kickstarter, exceeding their goal of $15,000. CBW's slogan is "Embeer Buffalo," signifying the desire to improve the beer culture of Buffalo, hoping to one day transform it into a premier beer destination.

CBW makes four beers year-round and a variety of seasonal and special releases. **The Jam** beers are a series of brews that are made only once and last about two weeks, only available at the brewery's taproom. Brews in the Jam series have included several IPAs, a Barleywine with brettanomyces, and a collaboration beer with Rochester's Roc Brewing, cleverly dubbed **Nano Nano.** For Buffalo's Beer Week and CBW's first anniversary, the brewery made a handful of

Frank
Style: American Pale Ale
ABV: 4.6%
Availability: On draft at CBW
and locations in Buffalo

In Buffalo and its surrounding areas, the name Frank is pretty common. The team at Community Beer Works decided to apply that name to what they feel is the most ubiquitous beer style: the American Pale Ale. Watkins brews Frank with Zeus, Centennial, and Zythos hops in the boil and in dry hopping. With citrus and pine on the nose, Frank is a hop-forward brew with a strong but drinkable bitterness.

special releases. **The Whale,** one of the brewery's year-round offerings, is a Brown Ale made with English brown malt and two types of chocolate malt, pouring a deep brown color. You'll find aromas of nuts, malt, coffee, and chocolate on the nose, which lead to more malt and chocolate flavors on the palate. A manageable 5.9 percent ABV, The Whale offers easy drinking with a smooth mouthfeel. **De Maas** is CBW's Belgian Amber, a balanced brew with caramel, malty aromas and a refreshing palate with notes of caramel and toast. At an almost-sessionable 5.1 percent ABV, De Maas is a great example of a Belgian-style beer.

Brewmaster Rudy Watkins makes the beer on a 1.5-barrel brewing system, a true nano size. When you visit the taproom, if it's too crowded for a tour, you can spot some of the brewing equipment in the space. Community Beer Works brews can be found only on draft at various beer bars throughout Buffalo and in some locations near the city. The team is also on hand every Saturday at the Elmwood-Bidwell Farmers' Market, pouring brews from 8 a.m. to 1 p.m.

ELLICOTTVILLE BREWING COMPANY

28A Monroe St., Ellicottville, NY 14731; (716) 699-2537; EllicottvilleBrewing.com; @EBCwny

Founded: 1995 **Founders:** Allen and Walter Yahn, Peter Kreinheder **Brewer:** Dan Minner **Flagship Beer:** Blueberry Wheat **Year-round Beers:** EBC Pale Ale, Nut Brown, EVL Amber Ale, Black Jack Oatmeal Stout, Blueberry Wheat, Monroe Street Pilsner **Seasonals/Special Releases:** Mowmaster, EVL Blizzard, Summer Wheat, Winter Witte, Pantius Droppus, Hop Bomb, Hey Guy Rye Pale Ale, Black Hops, Chocolate Cherry Bomb, E.S.B., Hopicity, Raspberry Beret, German Stein Beer, Chinook Porter, Nitrous Hopcide, Octoberfest Lager, Boozies Belgian Brutal, Bees Knees Belgian Ale, Catt County Cuvee, St. Jacobs Oak Aged Stout, Anniversary Ales, Bourbon Barrel **Tours:** No **Taproom:** Yes

Thanks to Ellicottville Brewing Company, the town of Ellicottville is known for more than just skiing. Opened as a brewpub in 1995, the company has since added a second brewpub in Fredonia, New York, and expanded the original Ellicottville location. The community has embraced recent expansions because they have created new jobs and increased activity in the town. The expanded brewpub is one of the best places around to kick back for a meal and some beers. The spotless space is quite large, and large windows make the brewing equipment easily visible

to patrons. On warm days patrons who sit at the covered outdoor bar or open patio area are treated to views of the surrounding mountains while sipping their pints.

The brewery makes a staggering number of beers throughout the year, spanning many styles from a traditional Oktoberfest-style Lager to a bourbon barrel–aged IPA. The top-selling **Blueberry Wheat,** marketed as an introduction to craft beer, is served at the brewery with a couple of blueberries in the glass. Blueberries dominate the beer's aroma, but the flavors are more along the lines of a sweet Wheat Beer. While the Blueberry Wheat is the brewery's top seller, Brewer Dan Minner's real talent lies with beers that step outside the box. Many brewers have a Witte for a summer seasonal, but Minner brews a **Winter Witte** with an oats addition to the traditional barley, wheat, coriander, and orange peel for a creamy mouthfeel that suits the season. Riffing on the bourbon barrel–aged Imperial Stout craze, Ellicottville took the **Pantius Droppus Imperial IPA** and aged it in bourbon barrels for a smoother taste that mellows out the beer's intense 95 IBUs.

The food at the pub hits classics like steamed mussels and a pulled pork sandwich, but you can also try dishes like sesame tuna wontons or orange rum-glazed salmon if you are looking for an alternative to pub-style eats. You can usually find a nice pairing for your food among the wide range of beers.

Beer Lover's Pick

Nitrous Hopcide
Style: IPA
ABV: 5.0%
Availability: Limited Release
Ellicottville took a hoppy IPA with a restrained 5.0% ABV and made it even more drinkable by serving it on nitrogen. The nitrogen gives the beer a smoothness that is unusual for an IPA. It takes the bite out of the bitterness, leaving the aroma and earthy qualities of the hops layered over the lightly sweet English malted barley.

THE FAIRPORT BREWING COMPANY

99 Main S. Street, Fairport, NY 14450; (585) 678-6728; FairportBrewing.com; @FairportNY

Founded: 2012 **Founders:** Tim Garman, Paul Guarracini **Brewer:** Paul Guarracini **Beers:** Peter J. IPA, Apollo 8, Olde Ezra Wee Heavy, Scum Jumper Ale, Red Rye IPA, Blackwatch Braggot, Fair Porter, Jordan Saison, William's Altbier, Trail Town Nut Brown, Pure Oil Strong Ale, Gutterwalker Stout, Millstone Blonde, Raider's Red, Common Folk, Brothers' Belgian, White Buck Ale, Oxbow ESB, Picnic in the Park Pale Ale **Tours:** Yes **Taproom:** Yes

Tim Garman and Paul Guarracini opened The Fairport Brewing Company in 2012. Garman, a Fairport native, wanted to bring together two things he loves: beer and his hometown. He aimed to start a brewery that was small enough to allow creativity with its brews and make use of the best ingredients he and Brewer Guarracini could get their hands on. Garman has had community involvement in his brewery, enlisting the help of Fairport's Facebook fans to suggest beer names and looking for monikers that are inspired by the community. One of the more memorable beer names is **Scum Jumper Ale,** a tribute to a long-standing tradition in Fairport of jumping off the Fairport Lift Bridge into the Erie Canal below, where you'd be submerged into some pretty interesting scum.

Picnic in the Park
Style: Pale Ale
ABV: 4.7%
Availability: Limited
Fairport Brewing Company made Picnic in the Park, a watermelon Pale Ale, specifically for Rochester Beer Week. The limited-edition brew is sessionable and refreshing. A light-bodied beer, Picnic in the Park has strong, but not overpowering flavors and aromas of watermelon and a pleasant sweetness.

Guarracini brews creative and interesting beers. His **Jordan Saison** is a refreshing and light-bodied beer with notes of pepper. The **Oxbow ESB** is an excellent example of the style, which isn't always so popular in the United States. Caramel with an earthy bitterness, the ESB pours an amber color and is complemented by English hops. **Apollo 8** is Fairport's Double IPA, and strong flavors of grapefruit and melon come through from the hops. This beer has overarching flavors of malt and clocks in at 8 percent ABV.

After only a short while in business, The Fairport Brewing Company's demand exceeded its supply, and its space. Originally opened in a small studio-like room in an office complex on the outskirts of town, they found a new home, an historic white cottage on Main Street. Built in 1934 as a Pure Oil corporate gas station, it has most recently been home to a local insurance company. The brewery had its new space, but there was one problem: funds to purchase a larger brewing system. Garman and Guarracini turned to the community, launching a Kickstarter campaign to raise money. The campaign exceeded its fund-raising goal of $25,000, with not only the help from individuals and beer fans, but also many Fairport businesses.

FLYING BISON BREWING COMPANY

491 Ontario St., Buffalo, NY 14207; (716) 873-1557; FlyingBisonBrewing.com;
@FlyingBison

Founded: 2000 **Founders:** Phil Internicola, Tim Herzog **Brewer:** Tim Herzog **Flagship Beer:** Rusty Chain **Year-round Beers:** Aviator Red, Rusty Chain, Buffalo Lager, IPA **Seasonals/Special Releases:** Buffalo Kolsch 716, 11th Anniversary Pale Ale, Barnstormer Pale Ale, Barrel Roll Bock, Bisonfest, Blackbird Oatmeal Stout, Blizzard Bock, Buffalo Brindle Porter, Polonia Pils, Skye Pilot Scotch Ale, Sunrise Amber, Warbird **Tours:** Yes; Thursday at 5 p.m., Friday at 6 p.m., Saturday at noon and 2 p.m. **Taproom:** Yes

For Tim Herzog, a gag gift he got from his wife turned into a passion and a lasting career. When he was younger and spending time with friends, he didn't like beer because all they drank was American adjunct Lagers. However, the first time he tried a beer imported from Ireland, he was a convert. The year they married, Herzog's wife gave him a homebrewing kit as a joke gift for his birthday. After that Herzog started homebrewing and didn't look back, opening Flying Bison Brewing Company in 2000. It was the first stand-alone brewery to operate in the city of Buffalo since Iroquois Brewing closed in 1972. Flying Bison beers are brewed on a 20-barrel system

Rusty Chain
Style: American Amber/Red Ale
ABV: 5.0%
Availability: Year-round, on draft and in bottles
Rusty Chain was originally slated to be a limited-release beer and, in partnership with Go Bike Buffalo, to support the Commercial District Bicycle Parking Program. The program is supported by the city of Buffalo to provide bike racks. The beer was so popular that Flying Bison decided to keep it on. Aromas of buttery toast on the nose carry through to the palate, which also has notes of caramel, sweet floral notes, and a spiciness from the hops.

in Buffalo's Riverside neighborhood, and in 2004 a bottling line was installed in the facility. In 2010 financial difficulties caused the brewery to suspend production, and it was purchased that year by Matt Brewing Company, as a subsidiary, though production remained in Buffalo.

Flying Bison's **Aviator Red** is one of its year-round offerings, an easy-drinking Amber/Red Ale that comes in at a manageable 5.25 percent ABV. Toasty, malty aromas lead to similar flavors, with notes of light caramel and toffee. **Buffalo Kolsch 716,** which used to be known as Dawn Patrol Gold, has notes of toast and malt on the nose. Crisp and refreshing, this Kolsch brew is smooth and light bodied with flavors of citrus. The **Buffalo Lager,** a near-sessionable 4.7 percent ABV, pours a golden color with a thick foamy head. Clean and drinkable, Buffalo Lager has a slight fruitiness and dry quality.

Herzog intended to foster and renew beer brewing in Buffalo, once a flourishing industry. The name "Flying Bison" also recalls Buffalo's history in aviation manufacturing. The brewery's beers are distributed throughout its home city and throughout Erie, Niagara, and Chautauqua Counties, on draft and in bottles.

Western New York

GENESEE BREWING COMPANY

25 Cataract St., Rochester, NY 14605; (585) 263-9200; GeneseeBeer.com;
@GeneseeBrewery @DundeeBeer
Founded: 1878 **Founders:** Wehle Family **Brewer:** Dean Jones **Flagship Beer:** Cream
Ale **Year-round Beers:** Genesee Beer, Genny Light, Genesee Cream Ale, Genesee Ice,
Genesee Brew House Pilot Series, 12 Horse Ale, J.W. Dundee's Original Honey Brown
Lager, J.W. Dundee Stout, J.W. Dundee Porter, J.W. Dundee English Style Ale, J.W. Dundee
Pilsner, J.W. Dundee Pale Ale, J.W. Dundee India Pale Ale **Seasonals/Special Releases:**
J.W. Dundee Kolsch Style Ale, J.W. Dundee Summer Shandy, J.W. Dundee Pale Bock Lager,
J.W. Dundee Oktoberfest, J.W. Dundee Nut Brown Ale, J.W. Dundee Irish Red Lager **Tours:**
Yes; every hour **Taproom:** Yes

Along with Matt Brewing Company in Utica, Genesee Brewing Company represents the history of brewing in New York State. That history involves industrialization, immigration, consolidation, and its near destruction by Prohibition. Founded in 1878, the Genesee Brewery was one of the few to survive Prohibition, reopening in 1932 as Genesee Brewing Company. The brewery made a name for itself with its iconic **Cream Ale** that it introduced in 1960 to cross the smoothness of

Genesee Cream Ale
Style: Cream Ale
ABV: 5.2%
Availability: Year-round
Once referred to as the "Male Ale" the Cream Ale sought to cross the characteristics of Ales and Lagers in America. The light body, golden color, and slightly sweet flavor have made Genesee Cream a favorite first beer for many drinkers and a nostalgic return for older drinkers. Craft beer geeks might scoff at the beer in many settings in favor of more flavorful beers, but the Cream Ale still has a place in the modern beer market.

Lagers that dominated the market with the flavor of Ales. For more variety in its offerings, the brewery introduced the **J.W. Dundee** line, starting with the **Honey Brown Lager,** in 1994. Unfortunately the late 20th century was difficult for the brewery, and the Wehle family was forced to sell after Ted Wehle, who ran the company, died in 2000. The sale amounted to an employee buyout that formed High Falls Brewing Company. In 2009 the company was then bought by KPS Capital, who merged the company with Labatt USA into North American Breweries and changed its name back to Genesee Brewing Company. Cervecería Costa Rica purchased North American Breweries in 2012.

Under the new ownership the brewery (though no longer technically craft) is reclaiming much of its heritage. Next to the sprawling industrial compound, the brewery built a new brewhouse that functions as a pub, pilot brewery, and museum. Those with nostalgia for Genesee Cream Ale, **Genny Light,** or **12 Horse Ale** can take in the historical can and bottle collection (look for the classic green Cream Ale cans). If you are interested in how breweries fit into the city of Rochester over time, you can view a map and illuminate lights to show the number and location of breweries in the city. The pilot brewery hosts tours and tastings at a bar overlooking a 20-barrel brewing system. The bar serves the Genesee, Dundee, and Honey

Brown beers and experimental brews from the pilot system, made by Brewmaster Dean Jones. The pub offers indoor seating and a balcony with a view of Rochester's waterfalls. Try the beef on weck with a Cream Ale.

ROC BREWING COMPANY

56 South Union St., Rochester, NY 14607; (585) 794-9798; RocBrewingCo.com; @RocBrewingCo

Founded: 2011 **Founders:** Chris Spinelli, Jon Mervine **Brewer:** Jon Mervine **Flagship Beer:** Golden Pale Ale **Year-round Beers:** Golden Pale Ale, Dark Mild, Cullinan's Revival **Seasonals/Special Releases:** Vague IPA, Lil' SIPA, Down Unda IPA, What the Fuggle IPA, ThreeNinety Bock, Big DIPA, Don't Fear the RIPA, Belgian Blonde, Cadejo Blanco, Cadejo Negro, Vern, Kyoto Protocol, Wet Smash, Drogo's Plight, Union 56, Sex Panther, Nano Nano **Tours:** Yes; by request **Taproom:** Yes

For Chris Spinelli and Jon Mervine, friends and homebrewing partners, Roc Brewing isn't about just selling beer—it's about selling the experience. The pair strike up conversations and get to know each person who stops into their taproom to try their beers. They had started homebrewing at a suggestion from Spinelli's mother, who took them to buy their first kit in May 2009. By the end of 2009 the friends, who had met while studying at Rochester Institute of Techology, had so many requests for their brews that they decided to go pro, partnering up with

Dark Mild
Style: Dark Mild
ABV: 4.0%
Availability: Year-round on draft
In keeping with Mervine's commitment to brew sessionable beers, his Dark Mild beer has hallmark flavors of big roasted beers, but comes in at a manageable 4 percent ABV. On the palate you'll taste flavors of malt, toasted bread, and chocolate. Notes of coffee contribute to a dry, yet nutty finish. Roc's Dark Mild is a big beer that's small and incredibly easy drinking.

Spinelli's mother to start their business. In 2010 Spinelli and Mervine quit their jobs, found a location for Roc Brewing, and completed construction on it in mid-2011, when they officially opened.

Mervine is the brewmaster and focuses his recipes on more sessionable beers, rarely brewing something very big; the biggest being an 8 percent **Belgian Blonde.** The **Golden Pale Ale** is light to medium bodied with moderate hop bitterness. Floral and pine notes on the nose, this brew finishes dry with a hint of honey. A great gateway beer for those who don't think they like craft brews, the Golden Pale Ale is crisp and refreshing. **Cullinan's Revival** is a Red Ale, a balanced beer and great example of the style. Notes of toffee and malt on the light body lead to a slight bitterness. Roc beers are available only on draft in and around the Rochester area.

The team at Roc Brewing applied for and was accepted to the Brewing the American Dream Program held by Sam Adams. The benefits of the program included a micro loan and a mentorship. Since becoming a part of Brewing the American Dream, Spinelli and Mervine have been able to reach out to Sam Adams for help when needed. When they mentioned they were going to barrel age beers, Sam Adams sent them 10-barrel racks, and the brewery welcomed them to look through their hop selection when they needed more. Roc Brewing also made a collaboration beer with Sam Adams, called **ThreeNinety Bock**—so named for the distance between the two breweries—a Maibock released in 2013, making Roc one of only a handful of breweries to brew a collaboration with the craft beer giant.

ROHRBACH BREWING COMPANY

97 Railroad St., Rochester, NY 14609; (585) 546-8020; Rohrbachs.com; @Rohrbachs
Founded: 1992 **Founder:** John Urlaub **Brewer:** Mitch LaGoy **Flagship Beer:** Scotch Ale **Year-round Beers:** American Lager, BlueBeary Ale, ESB, Flaherty's, Highland Lager, Kolsch, Next Door Ale, Old Nate's Pale Ale, Railroad Street Ale, Red Wing Red, Sam Patch Porter, Stock Ale, Vanilla Porter **Seasonals/Special Releases:** Altbier, American Amber, Belgian Dubbel, Black IPA, California IPA, Gregory St. Lager, Imperial Scotch Ale, Kacey's Kristmas Ale, Nightfrost Porter Oatmeal Stout, Oktoberfest, Pineapple Wheat, Pumpkin Ale, Rye Pilsner, Saison, Winter Wassail **Tours:** Yes; Saturday on the hour from 9 a.m. to 3 p.m. **Taproom:** Yes

John Urlaub might not be one of the well-known brewery founders from the first generation of craft brewers, but he seems to be the personification of the country's beer history for the last 25 years. Urlaub originally fell in love with beer when he tried the classic craft beer Anchor Steam while working for Kodak in San Francisco. His transfer to New York City brought him into contact with the venerated

but unsuccessful Manhattan Brewpub, where Urlaub witnessed his first brewpub in action. After the two experiences, he had a stint living in Rohrbach, Germany, near Heidelberg, which sealed the deal. Without a way to get the beers that he loved from Germany and having experienced the infant American craft brewing community, Urlaub started out on his own with a brewpub in downtown Rochester that eventually became Rohrbach. He added a new brewpub location on Buffalo Road in 1995, closing the first, and then the 20-barrel brewery Railroad Street location near the busy Public Market.

The brewery pumps out a wide range of classic beer styles like its flagship **Scotch Ale,** which has a deep ruby color and the style's trademark sweetness. The **Vanilla Porter** combines the dark chocolate and coffee notes of roasted grains with a strong vanilla flavor from the addition of vanilla extract.

The Railroad Street location houses Rohrbach's main production facility and has a large taproom for tastings and events. Tours are available on the hour on weekends (just don't expect them to start on time). The Buffalo Road brewpub (3859 Buffalo Road; 585-594-9800) serves German dishes like schnitzel, liverwurst, and sauerbraten, as well as familiar pub foods like chicken wings and burgers. In addition to making its own offerings, Rohrbach contract brews beers for other breweries.

Railroad Street IPA
Style: IPA
ABV: 6.5%
Availability: Year-round

This Amber IPA carries a stronger malt backbone than most IPAs that stands up to the hop bitterness. The heavy hop additions impart citrus notes and a low-level piney character to Railroad Street IPA. Toasted malt flavors come through the citrus and pine to create a balanced finish to the beer.

SOUTHERN TIER BREWING COMPANY

2072 Stoneman Circle, Lakewood, NY 14750; (716) 763-5479; STBCBeer.com; @STBCBeer
Founded: 2002 **Founders:** Phineas DeMink, Allen "Skip" Yahn **Brewer:** Dustin Hazer
Flagship Beer: IPA **Year-round Beers:** IPA, Phin & Matt's, 422 Pale Wheat, Porter, 2XIPA, 2XStout, Live Pale Ale, UnEarthly, Iniquity **Seasonals/Special Releases:** Eurotrash Pilz, Hop Sun, Harvest, Old Man Winter, 2XSteam, 2XRye, 2XMas, Back Burner, Compass, Pumpking, Krampus, Plum Noir, Crème Brulee, Warlock, Choklat, Oat, Oak Aged UnEarthly, Jah*va, Farmer's Tan **Tours:** Yes; Saturday 1 p.m., 2:30 p.m., 4 p.m.
Taproom: Yes

Southern Tier is undoubtedly the most widely known brewery in Western New York. Lakewood, two hours south of Buffalo, seems an odd location for such a large and popular brewery, but Southern Tier has called the town home since it opened in 2002. Founders Phineas DeMink and Allen "Skip" Yahn (also a founder of Ellicottville Brewing Company) sought to bring more brewing to an area whose only outpost at the time was Ellicottville. The pair didn't start just any brewery, however. Explosive growth during just over a decade in business has put the brewery at number 37 on the Brewers Association's 2012 list of the largest craft brewers in the United States. The production looks only to increase, since in 2013 construction was completed on a 110-barrel brewhouse and also to double the capacity of the beer cellar. Equally impressive to the growth is that Southern Tier has maintained the high quality of their beer while rapidly increasing production.

Hop Sun
Style: Wheat Beer
ABV: 5.1%
Availability: Spring and summer seasonal,
   in bottles and on tap

Hop Sun is one of the most thirst-quenching summer seasonals available. The Wheat Beer is crisp and light bodied but full of flavor. The addition of hop flowers keeps the beer bright and snappy with notes of lemon zest and a pleasant dry finish.

Southern Tier's operation is what you might think of when describing an ideal brewery. The large wood-covered facility is spotless; the taproom and shop—dubbed "The Empty Pint"—bustles on weekends. Locals drop in for pints, growlers, and cases of beer. Naturally, the tap list is long and spans flavors from the intense bitterness of the **2X IPA** to the supersweet and dark **Crème Brulee.** Special-release beers like the ever-popular fall seasonal **Pumpking**—think sweet pumpkin pie—and the creative **Plum Noir**—made using Italian plums—are available at the taproom for purchase by the bottle. The food menu is limited to pulled pork sandwiches and homemade chips, but you can also bring in outside food.

The brewery's back patio area is one of the most relaxing places in the state to grab a pint. Patrons are treated to live music in the summer and can participate in the game of Stones, as Southern Tier is home to the first public course. Stones is a ball sport similar to bocce, but it's played on a course with obstacles. The brewery runs a summer Stones league and tournament for those who get competitive.

THREE HEADS BREWING

164 Chelmsford Rd., Rochester, NY 14618; (585) 360-4342; ThreeHeadsBrewing.com/
ThreeHeadsBrewing; @3HeadsBrewing

Founded: 2010 **Founders:** Geoff Dale, Todd Dirrigl, Dan Nothnagle **Brewer:** CB Craft
Brewers **Flagship Beer:** The Kind IPA **Year-round Beers:** The Kind IPA, The Blimey
English Style Pale Ale, Skunk Black IPA, Java Sutra Coffee Porter **Seasonals/Special
Releases:** Loopy, Common Man, Ontario Coast IPA, Bromingo Smoked Maple Amber Ale,
Big Head Stout, Country Shweat Imperial Wheat, Rochestafarian, Too Kind Double IPA,
Cobbs Hill Black Lager **Tours:** No **Taproom:** No

In a familiar type of story, Three Heads Brewing grew first out of years of home-brewing by founders Geoff Dale, Todd Dirrigl, and Dan Nothnagle. The crew attended classes at the Siebel Institute on how to start a craft brewery and decided to take recipes developed by their homebrewing and leave the brewing up to Custom

Beer Lover's Pick

**Country Shweat Imperial
Wheat**
Style: Imperial Wheat Ale
ABV: 7.6%
Availability: Limited
Three Heads took their bold
approach to the normally
restrained Wheat Ales with their
Country Shweat Imperial Wheat
that they released for Rochester
Real Beer Week. Golden and hazy
with a white head, the beer has
a creamy feeling and is very
drinkable despite the 7.6% ABV.
The Caliente hops used give the
beer a fruity melon flavor that
doesn't overpower the mellowing
character of the wheat.

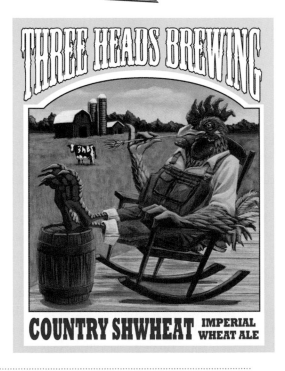

BrewCrafters in Honeoeye Falls just outside of Rochester (now known as CB Craft Brewers). The partners are focused on marketing and logistics, and in just three years the brewery has covered the state and launched into two of the largest beer markets in the country, Chicago and then New York City. The brewery's motto "Ales with Character. Characters with Ale" is taken to heart, as the beer names often poke fun at brewing conventions and the labels give a nod to hops' cousin marijuana. In 2012 the brewery teamed up with Massachusetts-based brewer Clown Shoes, another brewery known for tongue-and-cheek beer names and labels, to brew **Third Party Candidate,** an Imperial Amber Ale the summer before the national election.

Three Heads brews four year-round beers, **The Kind IPA, The Blimey English Style Pale Ale, Skunk Black IPA,** and **Java Sutra Coffee Porter.** The beers have big bold flavors and usually come in above 6% ABV. The Skunk Black IPA is full of citrus aromas and a piney, resinous flavor dominates, but the style's characteristic roast comes through on the back end to take things up a notch. Fans of the smooth mouth-feel from the use of oats will like the **Loopy,** an oatmeal Red Ale that also has strong flavors of pine and citrus. In early 2013 the brewery released **Too Kind Double IPA,** an 8.5% ABV Imperial version of their flagship The Kind IPA. Aggressively hopped, the beer includes the new Meridian hop that imparts extra fruitiness.

WOODCOCK BROTHERS BREWING COMPANY

638 Lake St., Wilson, NY 14172; (716) 333-4000; WoodcockBrothersBrewery.com
Founded: 2012 **Founders:** Mark, Andrea, Tim, and Debbie Woodcock **Brewer:** Tim Woodcock **Flagship Beer:** Amber **Year-round Beers:** Amber, American Pale Ale, India Pale Ale, Porter, Cold Storage Ale **Seasonals/Special Releases:** Summer Ale, Hoppycock IPA **Tours:** No **Taproom:** Yes

Located inside an old renovated cold-storage building just off of Lake Ontario is Woodcock Brothers Brewing Company. Mark Woodcock, his wife Andrea, and his brother Tim and his wife Debbie started the brewery as their second family venture; Mark and Tim work as owner and foreman of Ricmar Electric in North Tonawanda, a business started by their father over 30 years ago. They retrofitted the facility that used to store apples into a brewery and restaurant that seats over 100. The bar top is made from repurposed floor joists, and the stones that make the base of the bar were also repurposed from the structure, which is 100 years old. Enjoying your brews, you can look through ceiling-high windows opposite the bar at the brewing operation below. Patrons can enjoy their beer at seats inside or outside on a large patio area in front of the building.

A homebrewer for over 10 years, Tim adapted many of his recipes to work on a larger scale. His brews are sessionable and drinkable across the board, with the biggest beer—the **Porter**—clocking in at a still-manageable 5.8 percent ABV. Though the brewery officially opened in November 2012, the Woodcocks held a grand opening party in May 2013. To celebrate the grand opening, Tim brewed a special beer, the **Hoppycock IPA,** a hop-heavy beer with an earthy bitterness and the citrusy, floral notes present in many IPAs. The flagship **Amber Ale,** at a sessionable 4.1 percent ABV, is brewed with Fuggle and Northern Brewer hops. The beer pours an amber color and has caramel, toffee, and malt flavors with a subtle hop finish. The **Cold Storage Ale,** named for the building's history, is only available at the brewery. Crisp and refreshing, this beer is made with 2 Row malt and Cascade and Centennial hops that lend it a citrusy finish.

The menu features pub snacks such as spinach artichoke dip and fresh clams, an assortment of salads, chicken wings, and wood-fired pizzas topped with vegetables, meats, or just cheeses. Woodcock Brothers also uses its spent grain to make pretzels and bread for its dining room, a delicious way to reuse their malt. The beers are available on draft at their brewery and restaurant, but also at a variety of locations around Niagara County and some in Buffalo.

Porter

Style: Porter

ABV: 5.8%

Availability: Year-round, at the brewery and distributed locally

While the Porter is the biggest beer from Woodcock Brothers Brewing Compay at 5.8 percent ABV, it's still a deliciously drinkable brew. Made from several different malts—2 Row, Chocolate, Caramel 20 and 60, Black Malt—and Warrior and Willamette hops, the flavors are rich, roasty, and malty. The Porter pours a solid black color and has notes of coffee and toffee on the palate. This beer finishes with a slight roasted bitterness.

Western New York

Brewpubs

BECKER BREWING COMPANY

3724 Quaker Rd., Gasport, NY 14067; (716) 772-2211; BeckerFarms.com; @BeckerFarms
Founded: 2009 **Founder:** Oscar Vizcarra **Brewer:** Tim Herzog **Year-round Beers:** Pony Pale Ale, Rooster Red, Local Lager, Art's Amber, Black Stallion Stout **Seasonals/Special Releases:** Kolsch Summer Ale, White IPA, Blueberry Wheat, Frank's Octoberfest, IPA, Irish Dry Stout

Traveling around Upstate New York, you'll spot farm stands selling homegrown produce, farms that allow you to pick your own fruit, and vineyards offering wine tastings. What about a place that offers not only all three of those experiences, but also a taproom with fresh beer? Enter Becker Farms: a vineyard, farm, and brewery all rolled up into one, dubbed an agri-tourism mecca. In 1979 Melinda and Oscar

Vizcarra took over Becker Farms (originally established in 1894), which at that point had only a few tart cherry trees to its name. Since then the couple has revitalized the business, transforming it into a Western New York destination and events space. As their products expanded to include wine, the Vizcarras noticed a lot of people asking about beer. Oscar Vizcarra brought in Tim Herzog, the brewer at Flying Bison Brewing Company, to help start up microbrewery Becker Brewing Company, which launched in 2009.

The beers right now are brewed at Flying Bison in Buffalo, with plans to eventually move the brewing operation to Becker Farms, where it will be run by Oscar's son Andres. In the meantime, you can taste Becker beers at a taproom on the farm. **Art's Amber** has roasted caramel aromas and malty flavors. You'll find hints of toast and hops in this malty beer, which comes in at a sessionable 4.2 percent ABV. The **Pony Pale Ale,** a year-round offering, pours an amber color and is brewed with Cascade hops. The hops lend it a floral nose and spice characters to the palate. Becker's **Local Lager** is an easy-drinking, light-bodied beer at 4.8 percent ABV with clean flavors. The biggest brew on tap, at 7 percent ABV, **Black Stallion Stout** is full bodied with a smooth mouthfeel and rich chocolate and malted flavors.

At the taproom you can purchase pints, flights, pitchers, or growlers of beer and also enjoy a local lunch. The meals are made from locally grown ingredients and paired with your preferred brew. The menu changes depending on the season. You could spend all day at Becker Farms, tasting beer, picking raspberries and blueberries, and enjoying fresh, local food. In the summer the brewery is open daily at 11 a.m., and in winter is open at noon every day but Tuesday.

PEARL STREET GRILL AND BREWERY

76 Pearl St., Buffalo, NY 14202; (716) 856-2337; PearlStreetGrill.com
Founded: 1997 **Founders:** A group of investors **Brewer:** Phil Internicola **Year-round Beers:** Lake Effect Pale Ale, Lighthouse Premium Blond, Saber's Edge Double IPA, Street Brawler Stout, Trainwreck German Amber, Wild Ox Wheat, St. Pearlie Girl's Persuasions, Horace's Private Stock **Seasonals/Special Releases:** Rye Wist of Fete, Lune' d'bleu, Maestro's Muse, Spirit of Buffalo Summer Lager, Haar van de Hond Oud Bruin, Perlenstrasse Oktoberfest, Moonshadow Pumpkin Ale, Lord Lupulin , Don Cherry Cherry Wheat

Buffalo's recent renaissance is palpable in the downtown area, where the harbor and the city's sports venues keep a constant flow of visitors—at least when there isn't a blizzard. The Pearl Street Grill and Brewery, opened in 1997, lies right in the middle of the action. The brewpub resides in the massive space of an old sewing factory (check out the ceiling fans that run with a continuous belt between them)

with enough space for a 15-barrel brewhouse, a dining room, a bar, and pool tables (on two levels).

For a brewpub, Pearl Street keeps a large selection of house-brewed beers available on draft. Many of the beer names have a connection to Buffalo, like the **Lake Effect Pale Ale** or **Saber's Edge Double IPA.** In addition to a lineup of year-round beers the brewpub also branches out into specialty beers like **Haar van de Hond Oud Bruin** (Hair of the Dog Flanders Brown Ale) a rare example of a sour beer brewed in Western New York.

The brewpub serves a wide selection of dishes that seem designed for the cold weather and utilize many of its beers. Start with the potato pancakes, a good example of a classic and served with apples stewed in Don Cherry Cherry Wheat along with the traditional sour cream. The pot roast is braised in their Trainwreck ale and the kielbasa is served with mustard made with their Lake Effect Pale Ale. The restaurant also serves the standard pub food like burgers, salads, and pizzas.

Beer Bars

AURORA BREW WORKS
191 Main St., East Aurora, NY 14052; (716) 652-2337;@AuroraBrewWorks
Draft Beers: 6 **Bottled/Canned Beers:** Hundreds

When you walk into Aurora Brew Works (ABW), the first thing you see is a giant sign on the back wall that says BEER in bright red light bulbs. It evokes a feeling that you're at a carnival. Which you kind of are. Aurora Brew Works is practically a beer paradise, a magical emporium with hundreds of bottles and cans that you could pore over for hours. In the front of the shop is a small bar with six taps and a lounge-like area to enjoy your beers.

This is exactly what Darryl Howe and Michael Lundeen had in mind when they opened Aurora Brew Works in 2012. Patrons at ABW can choose from six draft beers

to purchase pints or a flight. If the options on tap don't satisfy you, you're free to roam about the store to purchase a bottle or can to enjoy at the bar or on the patio in front of the shop. There is also a selection of beer cocktails on the menu, a vanilla Porter float or Festina Peche mimosa for example.

ABW holds tastings for established breweries and also brand-new up-and-coming local ones. You're guaranteed to find your favorite craft beers from breweries like Great Lakes, Captain Lawrence, and Troegs, as well as rare and limited releases, like Founders KBS. Tuesday is Game Night at ABW, where you can play games on a classic Nintendo NES. Though Aurora Brew Works doesn't have a food menu, food trucks will often park and serve up eats right out front.

BLUE MONK

727 Elmwood Ave., Buffalo, NY 14222; (716) 882-6665; BMBflo.com; @BlueMonkBflo
Draft Beers: Over 30 **Bottled/Canned Beers:** Over 70

Strolling down Elmwood Avenue in Buffalo, you'll find various boutiques selling artsy and handmade wares, restaurants, a chocolate shop, a beer bottle shop, and several bars. While many of the watering holes on Elmwood could be characterized as "divey," that's not an adjective you'd attach to Blue Monk. The bar is owned by friends Mike Shatzel (who also owns Coles) and Kevin Brinkworth Jr., who after a trip to Philadelphia wanted to re-create the Belgian-influenced experience they had at bars there, in Buffalo. Named for jazz musician Thelonious Monk's hit "Blue Monk," the bar's extensive draft and bottle list has a Belgian spin.

Great offerings include Ommegang's Abbey Ale and Three Philosophers, Orval, Westmalle Dubbel and Tripel, and several selections from Unibroue. You may also find some rarer brews like BFM Abbaye De St. Bon Chien Grand Cru 2011, Stillwater Premium Forty Faave, Evil Twin Imperial Biscotti Break DeCicco's Version, and New England Bhandi-Bot Double IPA, which isn't widely available in New York State.

The Belgian flair of Blue Monk extends to the menu. Belgian-style frites are served with aioli in unique flavors such as honey-cayenne, sea salt, Thai curry ketchup, and smoked chili. Standard upscale bar fare such as plates of charcuterie or artisanal cheeses are on the menu, as well as a variety of mussels. Each dish of one pound of mussels is steamed in a Belgian-style Ale such as Delirium Tremens, Ommegang Hennepin, or Ommegang Witte. Ommegang also appears on the sandwich section of Blue Monk's menu, in a Rare Vos–braised short rib sandwich. If you're going to sit and enjoy some food, prepare for some slow service.

COLES

1104 Elmwood Ave., Buffalo, NY 14222; (716) 886-1449; ColesBuffalo.com;
@Coles_Elmwood
Draft Beers: 36 **Bottled/Canned Beers:** 100

Elmwood Avenue in Buffalo is the city's main artery for shops and restaurants. Coles, now owned by Mike Shatzel (who also co-founded Blue MonkBlue Monk"), has been one of the old standbys for craft beer drinkers and college students from nearby Buffalo State University.

The classic bar opened in 1934 in the wake of Prohibition and added taps a few at a time over the years, culminating in the current 36 selections. The bar has a vintage black-and-white checked floor and is decorated with interesting old tap handles. Despite the old sports memorabilia and photos, the bar stays current with its selection of seasonals like Dogfish Festina Peche and special brews like Southern Tier Plum Noir. Ithaca Beer Company, Ellicottville Brewing Company, Community Beer Works, and other New York brewers have a strong presence at the bar along with the popular out-of-state brewers like Great Lakes and Bear Republic.

If you need help with picking your beers, the draft menu has some flavor profiles and ABVs. The bar also runs tap takeovers from popular brewers and a popular Geeks Who Drink trivia night on Wednesday. The restaurant menu offers up a wide variety of burgers and of course Buffalo wings.

DONNELLY'S PUBLIC HOUSE

1 Water St., Fairport, NY 14604; (585) 377-5450; DonnellysPH.com; @DonnellysPH
Draft Beers: 33 **Bottled/Canned Beers:** 40 to 50

Donnelly's Public House, in the small town of Fairport on the Erie Canal, is a pub with a classic feel but a serious beer list. Owner Scott Donnelly keeps some of the best craft breweries on the taps, and for a bar outside the city of Rochester, he manages to run some great brewery events at the bar. Limited-release beers such as Founders Brewing Rubaeus and Scorcher #366 from Brooklyn Brewery can be found among the drafts. If you are interested in New York's burgeoning cider industry, you can also sample ciders from nearby producers like Black Bird in Baker, New York. For those looking for an introduction to craft beer, the friendly bartenders are armed with tablets showing the beers on tap with styles and additional information.

Donnelly tries to keep his patrons connected to the region's community of brewers with events and blog posts on the pub's website. The pub has made an effort to support some of the state's smallest breweries like Buffalo's Community Beer Works and Canadaigua's Naked Dove Brewing. For the 2013 Rochester Real Beer Week, the bar hosted a beer-pairing dinner with Good Nature Brewing of Hamilton, New York, one of the few breweries operating with a farm brewery license. On Tuesday the bar features two New York State beers for $3 a pint.

EBENEZER ALE HOUSE

4348 W. Seneca St., West Seneca, NY 14224; (716) 674-BEER; EbenezerAleHouse.com; @EbenezerAle
Draft Beers: 20 **Bottled/Canned Beers:** 50 to 60

Buffalo-area natives Nathan Springer and Shawn Schweis opened Ebenezer Ale House in 2011 to bring an affordable restaurant and bar with quality beer and food options to West Seneca. With 20 taps, the bar mixes craft brewers in with mass-produced beers like Labatt that have an especially strong hold in the area. Large-screen TVs are positioned above the bar for the passionate fans of Buffalo's sports teams. Brews like Great Lakes Lake Erie Monster, Founders Oatmeal Stout, and Victory Donnybrook Stout share space with local brewers like Flying Bison and Ithaca Beer Company. There are a few reasonably priced large-format bottles like Brooklyn Black Ops and Southern Tier Pumpking on the beer list.

Ebenezer Ale House is a large space with a wraparound deck for warm days. The food menu is predominantly burgers, sandwiches, and pizzas. Almost everything on the menu is an affordable $10 or under. More Ale houses like Ebenezer will help improve the beer options in the areas surrounding Buffalo.

THE LEWISTON VILLAGE PUB

840 Center St., Lewiston, NY 14092; (716) 405-7017; LewistonVillagePub.com; @PUBLIFE14092
Draft Beers: 40 **Bottled/Canned Beers:** Over 150

In 2008 Ken Scibetta and Ed Webster opened The Lewiston Village Pub and Wing Company, the two of them running the bar and subleasing the kitchen to the Wing Company, which left shortly thereafter. Scibetta and Webster took over the food operation, starting out with pizza and subs. Now items on Lewiston's extensive menu include crab cakes, salads, lobster, burgers, steak, and *Mestolos*. A dish original to The Lewiston Village Pub, *Mestolos* are made of homemade stretched dough topped with fresh ingredients, rolled up, baked, then sliced and served with sauce.

The Lewiston Village Pub has evolved into a relaxed neighborhood spot, called simply "The Pub," and Scibetta and Webster are committed to improving the surrounding community. In 2009 Scibetta launched PUBFEST, which has grown into a three-day festival with music, food, and beer, proceeds of which go to local charity Variety Kids Telethon.

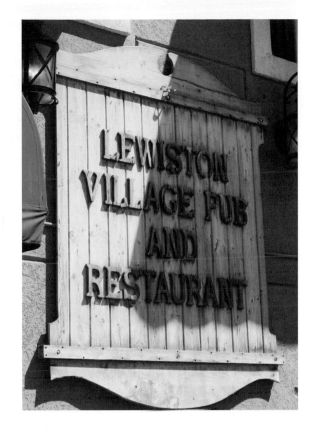

The pub's beer list is categorized by style and features many New York breweries including Southern Tier, Ithaca, Ommegang, and Lake Placid. The bar offers a mug club, where members get a personalized mug for $10; they then pay just $6 for all subsequent refills.

LOVIN'CUP

300 Park Point Dr., Ste. 101, Rochester, NY 14623; (585) 292-9940; Lovincup.com; @LovincupRoc
Draft Beers: 10 **Bottled/Canned Beers:** Over 50

Ed Ward, Leslie Zinck, Bob Zinck, John Nichols, and Clay Carpenter opened Lovin'cup in 2008. Located on the edge of the Rochester Institute of Technology campus, Lovin'cup is at once a bar, restaurant, music venue, and coffee shop. A space large and comfortable enough to accommodate tons of people, Lovin'cup has a comprehensive menu with bar snacks like chicken wings, quesadillas, buffalo sliders, and meat and cheese plates. Choose from healthy options like salads and wraps, or heartier fare like burgers, sandwiches, and paninis. An assortment of gourmet coffee drinks served in the morning makes Lovin'cup not only a place to enjoy an evening out, but also where you can nurse your hangover the next day.

Affixed to the wall opposite the bar in the front of the space is a large steampunk-style sculpture that doubles as a wine rack. Metal is fabricated in shapes of piano keys and music notes, with slots for wine bottles scattered throughout. The beer menu features draft and bottled brews, which are characterized by style. The tap offerings change frequently and—except for the macro mainstays such as Guinness, Blue Moon, and Labatt—feature some local breweries like Southern Tier and 3 Heads Brewing. The bottle list is made up of mostly American beers, with some imports like Fuller's and Chimay. Lovin'cup is definitely a fun place to enjoy some brews, food, and tunes.

MACGREGORS' GRILL AND TAP ROOM

300 Jefferson Rd., Rochester, NY 14623; (585) 427-8410; MacGregorsGrillAndTapRoom.net
Draft Beers: 70+ **Bottled Beers:** About 12

The Rochester-based chain MacGregors' Grill and Tap Room has expanded over the years to include three locations in Rochester, one in Amherst, and one in Canadaigua. The goal here is getting as many beers into the hands of beer drinkers as possible. Beer lists can range upward of 70 beers from local brewers like Naked Dove and Three Heads and larger brewers including Harpoon, Brooklyn, and Dogfish Head. Mass-produced beers from the likes of AB InBev and Coors make up a significant chunk of the menu, but the good outweighs the bad. The bars also run vintage nights, comparing beers like Dogfish Head 120 Minute IPA from different years.

The bars carry their own English-style Pale Ale, using British grains and hops. The Pale Ale is brewed for the bars by Harpoon Brewery in Boston. Regular drinkers from the area can take advantage of the bar's Beer Club card that works like frequent flier miles. Points can then be applied toward the purchase of beers.

MR. GOODBAR

1110 Elmwood Ave., Buffalo, NY 14222; (716) 882-4000; MrGoodbarBuffalo.com
Draft Beers: 30 **Bottled/Canned Beers:** Over 30

Chicken wings are a Buffalo institution. If you live there or ever have, chances are you have your go-to place to eat them, and if you're visiting, wings are a must-eat for at least one meal. Mr. Goodbar, a mainstay on Elmwood Avenue since 1986, is well-known for its chicken wings, made with a choice of 15 flavors, one of the most popular being Cajun Stout. Dominic Massaro purchased the bar in 1995 and brought on managers Amanda and Bobby Rabb, who have since taken over ownership. The husband-and-wife team reinvigorated the atmosphere and energy of the

place, which now has live music from local up-and-coming bands every Friday, open mic comedy night every Wednesday, and a monthly beer club spearheaded by Robby.

Each month the bar hosts its Goodbar Goodbeerclub, a beer-tasting event with brews along various themes with food accompaniments. Goodbar has one cask offering, pouring craft and imported cask ales. The beer selection often features New York breweries such as Flying Bison, Community Beer Works, Southern Tier, and Ithaca. Though the bar is dark and a bit divey, it's a fun neighborhood spot to meet friends, shoot some pool, watch a local sports game, chow down on wings, and listen to top regional bands.

THE OLD TOAD

277 Alexander St., Rochester, NY 14607; (585) 232-2626; TheOldToad.com; @TheOldToad
Draft Beers: 15 on tap, 4 on cask **Bottled/Canned Beers:** 80 to 90

English pubs have a special and nostalgic place in beer culture. Since 1990, The Old Toad has sought to capture some of the English pub's magic and transport it to Rochester. Opened by Englishman David Wicket and Rochester native John Roman, the bar is highly regarded by the local beer community for the beer, service, and eclectic crowd. The servers are students from United Kingdom universities like

Edinburgh and Manchester participating in The Old Toad's training program for the food and drink industry. Not only does the staff come from Britain, but the physical bar itself does too.

Surprisingly the majority of beers on tap are American, made by brewers like Uinta and Lagunitas. The Old Toad is a pioneer in serving cask Ale to the Rochester community and offers several beers via this traditional method of storing and serving beer. The cask Ale program often offers fresh casks of English styles by Middle Ages Brewing—just an hour's drive east on I-90. You can catch some great casks at the bar's popular "Firkin Friday" event.

THE OWL HOUSE
75 Marshall St., Rochester, NY 14607; (585) 360-2920; OwlHouseRochester.com; @TheOwlHouse
Draft Beers: 12 **Bottled/Canned Beers:** Over 20

The Owl House can be found on a residential street in Rochester, and you might just drive by it the first time you visit, as it looks like a regular house. In fact the home was built in 1867 for Rochester's deputy sheriff. A cozy setting, The Owl House, opened in 2010, has a beer list of 12 on tap and more than 20 bottle and can picks that are curated with local and specialty craft brews. Draft selections have included offerings from New York brewers like Naked Dove, Roc Brewing, and

Three Heads, and in bottles you might find BFM Abbaye De St. Bon Chien 2009, Bayerischer Bahnhof Leipziger Gose, De Glazen Toren Cuvee Angelique, or Dogfish Head Tweason'ale (for those who can't digest gluten).

The food menu consists of dishes using locally sourced ingredients: sandwiches, soups, salads, small plates, and bar snacks. Brunch selections are offered on Saturday and Sunday from 11 a.m. to 3 p.m. You don't normally find beer bars that accommodate different dietary restrictions, but owner Jeff Ching decided to offer vegan, vegetarian, and gluten-free options after working at a Boston eatery that did. On the menu you'll find items such as vegan cheese, smoked tofu, a lentil patty sandwich, and gluten-free bread. All of the desserts are vegan, and everything that can be made by hand, is.

PIZZA PLANT

5110 Main St., Williamsville, NY 14221; (716) 626-5566; PizzaPlant.com; @PodGuy
Draft Beers: Transit Road has almost 30, with 1 on cask, Main Street has over 10 with 1 on cask **Bottled/Canned Beers:** Over 20 at each location

In 1980 brothers Daniel, Robert, and James Syracuse decided to open a pizzeria. When thinking about the name "Pizza Plant," they debated whether it would mean "pizza factory" or "a pizza thing that grows." Eventually they decided that their pizza plant would come from the ground. This led to the name they gave their

calzone-like creation, the Pod. The trio wanted a pizza-like food item that would be handheld and customized. Visitors to Pizza Plant can choose Pods—shaped a little like footballs—with countless different fillings, like chicken souvlaki, meatballs, or Sicilian steak, or they can customize their own. Other menu items include regular pizza, stuffed pizzas, pasta, sandwiches, and salads (which can be served in a bread bowl). Pizza Plant also offers vegetarian and gluten-free options.

Since Daniel was a craft beer lover, the brothers decided to incorporate fine craft beer in their pizzerias, which have had several locations over the years and in 2013 began the process to franchise. They've been committed to serving the local craft beer community, often holding tastings for new up-and-coming area breweries. Beer-focused events held at Pizza Plant have included sour beer tastings, hoppy beer tastings, Christmas in July, Imperial Stout days, and an Ommegang and chocolate beer tasting. The menu and atmosphere are a bit overly quirky, but Pizza Plant is a great place to get pizza (or a Pod) and a beer. A second Williamsville location is at 7770 Transit Road (716-632-0800).

THE REVELRY

1290 University Ave., Rochester, NY 14607; (585) 340-6454; TheRevelryRoc.com; @TheRevelryRoc
Draft Beers: 5 **Bottled/Canned Beers:** Almost 20

Josh Miles founded The Revelry in the Neighborhood of the Arts in Rochester in 2013, with a focus on hospitality. Walking into the bar/restaurant, you can feel that this focus has paid off. It's a luxurious space with dark hardwood floors and chandeliers. Everyone, from the hosts to the servers to the bartenders, looks dapper in dresses, button-down shirts, vests, and ties. You feel taken care of from when you walk in to when you leave—though if you don't have a reservation, you might not be able to eat in the dining room. But sitting at the bar is a great alternative. The surface of the bar is polished and black, so shiny that you can see your reflection. While there are only five taps, the beer selection is highly curated, featuring fine Belgian beers from breweries like Delirium and Dupont, local offerings such as Roc Brewing's Dark Mild, and craft favorites including Evil Twin and Victory. The bartenders are knowledgeable about the selections and will ask what types of beers you like if you're stumped about what to order.

The Revelry's menu is designed to honor South Carolina's Lowcountry, as Miles is a native of Greenville, South Carolina. You'll see fried okra, fried chicken, local greens and heirloom veggies, cast-iron corn bread, fried green tomatoes, and pink

beet deviled eggs. A modified menu is available to choose from at the bar. There's an extensive collection of wines and a menu of artisanal cocktails if beer isn't your thing. But either way, The Revelry is a lovely spot to spend an evening and an excellent place to visit in your finest duds.

STONEYARD BAR AND GRILL

1 Main St., Brockport, NY 14420; (585) 637-3390; StoneyardBarAndGrill.com;
@Stoneyard_Bar
Draft Beers: 21 **Bottled/Canned Beers:** 30 to 40

The quiet town of Brockport isn't too far from Rochester, but it feels a world away with a quaint and sleepy main street that doesn't have much in the way of craft beer options. The brightest beer spot is Stoneyard Bar and Grill, located right on the Erie Canal. From the façade you might not think that there is a serious beer menu inside, but you'll be pleasantly surprised once you check out the menu and see Great Lakes Brewing, Roc Brewing, and Stillwater Artisanal Ales on the tap list. The food menu is quite large, so you can put together some interesting pairings. The bottle list mixes in some of the larger and well-known American craft brewers like Lagunitas, Oskar Blues, and Bear Republic.

On nice days you can sit outside on the patio on the lower level, observe the murky waters of the Erie Canal, and maybe catch a little boat traffic. On the last Wednesday of every month, the bar runs "Beer Master's University" to educate drinkers about the finer details of beer. Styles and brewing techniques have been among the topics discussed, and the tastings sometime feature local brewers. Members of the Beer Master's Club (a $20 annual fee) pay $5 for the "Beer Master's University" events, while nonmembers pay $10.

TAP & MALLET

381 Gregory St., Rochester, NY 14620; (585) 473-0503; TapAndMallet.com;
@TapAndMallet
Draft Beers: 30 on tap, 1 on cask **Bottled/Canned Beers:** Over 150

England native Joe McBane came to the United States in 2000, when he managed Rochester British pub The Old Toad. He opened Tap & Mallet with Casey Walpert (who also opened The Bug Jar and owns Mex) in 2007 to be the best destination for beer and pub food in Rochester. In 2012 the duo opened Tap & Table, a more food-forward spot with the same commitment to beer selection as their first venture. Tap & Mallet is upscale but has a relaxed pub atmosphere, and with 30 beers on tap and 1 on cask, it's a great place to get fresh beer. The draft list features many beers from nearby breweries like Ommegang, CB Craft Brewers, Empire, and Southern Tier. The bottle and can list is categorized by style, offering American craft favorites such as Dogfish Head, Sierra Nevada, and Stone, alongside imported brews including Fullers, Sam Smith's, and Duvel. You can enjoy your brews at the pub or fill growlers to take home. The menu is comprised of elevated pub fare and comfort food.

TAP & TABLE

284 Exchange Blvd., Rochester, New York 14608; (585) 329-3388; TheTapAndTable.com;
@TapAndTableROC
Draft Beers: 30 **Bottled/Canned Beers:** 10-20

After the success of Tap & Mallet, owners Joe McBane and Casey Walpert opened Tap & Table in 2012. Located on the Genesee River in Rochester, Tap & Table has embraced quality beer as the accompaniment to fine food. With large windows and a patio, diners and drinkers can take in a view of the river and the city while enjoying a pint and a meal. The bar boasts 30 rotating tap lines. Small local brewers like Naked Dove, just south of Rochester in Canadaigua, and Rochester's 3 Heads Brewing are regularly on tap, along with Sierra Nevada, Victory, and other larger craft brewers. The staff takes their beer seriously, serving each brew in its proper glassware.

The food menu at Tap & Table stands up well to the beer menu. Try the perfectly prepared pork belly and scallops or the ricotta gnocchi. Each dish has suggested beer pairings listed on the menu, so you may want to hold your drink order until you choose your meal.

VICTOIRE BELGIAN BEER BAR AND BISTRO

120 East Ave., Rochester, NY 14604; (585) 325-3663; VictoireBar.com
Draft Beers: 24 **Bottled/Canned Beers:** 40 to 50

It seems that every good beer town must have a good Belgian beer bar. Buffalo has Blue Monk, New York City has Burp Castle, and Rochester has Victoire. Located in the heart of downtown Rochester, Victoire has a beer menu of almost exclusively Belgian imports and North American versions of Belgian styles. The bar and restaurant maintain over 20 taps of Belgian-style favorites from Ommegang and Unibroue along with imports from Belgium such as Delirium Tremens and Duchesse De Bourgogne. Tap beers are written vertically on the chalkboard above their draught lines behind the immaculate wooden bar. The bottles are separated by styles, i.e., Dubbels, Saisions, and Lambics. The bar suggests several flights that highlight different groups of beers, or you can choose your own four beers for a tasting flight.

Like any good Belgian bistro, the menu of course offers classic varieties of Moules Frites and also cheese and charcuterie plates. Wednesday you can try your hand at some unusual pairings, when the bar has its weekly wild game night. The space itself is dimly lit, with several rooms that can accommodate large groups. Outdoor seating is available just far enough below street level to feel separated from the city.

Pub Crawls

Buffalo

Walking along Elmwood Avenue is a must if you're visiting the city. Home to dozens of shops, boutiques, restaurants, and bars, it's an awesome place to spend a weekend day drinking beers.

A pub crawl is a great way to see multiple places in one day and allows you to do so safely, as long as you walk, take a cab, or find someone willing to be your designated driver.

Mr. Goodbar, 1110 Elmwood Ave., Buffalo, NY 14222; (716) 882-4000; MrGoodbar Buffalo.com

Start out for lunchtime at Mr. Goodbar, home of an extensive beer list and some of the most highly rated chicken wings around, available in a variety of flavors. If you happen to stop by on a Sunday, wings are 50 cents each.

Coles, 1104 Elmwood Ave., Buffalo, NY 14222; (716) 886-1449; ColesBuffalo.com

Once you leave Mr. Goodbar, walk a few steps to Coles, which can be found right next door. A historic bar that opened in 1934 after Prohibition, Coles is an Elmwood Avenue institution. Check out the tap handle decoration as you sidle up to the bar, which has a great selection of local and regional brews.

Blue Monk, 727 Elmwood Ave., Buffalo, NY 14222; (716) 882-6665; BMBflo.com

Walk about 15 minutes up Elmwood, and you'll happen upon Blue Monk, under the same ownership as Coles. Enjoy the bar's large selection of Belgian and Belgian-style beers with Belgian food.

The Village Beer Merchant, 547 Elmwood Ave., Buffalo, NY 14222; (716) 881-1080; Facebook.com/TheVillageBeerMerchant

A few more blocks north on Elmwood will take you to the Village Beer Merchant, where you'll find a well-curated selection of beer in bottles and cans. While you can't drink these brews on-site, you can definitely load up on some of your favorites to bring home.

Continued . . .

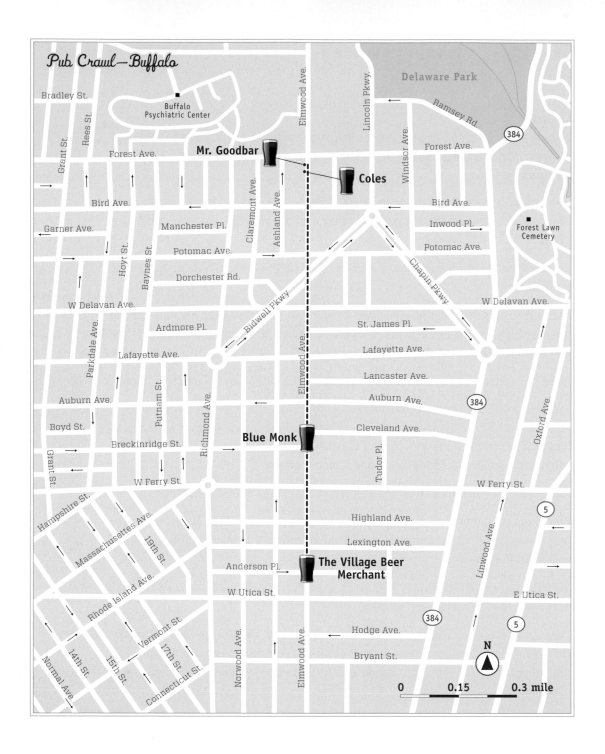

Pub Crawl—Buffalo

Bradley St.
Rees St.
Grant St.
Buffalo Psychiatric Center
Forest Ave.
Bird Ave.
Garner Ave.
Hoyt St.
Baynes St.
Manchester Pl.
Potomac Ave.
Dorchester Rd.
W Delavan Ave.
Parkdale Ave.
Ardmore Pl.
Lafayette Ave.
Putnam St.
Auburn Ave.
Boyd St.
Breckinridge St.
Grant St.
W Ferry St.
Hampshire St.
Massachusettes Ave.
19th St.
Rhode Island Ave.
Vermont St.
17th St.
14th St.
15th St.
Normal Ave.
Connecticut St.
Norwood Ave.
Anderson Pl.
W Utica St.
Hodge Ave.
Bryant St.

Claremont Ave.
Ashland Ave.
Elmwood Ave.
Bidwell Pkwy
Elmwood Ave.

Mr. Goodbar
Coles
Blue Monk
The Village Beer Merchant

Delaware Park
Ramsey Rd.
Lincoln Pkwy.
Windsor Ave.
Forest Ave.
Bird Ave.
Inwood Pl.
Potomac Ave.
Chapin Pkwy
W Delavan Ave.
St. James Pl.
Lafayette Ave.
Lancaster Ave.
Auburn Ave.
Cleveland Ave.
Tudor Pl.
W Ferry St.
Highland Ave.
Lexington Ave.
E Utica St.
Hodge Ave.

Forest Lawn Cemetery
Oxford Ave.
Linwood Ave.

384
384
5
384
5

N

0   0.15   0.3 mile

Rochester

Home to Genesee Brewing Company, one of the oldest and most historic breweries in the state, Rochester has undergone a craft beer resurgence in recent years. With the exception of Genesee, the rest of the spots on this crawl are within walking distance of each other.

Genesee Brew House, 25 Cataract St., Rochester, NY 14605; (585) 263-9200; Genesee Beer.com/Brew-House

At Genesee Brew House you'll be able to not only taste beer history, but view it as well. The ground floor of the newly built establishment is home to a gift shop and craft beer museum. Take a look at the pilot brewery in the back and try some brews before moving on to your next stop.

The Owl House, 75 Marshall St., Rochester, NY 14607; (585) 360-2920; OwlHouse Rochester.com

A short drive from Genesee is The Owl House, a craft beer bar that is highly regarded for its food, with many vegan and gluten-free options available. It's a cozy spot to enjoy lunch.

Roc Brewing Co., 56 S. Union St., Rochester, NY 14607; (585) 794-9798; RocBrewing Co.com

Next, travel a few blocks away from The Owl House to hit nanobrewery Roc Brewing Company. Chat with owners Chris Spinelli and Jon Mervine about their hand-crafted brews, and check out some local art on the walls.

The Old Toad, 277 Alexander St., Rochester, NY 14607; (585) 232-2626; TheOldToad .com

Three blocks from Roc Brewing Co., you'll be transported to England at The Old Toad, modeled after a traditional British pub. Grab a pint of the brew that's on cask and enjoy some bar snacks before moving on.

MacGregors' Grill and Tap Room, 355 East Ave., Rochester, NY 14604; (585) 413-3744; MacGregorsGrillAndTapRoom.com

Around the corner from The Old Toad, you'll find MacGregors' Grill and Tap Room, where you can try out the house beer, an English Pale Ale brewed for the bar by Harpoon Brewery in Boston.

Victoire Belgian Beer and Bistro, 120 East Ave., Rochester, NY 14604; (585) 325-3663; VictoireBar.com

Continued . . .

Finally, walk six and a half blocks west from MacGregors' and you'll come upon the basement-level Victoire, a Belgian-style bar. Walk in the bistro entrance for dinner, where you'll see more inspiration from Belgium on the menu, with mussels and duck fat frites.

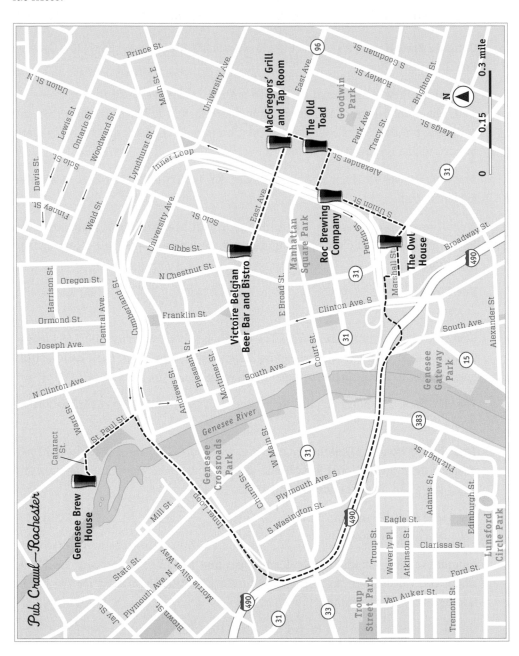

Beer Festivals

Whether you're a craft beer expert or novice, the best way to try a bunch of beers you've never had before is at a beer festival. Attending one of these events means you have dozens of beers at your fingertips, and you only have to try a little bit at a time. So if you don't like it, you don't have to suffer through the rest of the pint. New and rare brews are often poured at beer festivals, so you don't have to go on a hunt for that new sought-after release. What follows are some of the best festivals in New York.

Year-Round

GET REAL PRESENTS
Various locations; GetRealPresents.com

Get Real Presents is a crew of eight craft beer aficionados in New York City who hold beer and food festivals with the goal of fostering the growth of craft beer while supporting local food purveyors. They've held a number of festivals in New York City, including a Belgian-inspired event, a Farmhouse Fest, and a tasting of cask ales. In 2013 the group spearheaded a Get Real Beer Week, producing seven events over seven days to showcase the growth of craft beer in New York City. They've also created popular events that have returned to become annual festivities: aPORKalypse Now and Beer Balls. aPORKalypse Now features fine craft beers paired with pork-inspired dishes from local artisans and restaurants. At Beer Balls, many different types of meatballs accompany the beers.

NYC CRAFT BEER FESTIVALS
Various locations; NYCCraftBeerFest.com

The Hand Crafted Tasting Company, a division of event company Mad Dog Presents, has been producing beer-tasting events since 2012. Hand Crafted Tasting holds several NYC Craft Beer Festivals a year at various locations throughout New York City. Whether at the Lexington Avenue Armory, Basketball City, or Webster Hall, these festivals showcase beer from over 70 breweries and food from local restaurants and purveyors. Free seminars at each event have covered topics such as women in beer, barrel aging, or pairing beer with cheese. Tickets to the NYC Craft Beer Festivals are sold in three tiers: Connoisseur, VIP, and General Admission. Connoisseur and VIP tickets get event goers an extra hour to taste beers, and Connoisseur ticket holders have access to an exclusive lounge with special beers, often rare or limited releases. At afternoon or evening sessions, attendees can experience the best in craft beer.

February

BREWER'S CHOICE

City Winery, 155 Varick St., New York, NY 10013; nycbeerweek.com

When you attend a beer festival, it's often the case that people pouring the beer don't know much about it. It's rare to have a brew poured by someone involved in making it, rarer still to have the brewmaster pouring his or her own beer and describing it to you. This is the premise of Brewer's Choice, a featured event in New York City Beer Week. Launched in 2010 by Jimmy Carbone, the owner of craft beer bar Jimmy's No. 43 and founder of Good Beer Month (see below), Brewer's Choice is a chance to not only meet the people who make your favorite beers, but also taste brews they themselves have chosen to pour for you. It's common at Brewer's Choice to have Garrett Oliver, brewmaster of Brooklyn Brewery, pour samples from rare "ghost bottles" he brought to the event—his private reserve of experimental, bottle-conditioned Ales. Most of the breweries in attendance are from New York State, and you'll also taste artisanal foods, often from local farms.

April

TAP NEW YORK CRAFT BEER & FINE FOOD FESTIVAL

Hunter Mountain Base Lodge, 7740 Main St., Hunter, NY 12442; TAP-NY.com

What began as the Hudson Valley Beer and Food Festival, founded in 1997 by Bill Woodring and Nat Collins, has evolved into the premier craft beer event in New York State, named TAP when brewers from Long Island and Buffalo were invited in 2001. Almost all the breweries in attendance pouring their beer are from New York, from the tiniest nanobreweries to large-production scale operations. But the indoor/outdoor event doesn't only showcase beer, it's also about food. Event goers can witness cooking demonstrations and experience food and beer pairings from some of the best chefs. TAP is also a beer competition; each year breweries are chosen for the Matthew Vassar Cup, given to the best Hudson Valley brewery, the F.X. Matt Memorial Cup, given to the best craft brewery in the state, and the Governor's Cup, given to the best craft beer in the state. A two-day event held every year at

Hunter Mountain in April (usually the last full weekend of the month), TAP New York showcases the exploding craft beer movement in New York State.

BUFFALO ON TAP
Buffalo Niagara Convention Center, 153 Franklin St., Buffalo, NY 14202; townsquareliveevents.eventbrite.com/

While TAP NY is certainly the leading beer festival in the state in the month of April, Western New Yorkers can enjoy an event in their region at the end of the month. Buffalo on Tap started in 2013 at the Buffalo Niagara Conventin Center, right in the middle of downtown Buffalo with over 100 beers from over 70 breweries. The festival also carries ciders and a selection of gluten free brews. Local New York brewers are heavily represented, including Rohrbach from Rochester and Buffalo's own Flying Bison. A wide variety of quality imports are also available for sampling, such as trappist breweries Orval, Rochefort, and Westmalle. The festival is the largest of its kind in Western New York. Live music is sponsored by local radio stations and barbeque is served up to pair with beers.

June

SARATOGA BREWFEST
Saratoga County Fairgrounds, 162 Prospect St., Ballston Spa, NY 12020; SaratogaBrewfest.com

The Saratoga County Fairgrounds are the setting for antique car shows, dog shows, family fun days, and each June, the annual Saratoga Brewfest. The quaint and picturesque city of Saratoga is home to the area's largest celebration of craft beer, founded in 2010. Originally held at the Elms Family Farm, the event was moved to the Fairgrounds in 2012. Over 150 beers are available to sample at the festival, from regional breweries and others from across the country. Attendees can taste beer while sampling some local eats and enjoying live music. Tickets for this one-day celebration are sold in two levels: VIP and General Admission, with VIP ticket holders entitled to early admission to the event, rare and limited brews, and the chance to meet the brewers.

July

EMPIRE BREWFEST
Clinton Square, Syracuse, NY; EmpireBrewfest.com

Clinton Square is located in the heart of downtown Syracuse and was historically a center of trading and business for the city. In 2001 it was turned into a venue for various festivals and events held in the city, one of which is the annual Empire Brewfest. The event was founded as the Empire State Brewing and Music Festival by David Katleski, owner of Empire Brewing Company. Event promoter The Results Group took over the celebration in 2011. In 2013 the Empire Brewfest featured beer from dozens of national and international breweries, with a special focus on New York State beer makers, from large breweries like Matt Brewing, to small, brand-new ones like Hopshire Farm & Brewery. There were two information sessions with start-up brewers, a mini Wine Trail, and a sampling of libations from five wineries. Other features of the event include a food pairing and an "Eggs & Kegs" breakfast the day after.

Craft Beer Weeks

February
Saratoga Beer Week,
SaratogaBeerWeek.com

The City Center in downtown Saratoga Springs is the setting for Saratoga Beer Week, which starts with a kickoff party and ends with the Saratoga Beer Summit. Other events include brewery tours of Olde Saratoga, beer specials and dinners at Druthers Brewing Company, tap takeovers, beer tastings, and seminars.

NYC Beer Week,
NYCBeerWeek.com

What started in 2008 as a series of pub crawls designed to support and encourage craft beer growth in New York City has turned into a full-fledged weeklong celebration. Run by the New York City Brewer's Guild, who took over from founder Josh Schnaffer in 2013, featured events include an opening night bash, Brewer's Choice, and a closing party. Participating bars offer specials, beer dinners, and tasting events.

May
Long Island Craft Beer Week,
LongIslandCraftBeerWeek.com

In recent years there's been an explosion of craft beer growth on Long Island,

GOOD BEER MONTH
Various locations, New York City; GoodBeerSeal.com

In response to the craft beer explosion in New York City, Jimmy Carbone, owner of Jimmy's No. 43, started the Good Beer Seal program. By awarding certain bars with a red square seal to display on their doors or windows, the seal aims to single out the special places, those that are independently owned, serve at least 80 percent craft beer, and give back to the community at large. An outgrowth of the Good Beer Seal program is Good Beer Month, which celebrates fine craft beer in New York City with beer dinners, panel discussions, festivals, and special events at the Good Beer

with new breweries and bars opening at a rapid clip. Long Island Craft Beer Week began in 2010 to foster this growth and raise awareness of craft beer culture on the island. An array of events include tap takeovers, beer dinners, meet the brewer nights, the Golden Tap Awards, and the Bay Fest kickoff party.

June
Rochester Real Beer Week,
RochesterRealBeer.com

Launched in 2012, Rochester Real Beer Week is a collaboration between the breweries and craft beer bars in the area. Its anchor event is the Rochester Real Beer Expo, a collection of the best craft beers and food from regional bars and restaurants. Other features of this beer week include special-release brews, tap takeovers, special beer dinners, and cask festivals.

September
Buffalo Beer Week,
BuffaloBeerWeek.com

New York's westernmost big city has been home to an annual beer week since 2008, a venture aimed at promoting the growing craft beer culture in Erie and Niagara Counties. Pub crawls, tastings, meet the brewer nights, and special dinners are just some of the activities during the 10-day celebration. Its banner events are a Collab Beer Fest, Brewbash at the Ballpark, and a BFLO Beer Geek FESTIVAL.

Seal bars. July Good Beer Month is given a proclamation by the mayor each year, and since its inception has expanded to the five boroughs of New York City, Long Island, and Jersey City.

August

BELGIUM COMES TO COOPERSTOWN
Brewery Ommegang, 656 County Hwy. 33, Cooperstown, NY 13326; Ommegang .com/#!cooperstown

Belgium Comes to Cooperstown, or BCTC, began in 2004 as a small gathering to appreciate Belgian and Belgian-style beers. Since then it has exploded into an epic Belgian beer extravaganza, what is likely the most loved and anticipated beer event in New York State. The two-day celebration is held by Brewery Ommegang, and takes places on the brewery's expansive grounds. It includes camping, live music, a VIP dinner, cooking competitions, brewing demonstrations, and lectures. You (and over 3,000 other attendees) can taste hard-to-find Ales from Belgium and Belgian-style Ales from across North America. Upwards of 75 breweries attend the event to pour 300 beers. The 2013 event even featured a Ferris wheel. There are three levels of tickets to this event: General Admission for the Saturday beer tasting only, a Tasting and Camping ticket, and a VIP ticket that gets you into a VIP dinner, the beer tasting, and two days of camping. The festival sells out quickly, so count yourself lucky if you happen to acquire a VIP spot.

NORTH FORK CRAFT BEER, BBQ & WINE FESTIVAL
Martha Clara Vineyard, 660 Herricks Ln., Riverhead, NY 11901; NorthForkCraftBeerFestival .com

With its gorgeous scenery, proximity to the water, and delicious eats, the North Fork of Long Island is a great place to attend a festival celebrating beer and food. Launched in 2006, the North Fork Craft Beer, BBQ & Wine Festival takes place every August. In 2013's event, there were more than 50 brewers in attendance serving 100 brews. While the wines and BBQ are local, beers come from breweries across the country and internationally, as well as from nearby businesses. Long Island mainstays such as Blue Point Brewing Company, Long Ireland Beer Company, and Port Jeff Brewing, along with new up-and-coming breweries, company pour their libations, and attendees can listen to live music while drinking and enjoying gourmet barbeque. Tickets are sold in two tiers for this event: VIP and General Admission.

VIP tickets garner you an extra hour of tasting and some special beers. The festival is outdoors and has raised money for charities, such as the Beer for Brains Foundation.

September

HUDSON RIVER CRAFT BEER FESTIVAL

Riverfront Park, 1 Flynn Drive, Beacon, NY 12508; hudsonrivercraftbeerfestival.com

Recently the Hudson Valley has exploded with craft beer growth. In late September Riverfront Park in Beacon is the setting for the Hudson River Craft Beer Festival, a celebration of New York State beer and Hudson Valley heritage. The tickets are available in three tiers: VIP, general admission and entertainment. VIP ticket holders spend an extra hour at the festival tasting beers, get a souvenir glass and t-shirt. General admission includes entry, beer tasting and a glass, while the entertainment ticket only includes entry, no beer samplings. Breweries pouring beer at the event are largely from New York State, including Chatham Brewing, Sloop Brewing, Newburgh Brewing Company, Brown's Brewing Co., Sixpoint, Butternuts Beer & Ale, Middle Ages Brewing Company and Southern Tier Brewing Company. In addition to beer and food from nearby purveyors, this festival festures live music from local bands.

OKTOBEERFEST

Saratoga County Fairgrounds, 162 Prospect St., Ballston Spa, NY 12020; oktobeerfestny .com

Starting in 2009, Saratoga.com has held its Oktobeerfest celebration at the end of September. The day-long event features authentic German beer and food, live music, contests and games. More than 20 seasonal beers are served up at the event. German brews have included Dinkelacker, Spaten Optimator and Warsteiner Oktoberfest, while New York breweries come out in strong force. Brooklyn Brewery, Brown's Brewery, Brewery Ommegang, Saranac and of course the local Olde Saratoga Brewing Company, are just some of those represented. All breweries bring their Oktoberfests, pumpkin brews and other fall seasonals. Tickets are under $20 and advance purchases include a German beer mug.

September–October

BEAR MOUNTAIN OKTOBERFEST

Bear Mountain State Park, Tomkins Cove, NY 10986; visitbearmountain.com

The traditional Oktoberfest celebration, which originated in Germany, runs from the end of September to the beginning of October. The Bear Mountain Oktoberfest at Bear Mountain State Park in Tomkins Cove, takes place on weekend between the middle of September to the middle of October: a month-long (weekend) celebration of German beer and food. Admission is free to this event, where you're sure to see folks in lederhosen and dirndls. Each weekend features different entertainment, from polka bands to German festival bands and dance groups. Belgian waffles, German sausages and pierogies are available for purchase at reasonable prices. Of course, there's also beer.

October

BROOKLYN POUR
Skylight One Hanson, 1 Hanson Pl., Brooklyn, NY 11217; microapp.villagevoice.com/Brooklyn-pour

The Williamsburg Savings Bank in Brooklyn's Fort Greene neighborhood is one of the coolest event venues. Now known as Skylight One Hanson, the building is a famous Brooklyn landmark, at one point was the tallest in the borough. The building was restored in keeping with its old character, with original bank windows, art deco accents and a downstairs vault. Starting in 2011 the *Village Voice* has held Brooklyn Pour in the space, a craft beer tasting even featuring over 100 brews. The curated beer list is accompanied by demonstrations, beer talks and a food court inside the old bank vault. Brews from New York breweries like Brewery Ommegang, Brooklyn Brewery, Rockaway Brewing Company, and Singlecut Beersmiths are among the libations poured. Tickets can be purchased in two tiers: VIP and general admission. VIP tickets get attendees an extra hour at the event, access to the VIP mezzanine, complimentary food and a gift bag. Both tickets include a souvenir tasting glass.

BYOB: Brew Your Own Beer

A rite of passage for any craft beer lover is learning to brew. There's something about spending a whole day in the kitchen or backyard (or wherever you are able to McGyver a homebrewing setup) and winding up with bottles or a keg of beer you made with your own hands. Maybe you like to brew with your friends, with all of you gathered around the boil, smelling the delicious bready aroma of hot wort; or you prefer to brew by yourself, for the enjoyment or to enter into competitions. Or maybe you don't know how to make beer and always wanted to start.

Whatever category you fall into, there are plenty of homebrewing shops around New York for you to obtain supplies, get advice and recipes, or even take classes. Here are some of them, followed by a handful of five-gallon batch beer recipes.

Home Brew Shops

BITTER & ESTERS

700 Washington Ave., Brooklyn, NY 11238; (917) 596-7261; BitterAndEsters.com

B rewers and friends John LaPolla and Douglas Amport opened Bitter & Esters in mid-2011. They originally wanted to start a brewpub, but the high startup cost deterred them. It turned out for the best, though, because Bitter & Esters has become a valuable community space for homebrewers. Not only can you purchase everything you need to cook up a batch at home, but LaPolla and Amport will also help you in either formulating your own recipe or choosing one from their extensive beer library. The pair holds classes for homebrewers of all levels, from beginner to pro. If you know how to brew but don't want to do it at home (it can get pretty messy), you can pay Bitter & Esters to brew at their facility. Your beer will be stored in the basement of the Prospect Heights location, and when its ready, staff members will transfer it to a bottling keg. You'll return to bottle, then take your creation home to condition and enjoy.

BROOKLYN BREW SHOP

BrooklynBrewShop.com

I n New York City you'd be hard-pressed to find a lot of unused space. But the thing about making your own beer is that it takes up a fair amount of space. This is where Erica Shea and Stephen Valand come in. In 2009 the business team and real-life couple launched the Brooklyn Brew Shop at the Brooklyn Flea Market. They sold one-gallon kits and all the materials—including the grain already measured and mixed—to brew at home. And for those new to brewing, they produced a series of instructional videos, posting them on their website. Since then they have expanded to a booming online store, and their kits are sold in stores all over the United States and even internationally. Shea and Valand aim to get people to love craft beer by making it themselves. Their one-gallon kits are the perfect place to start, or the perfect solution for the space-constrained brewer.

BROOKLYN HOMEBREW
163 8th St., Brooklyn, NY 11215; (718) 369-0776; Brooklyn-Homebrew.com

Brooklyn's reputation as a hotbed for homebrewing owes much to Brooklyn Homebrew. Before Danielle Cefaro and Benjamin Stutz opened the shop in 2009, New Yorkers had to order all their equipment and ingredients online. Cefaro and Stutz were tired of ordering from the Internet, so they opened the shop on Eighth Street in the Gowanus neighborhood of Brooklyn. The shop is well stocked with not only your basic ingredients but also specialty ingredients for the more adventurous brewers. In late August the shop teams up with local hop farms to get perishable fresh hops into the hands of local brewers. The shop also hosts monthly homebrewing classes to help beginners get started or experts hone their skills. Brooklyn Homebrew's semiannual Brooklyn Wort events celebrate local brewers with a competition that is open to the public and has professional regional brewers like Kelly Taylor of KelSo and beer journalists like Joshua Bernstein as judges.

DOC'S HOMEBREW SUPPLIES
451 Court St., Binghamton NY, 13904; (607) 722-2476; DocsBrew.com

For over 20 years Doc's Homebrew has been operating in Binghamton. Since opening in 1991 the store has been in three different locations—all on the same block. As is to be expected from such a homebrewing institution, Doc's has well-stocked shelves with all standard start-up equipment and a wide range of ingredients. The shop also carries winemaking supplies in case you'd like to branch out or experiment. While Doc's doesn't have a conventional online store, there's a form to place orders on the website, and you can always order by phone.

KARP'S HOMEBREW SHOP

2 Larkfield Rd., East Northport NY, 11731; (631) 261-1235; HomebrewShop.com

Chances are, at some point a piece of your homebrewing equipment will need jerry-rigging if you want to either improve your brews or just save one during a crisis. So it's a nice security blanket when your homebrew shop also happens to be one of the oldest family-run hardware stores in the area. Karp's was opened by Alan Karp in 1934 as a hardware store and was operated by Karp descendants until Alan Talman, Richard Karp's stepson, took over the business in the 1990s. That's when a homebrewing section was added in the back room with equipment, ingredients, and instructional books. It may not be as glamorous and sparkling as some other shops, but if you need help figuring out how to put together your own mash tun or false bottom, this is probably the best place to be. The store's long history as the area's go-to homebrew shop led to its recognition in 2013 as the Best Homebrew Shop on Long Island at the Golden Tap Awards.

PANTANO'S WINE GRAPES & HOME BREW

249 Rte. 32 S., New Paltz, NY 12561; (845) 255-5201; PantanosBeerWine.com

Jerry Pantano didn't originally intend to start a one-stop shop for all your fermenting needs, but that's just what happened. Years ago, on his way out of the grape-selling business, he decided to sell off his inventory when a friend suggested he sell wine-making equipment as well. The business became so successful that he continued. Another friend suggested he sell beer-making supplies as well, so he did, and hasn't looked back. His shop is located in a large warehouse space just outside quaint downtown New Paltz. You'll be able to find boiling pots, grains, hops, bottles, bottle racks, cappers, fermentation buckets, recipes, and pretty much anything else you could need for brewing. Pantano is also committed to the local brewing community, hosting the Montauk Homebrewer's Association in his store.

Clone Beer Recipes

BRONX PALE ALE

Since debuting in 2011, Brewer Damian Brown of The Bronx Brewery made his focus the Pale Ale and its many variations. The flagship Pale Ale is a blend of British malt and American ingredients for a full-bodied and flavorful Pale Ale. Brown is one of the most precise brewers you are likely to meet, and in just a few short years the Bronx Pale Ale has become one of the most respected and popular Pale Ales in the New York City market.

Malt

%	Amount	Name
78.9%	8.93 pounds	Muntons Maris Otter
6.4%	0.70 pound	Weyermann Caramunich I
1.9%	0.20 pound	Baird Crystal 70/80
4.3%	0.46 pound	Briess Vienna Malt
4.3%	0.46 pound	Briess Aromatic Malt
4.3%	0.46 pound	Briess Victory Malt

Hops

Amount	Name	Form	Alpha	Boil Time
0.6 ounce	Centennial	T90 Pellet	8.9	60 min.
0.11 ounce	Centennial	T90 Pellet	8.9	30 min.
0.11 ounce	Cascade	T90 Pellet	6.0	30 min.
0.37 ounce	Centennial	T90 Pellet	8.9	15 min.
0.37 ounce	Cascade	T90 Pellet	6.0	15 min.
0.48 ounce	Centennial	T90 Pellet	8.9	0 min.
0.48 ounce	Cascade	T90 Pellet	6.0	0 min.
0.64 ounce	Centennial leaf		8.9	dry hop
0.64 ounce	Cascadeleaf		6.0	dry hop

Yeast

White Labs 001 California Ale

Mash Schedule

Mash thickness: 2.5 pounds/ gallon (rough sediment, active carbon, and UV-filtered water)

Mash type: Single Step at 150°F, 30-minute rest, iodine saccharification test

Sparge water temperature: 170°F (rough sediment, active carbon, and UV-filtered water)

SG to kettle (kettle and boil loss dependent): 1.062

SG to fermenter: 1.064

Fermentation and Conditioning

Primary Fermentation: 7 days

Primary Temperature: 70°F

Transfer to conditioning tank warm; dry hop and leave at 70°F for 2 days

Crash in conditioning tank for 8 to 9 days at 32°F

Finishing

Carbonate to 2.5 vol. CO_2

COURTESY OF THE BRONX BREWERY (P. 5)

508 BANGIN' BERLINER

Chris Cuzme from 508 GastroBrewery has made a name for himself with his creative collaborations like this Berliner Weisse, the first beer in the "Pillow Talk" series of beers made with Mary Izett of Fuhmentaboudit! on Heritage Radio Network. The method produces a very clean lactobacillus flavor, uninhibited by other activity. This way, the lactobacillus lives and dies in the brew kettle, not threatening anything else. For extra complexity—with sound sanitary practices—try adding some brettanomyces after primary fermentation.

Starting Gravity: 1.038   Final Gravity: 1.007   IBU: 8.3   Target ABV: 4.1%

Malt

3.5 pounds	*Pilsner Malt, 50%*
3.5 pounds	*German Wheat Malt, 50%*

Hops

1.5 ounces	*Hersbrucker Hops (2.3% Apha Acid)*

Yeast

German Ale Yeast, Safale 05, Safale 04

Mash at 150°F and sparge. Transfer wort to kettle, cooling to 108°F.

Kettle Sour: When all wort has been transferred to the kettle and is at roughly 108°F, add about .25 pound per pound of unmilled Pilsner malt. Purge the headspace with CO2 and cover the top with plastic wrap and/or tinfoil, ensuring that no oxygen will meet the wort while you let the lactobacillus work. If you let oxygen in, unwanted activity will occur, creating nondesirable flavors. Without oxygen the lactobacillus naturally existing on the outside of malt will begin to sour the beer uninterrupted by "other stuff." Maintain a temperature of 108°F for between 30 and 40 hours by a) using a temperature control that monitors and controls your heat source, or b) finding that "sweet spot" with your oven and letting it sit. Taste it along the way until you have achieved the amount of sourness you find desirable (Cuzme and Izett shoot for a pH of between 3 and 3.5. You can use ph strips or a pH meter, both available at your local homebrew shop).

Bring to boil. Add hops, Irish moss, or whirl floc, yeast nutrient. Boil 15 minutes.

Chill beer to 65°F.

Pitch yeast and ferment for 2 weeks at 67°F.

COURTESY OF 508 GASTROBREWERY (P. 24)

508 EDDIE OYSTERS STOUT

In recent years Oyster Stouts have gotten more attention for their smoothness and rounded roast flavors. Long Island's waters provide great local oysters like the Naked Cowboy Oysters from the Long Island Sound that 508's Chris Cuzme uses in this beer, the Eddie Oysters Stout.

Starting Gravity: 1.055   Final Gravity: 1.018   IBU: 36.3

Malt

8 pounds	*Maris Otter Pale Malt*	*76.6%*
14.8 ounces	*Roasted Barley*	*8.9%*
6.7 ounces	*Simpsons English Brown Malt*	*4%*
6.1 ounces	*Chocolate Malt*	*3.6%*
6.7 ounces	*Flaked Oats*	*4%*
4.7 ounces	*Flaked Barley*	*2.8%*

Hops

.25 ounce	*First Wort Hops: Nugget*	*(12.1% AA) for 15.8 IBU*
.35 ounce	*60-Minute: Nugget*	*(12.1% AA) for 20.5 IBU*
.25 ounce	*Flame Out: Nugget*	*(12.1% AA)*
.20 ounce	*Whirlpool: Nugget*	*(12.1% AA)*

Yeast

London Ale Yeast (Wyeast 1028), Safale 04, or WLP013

Additional Ingredients

4-6 Whole Oysters
Irish Moss

Mash at 152°F.

Add First Wort Hops as the kettle comes to a boil.

When the kettle has come to a boil, add 60-Minute Hops.

Fifteen minutes later, or 45 minutes before the end of the boil, add 4 to 6 whole oysters within a cheesecloth or mesh bag. The oysters will naturally open up and expose the brine and oyster pulp within. The brine and shell add a saltiness that accents the roast, while the oyster pulp contributes to a silky smoothness.

After 30 minutes, or 45 minutes from the end of the boil, add Irish Moss or Whirl Floc and yeast nutrient. Boil 15 minutes more.

Remove oyster bag.

Chill beer to 65°F and transfer to fermentation vessel.

Pitch London Ale Yeast (Wyeast 1028), Safale 04, or WLP013. Ferment for 2 weeks at 67°F.

RECIPE COURTESY 508 GASTROBREWERY (P. 24)

GREAT SOUTH BAY BLONDE AMBITION

Great South Bay is making a name for itself with refreshing beers that are especially enjoyable in summer like their Massive IPA and Blood Orange Pale Ale. The Blonde Ambition might be the most drinkable of the bunch and is a crowd pleaser with its use of apricots.

Starting Gravity: 1.050   Final Gravity: 1.010   Target ABV: 5.3%   IBU: 15   SRM: 3

Malt

9.5 pounds German Pilsner malt

0.75 pound light (~2 L) European dextrine malt (of Weyermann Carafoam)

Hops

0.5 ounce Saaz 90 minutes at the start of boil

0.5 ounce Hallertau Mittelfruh 30 minutes before flameout

0.25 ounce Saaz 0 minute at flameout

0.25 ounce Hallertau Mittelfruh 0 minute at flameout

Yeast

American Ale Yeast

Additional Ingredients

2 lbs. fresh apricot puree or 4 oz. sweetened apricot flavoring

Mash at 150°F for 60 minutes. Boil for 90 minutes. Ferment with an American Ale yeast strain at suggested temperature. After krausen falls, add 2 pounds fresh apricot puree or 4 ounces sweetened apricot flavoring prior to bottling. Rack off and carbonate to 2.5 volume.

COURTESY OF GREAT SOUTH BAY BREWERY (P. 72)

NEWBURGH BREWING PEATED PORTER

Located in the Hudson Valley, Newburgh Brewing Company is making waves with flavorful, low-ABV beers. The Peated Porter is a great example of a porter with rich and interesting flavors without too much alcohol.

70% Mash Efficiency: 5 gallons   Starting Gravity: 1.043
Finishing Gravity: 1.013   Target ABV: 4.0%   IBU: 36

Malt

5.5 pounds Pale Malt   65%
0.8 pound Flaked Barley 10%
0.6 pound Aromatic Malt 7%
0.4 pound Roasted Barley 5%
0.4 pound Black Malt 5%
0.32 pound Peat Malt 4%
0.16 pound Wheat Malt 2%
0.16 pound Chocolate Malt 2%

Hops

0.9 ounce East Kent Goldings (5.5%aa) First Wort Hopping for 20 IBU
0.2 ounce English Fuggles (4.5%aa) First Wort Hopping for 5 IBU
0.9 ounce East Kent Goldings (5.5%aa) at 30 minutes for 7 IBU
0.2 ounce English Fuggles (4.5%aa) at 30 minutes for 4 IBU

Yeast

English Ale Yeast

Single infusion mash at 150°F for 60 minutes. Use an English Ale yeast strain with a high degree of attenuation. Ferment at 68°F.

COURTESY OF NEWBURGH BREWING COMPANY (P. 118)

COMMUNITY BEER WORKS THE WHALE

The tiny Community Beer Works in Buffalo is bringing fresh beer to the city in a big way. The Whale is a great brown ale to have at any time of year, especially in the fall.

70% Mash Efficiency: 5 gallons   Starting Gravity: 1.059
Finishing Gravity: 1.013   Target ABV: 5.9%   IBU: 28

Malt

9.5 pounds Canadian 2-Row Malt 83%
1.5 pounds Thomas Fawcett Brown Malt 14%
0.25 pound Thomas Fawcett Pale Chocolate Malt 2%
0.13 pound Briess Chocolate Malt 1%

Hops

1 ounce German Northern Brewer (7.5%aa) 60 min

Yeast

White Labs WLP001 or 11 grams properly rehydrated Fermentis Safale US-05 dry yeast

Single infusion mash at 154°F for 60 minutes. Boil for 60 minutes. Pitch with an appropriate starter of White Labs WLP001 or 11 grams properly rehydrated Fermentis Safale US-05 dry yeast.

Ferment at 66°F.

COURTESY OF COMMUNITY BEER WORKS (P. 224)

EMPIRE AMBER ALE

Empire's Amber Ale blends the brewery's American and English influences for an easy-drinking beer that focuses on balance. The play between the English Marris Otter 2-row backbone and the assertive qualities of the American Nugget and Cascade hops keeps the beer interesting.

Starting Gravity: 1058   Original Gravity: 1014   Target ABV: 5.5%   IBU: 28

Malt

9 pounds Thomas Faucet Marris Otter 2-row

1 pound Thomas Faucet Crystal 65

0.5 pound Thomas Faucet CaraMalt

Hops

0.75 ounce Nugget Hops for 60 minutes

0.5 ounce Nugget Hops for 30 minutes

0.5 ounce Cascade Hops at whirlpool

Yeast

American Ale Yeast

Single infusion mash at 148°F for 1 hour. Pitch an American Ale yeast and ferment at 68°F.

COURTESY OF EMPIRE BREWING COMPANY (P. 177)

BEEHAVE HONEY BLOND ALE

The recipe for Beehave from Hopshire Farm & Brewery was made specifically to be a 100 percent New York beer, with a low-alcohol content. Light grains and few hops create a base that features the delicate taste of honey. The grains are Pale and 20 L Crystal, which we can get from the malt houses that use New York grain. Hopshire used its own hops combined with those from nearby friends. Those who like lighter beers appreciate Beehave's lack of bitterness, while adventurous beer drinkers like the clean taste and subtle honey flavors.

Original Gravity: 1.050   Final Gravity: 1.008   IBU: 10   Target ABV: 4.2%

Malt

7 pounds Pale malt
.5 pound 20 L Crystal malt
1.5 pounds honey (use a light honey such as alfalfa, basswood or wildflower)

Hops

.2 ounce Williamette 60 minute
.25 ounce Williamette 30 minute
.5 ounce Williamette 20 minute

Yeast

White Labs California Ale (WPL 001)

Mash at 150°F for 60 minutes. Pitch yeast at 68°F.

RECIPE COURTESY HOPSHIRE FARM & BREWERY (P. 182)

In the Kitchen

Using beer while cooking, in the place of a broth or wine, can impart complex flavors into the food that you may not taste otherwise—there are so many different styles of beer that have their own unique characteristics. A handful of recipes you can cook up in your own kitchen follow. After making these, try your hand at creating some of your own recipes!

Food Recipes

SPENT GRAIN PRETZELS

It's always a shame to throw out your grain from a batch of beer you've brewed. Many breweries donate theirs to farms to feed animals; others bake with it. Use your own spent grain in these pretzels by Woodcock Brothers Brewing Company. They make a great snack.

1 package yeast
6 cups flour
1 cup dried and ground spent grain
1 teaspoon sugar
1 teaspoon salt
Warm water
5 tablespoons baking soda
Coarse salt for topping

Heat oven to 425°F. Combine all ingredients and knead. Do not leave dough to rise. Flour surface and then take a ball of dough, roll it out, and shape the pretzels into rods, about 5 inches long and 1 inch in diameter. Heat water in a large pot. Once the water is boiling, add the baking soda and drop the shaped pretzels in the boiling water. Once they are done cooking, they will float to the top. Remove them from the water, place on a greased cookie sheet, and sprinkle with coarse salt while still wet. Bake for about 15 minutes, until they start to brown on top. Transfer to a cooling rack. Makes 10 to 14 pretzels.

COURTESY OF WOODCOCK BROTHERS BREWING COMPANY (P. 241)

PORTER AND CARAWAY MUSTARD

This mustard from The Hop bottle shop and restaurant in the Hudson Valley is delicious on sandwiches, with sausage, or by itself spread on toast.

10 eggs
18 ounces Porter
¼ pound mustard powder
2 teaspoons Worcestershire
4 teaspoons kosher salt
¾ cup Champagne vinegar
½ pound brown sugar
2 tablespoons honey
2 tablespoons molasses
¼ cup whole caraway seeds
6 tablepoons whole mustard seeds

Whisk eggs in large mixing bowl. Add Porter, mustard powder, Worcestershire, salt, vinegar, brown sugar, honey, and molasses. Whisk until combined. Let rest, covered, for 1 hour.

Meanwhile, toast both seeds and then add to the mixture. Add water to a large pot that is wide enough to support the base of the mixing bowl. Bring to a simmer. Place mixing bowl over simmering pot and whisk again. Whisk occasionally until mixture congeals and thickens, about 40 to 45 minutes—don't overthicken, as mixture will thicken more when cool.

Jar and seal immediately, or cool in shallow dish before refrigerating.

COURTESY OF THE HOP (P. 131)

BEER BATTER FRIED MOZZARELLA

Fried food is a classic beer accompaniment. Often, brewpubs and breweries use their beer in the batter, whether it's for fish-and-chips, pickles, zucchini, or in this case, fried mozzarella.

> *Vegetable oil to fill wok halfway*
> *1 16 oz package fresh mozzarella, cut into .5 inch slices*
> *1 cup, plus 1 tablespoon white flour*
> *1 cup wheat flour*
> *2 cups BrickHouse Red (or any other Red Ale)*

Heat the vegetable oil in a wok or large pot over high heat. Cut the mozzarella into .5-inch slices. Mix together 1 cup white flour, wheat flour, and beer in a shallow bowl. Put 1 tablespoon of white flour in another shallow bowl. When vegetable oil is hot (test it by dropping water into it; if it's hot enough, the water will sizzle), coat mozzarella slices in white flour, then flour/beer batter, and then carefully drop them into the oil. Remove when batter is golden brown and the cheese just starts to peek out, a few minutes on either side.

COURTESY OF BRICKHOUSE BREWERY AND RESTAURANT (P. 92)

ALE AND ONION SOUP

Onion soup is a great way to warm up in the cold weather of New York's Adirondacks, and the use of Moose Island Ale in Lake Placid Pub & Brewery's version adds some extra depth to this dish.

1 onion, diced
3 stalks celery, diced
1 portabella (cap and stem)
4 cups Moose Island Ale
1 cube vegetable bullion
6 cups water
1 teaspoon basil
1 teaspoon oregano
3 teaspoons salt
1 teaspoon black pepper
1 teaspoon thyme
1 teaspoon Frank's RedHot
1 teaspoon onion powder

In a large pan sauté the onions, celery, and portabella over medium heat. Add the ale and reduce for 15 minutes. In 6 cups of water dissolve the vegetable bullion with a whisk. Add remaining seasonings. When beer is reduced, add stock and cook for 15 more minutes. Ladle into bowls and serve.

COURTESY OF LAKE PLACID PUB & BREWERY (P. 156)

BEEF AND BEER CHILI

Beer and chili make a natural combination, and the addition of a nice dark Ale like Ubu Ale from Lake Placid Pub & Brewery only enhances the richness of the chili and helps bring the ingredients together.

2 pounds ground beef
Olive oil to coat pan
2 cups diced onions
2 cups diced peppers
1 tablespoon minced jalapeños
3 stalks celery, diced
1 teaspoon chili powder
2 teaspoons onion powder
2 teaspoons garlic powder
1 teaspoon pepper
2 teaspoons salt
1 tablespoon cumin
2 tablespoons brown sugar
2 cups Ubu Ale
1 tomato, diced
1 tablespoon white vinegar
1 (15-ounce) can black beans, drained and rinsed

In a large saucepan, brown the ground beef well, drain, and set aside. In the same pan add a small amount of oil and sauté the onions, peppers, jalapeños, and celery for 5 minutes. Add all spices and brown sugar, and stir to coat vegetables. When vegetables are coated, add Ubu Ale and reduce by half. Add reserved ground beef, tomato, and vinegar and bring to a boil. Reduce heat to low and cook for 1 hour, stirring often. When chili is finished cooking, add black beans.

COURTESY OF LAKE PLACID PUB & BREWERY (P. 156)

GOUDA SOUP

Thick, creamy cheese soup is the perfect meal for a bitter, cold day. This recipe adds Pearl Sreet Grill and Brewery's Lighthouse Blonde Ale to the soup, for more depth and bite.

2 cups chicken stock
2 cups Lighthouse Blonde Ale
1 pound smoked Gouda cheese
2 cups heavy cream
6 tablespoons cornstarch
6 tablepoons cold water

Combine chicken stock and beer in a large stockpot and bring to a low boil. Add cheese and lower heat to prevent burning. After cheese has melted, add heavy cream. Combine cornstarch and water to make a slurry. Whisk slurry into simmering soup to thicken to desired consistency. Simmer until the starchy taste has cooked away. Cool and serve.

RECIPE COURTESY PEARL STREET GRILL AND BREWERY (P. 245)

STEAMED MUSSELS WITH HENNEPIN AND GINGER

In Belgium, it's a tradition to steam mussels in white wine. But at Belgian-themed bars, you'll often find them steamed in beer, creating a rich broth. Try this recipe using Ommegang Hennepin.

2 tablespoons butter
2 ounces bacon, finely chopped
1 cup scallions, finely chopped
½ cup celery, finely chopped
1 tablespoon fresh ginger, grated
4 pounds mussels, thoroughly cleaned and bearded
Freshly ground black pepper to taste
1½ cups Ommegang Hennepin
¾ cup heavy cream (optional)
2 tablespoons finely minced fresh cilantro or parsley

Melt the butter in a large pot (with lid). Add the bacon and cook over medium heat for 3 minutes. Add the scallions, celery, and ginger and simmer, stirring, for another 3 minutes. Add the mussels, and flavor with a generous grinding of black pepper. Pour the beer and cream over the mussels and cover the pot tightly. Bring to a boil over high heat and steam the mussels in the covered pot until they all open, 3 to 6 minutes, depending on their size. Shake the pot vigorously a few times to toss the mussels with the broth and to allow them to open. Discard any mussels that remain closed. Divide the hot mussels into soup bowls along with the broth. Garnish with the minced cilantro or parsley. Serve with a generous portion of Belgian-style fries or bread and Hennepin.

COURTESY OF BREWERY OMMEGANG (P. 170)

AMBER ALE BOLOGNESE

A version of this bolognese has been passed down by many cooks in the Annese family. The beer addition is a recent development. The dish is equally as good when made for two or for a big family feast.

1 onion, chopped
3–4 baby carrots, chopped
1–2 celery stalks, chopped
2 cloves crushed garlic, minced
Olive oil to coat bottom of pot
2 pounds ground beef
1 cup Amber Ale
1 6-ounce can tomato paste
Salt
Pepper

Over medium heat in a large pot, sauté the onion, carrots, celery, and garlic in olive oil. It should start to clarify. Break up the meat into small bits and add it to the pot, cooking just so that it's browned. Add the beer and tomato paste and cover with water. Simmer on low until the sauce thickens and the vegetables are soft (about 30 to 45 minutes). Season with salt and pepper to taste. Serve on its own or over pasta.

BY GIANCARLO ANNESE

ARTICHOKE RISOTTO WITH PROSCIUTTO AND HENNEPIN

Normally cooked down with broth, using beer in risotto makes the resulting dish creamier, with more depth of flavor.

6 cups vegetable broth

3 tablespoons butter

3 tablespoons olive oil

2 shallots, chopped

1 cup Arborio rice (this Italian short-grain rice is available at Italian markets and at many supermarkets nationwide) or medium-grain rice

1/2 cup Hennepin

16 ounces canned artichoke hearts

1/2 cup freshly grated Parmesan cheese (about 2 ounces)

4 ounces of prosciutto ham thinly sliced and diced

3/4 teaspoon chopped fresh thyme

1 lemon, juiced

Bring vegetable broth to a simmer in a medium saucepan. Reduce heat to low, cover, and keep broth hot. Melt butter with olive oil in a large heavy saucepan over medium heat. Add chopped shallots; sauté 2 minutes. Add rice and stir to coat. Add Hennepin and simmer until liquid is absorbed, stirring frequently, about 8 minutes. Increase heat to medium-high. Add 3/4 cup hot vegetable broth and simmer until absorbed, stirring frequently. Add the artichoke hearts and remaining hot vegetable broth 3/4 cup at a time, allowing broth to be absorbed before adding more and stirring frequently until rice is just tender and mixture is creamy, about 20 minutes. Stir in Parmesan cheese, proscuitto ham, chopped fresh thyme, and lemon juice. Serve warm.

COURTESY OF BREWERY OMMEGANG (P. 170)

GOLDEN RULE BLOND AND CHIPOTLE MARINATED SALMON

You don't often see fish that's been marinated. But Chef Sean Comiskey of Druthers Brewing Company—which consistently serves delicious food—takes chances. It's a unique and tasty way to use beer.

4 (6-ounce) salmon fillet, skinned an deboned

Marinade
2 pints Druthers Golden Blond
6 whole dried chipotle peppers
4 cloves garlic, hand crushed
2 peeled shallots, roughly chopped
10 sprigs cilantro
2 sprigs thyme

Mix ingredients together in a shallow bowl or plastic container and submerge salmon fillets. Marinate over night but no longer then 24 hours.

Salsa Verde Sauce
1/2 cup rice wine vinegar
Juice of 1 lemon
3 cloves garlic
1 shallot
1 anchovy
1 tablespoon whole mustard
1 teaspoon honey
1 cup olive oil, plus 1/2 cup
1/8 cup chopped cilantro
1/4 cup chopped mint
1/4 cup chopped flat-leaf parsley
Salt to taste
1/2 cup extra virgin olive oil

Salt
Fresh ground coarse black pepper
1/4 cup blended oil

Combine vinegar, lemon juice, garlic, shallot, anchovy, mustard, and honey in a blender. Slowly add 1 cup of oil with blender running to emulsify. Turn blender off, and add all the herbs. Turn blender back on, add extra virgin olive oil and chill immediately.

Heat oven to 350°F. Remove fish from marinade and pat dry. Season well with salt and fresh ground coarse black pepper. Heat a heavy-bottomed oven-safe sauté pan and add a thin layer of oil. As oil nears smoking point, slowly add salmon (skin side up). Fish is ready to flip when golden brown. Flip fish and then put entire pan in the oven. Cook 3 to 6 minutes, until fish is cooked to desired temperature. Remove fish from pan, and garnish with Salsa Verde Sauce. Eats well with salad, steamed vegetables, and/or light starch.

COURTESY OF DRUTHERS BREWING COMPANY (P. 161)

LOBSTER GUMBO

After Hurricane Katrina, Jimmy's No. 43 organized a gumbo fundraiser with several chefs. Jimmy learned a few key lessons: use a cast-iron skillet, make the roux with interesting fatlike bacon and/or duck, and use the "holy trinity of base": celery, onions, bell peppers. Then add in any combination of broth, meat, seafood, and spices.

> *2 lobsters*
> *2 tablespoons butter*
> *1 tablespoon bacon fat*
> *1 cup Empire IPA*
> *1 cup flour*
> *1 cup bacon or duck fat*
> *1 cup chopped onion*
> *1 cup celery*
> *1 cup chopped bell pepper*
> *Crushed red pepper to taste*
> *Dice jalapeño to taste*
> *2 sausages*

Boil lobsters in a stockpot, reserving some of the water as stock plus the carcasses (do this ahead of time).

Braise lobster carcasses in a skillet with butter and bacon fat. Brown carcasses until skillet has an "essence of lobster" to it. Add beer and reserved lobster cooking water to create a concentrated essence of lobster jus.

Add flour and bacon or duck fat to a cast-iron skillet over medium heat to create a roux. Keep stirring to build the base. Allow color to deepen to a coffee or chocolate brown color without burning. Add the "trinity" of onions, celery, and bell peppers to the dark roux. Cook until vegetables turn golden colored, then add crushed red pepper and a small amount of jalapeño to add spice; if using bacon fat, there is no need to add salt to the roux.

Gradually add warm lobster concentrate and beer as roux absorbs and grows. Once roux is sufficiently built, add sausage, lobster, and additional lobster/beer broth to create the gumbo. Cook at least 1 hour.

COURTESY OF JIMMY CARBONE, OWNER OF JIMMY'S NO. 43 (P. 44)

RARE VOS CHEDDAR CHEESE CAKE

Beer and cheese are meant for each other. Here, they're baked together in an indulgent cheesecake. How could you go wrong?

Crust

> 1 cup sifted flour
> ¼ cup sugar
> 1 teaspoon grated lemon rind
> ½ cup butter, softened
> 1 egg yolk
> ¼ teaspoon vanilla

Preheat the oven to 500°F. To prepare the crust, mix the flour, sugar, and lemon rind. Cream the flour mixture with the butter. Add the egg yolk and vanilla. Stir until a soft dough forms. Press ⅓ of the dough into the bottom of an 8-inch springform pan. Bake for 8 to 10 minutes or until lightly browned. Watch carefully, as it burns quickly. Let cool. Press the remaining dough around the sides of the pan, coming to within 1 inch of the top.

Filling

> 2 pounds cream cheese
> 1 cup finely grated cheddar cheese
> 1¾ cups sugar
> ¼ teaspoon vanilla
> ½ teaspoon lemon rind
> ½ teaspoon orange rind
> 4 eggs
> 2 egg yolks
> ¼ cup Rare Vos
> ¼ cup heavy cream

Beat the cream cheese until light and fluffy. Beat in the cheddar cheese until well blended. Add the sugar, vanilla, and lemon and orange rinds. Beat until smooth. Add the eggs and yolks, one at a time, beating well after each addition. Stir in the beer and heavy cream.

Pour filling into the prepared crust. Return to the 500°F oven and bake for 8 to 10 minutes or until lightly browned. Reduce the oven temperature to 250°F. Bake for an additional 1 to 1½ hours, or until a tester inserted in the center comes out fairly clean. Cool to room temperature. Serve warm or chilled with fresh fruit slices.

COURTESY OF BREWERY OMMEGANG (P. 170)

CHOCOLATE ABBEY ALE CAKE

A decadent chocolate cake made with Ommegang's flagship Abbey Ale. Sometimes there's nothing better than beer and chocolate.

Cake

$^3/_4$ cup, plus 2 tablespoons salted butter

$2^1/_2$ cups cake flour

2 teaspoons baking powder

$^1/_2$ teaspoon baking soda

$^1/_2$ teaspoon salt

3 eggs, separated, at room temperature

$1^1/_3$ cups sugar

3 ounces unsweetened Baker's chocolate, melted

1 cup Abbey Ale, flat

Preheat oven to 375°F. Lightly grease two 9-inch cake pans with 2 tablespoons butter and dust with $^1/_4$ cup of flour. Shake out and discard any excess flour; set pans aside. Mix the remaining flour with the baking powder, baking soda, and salt. Beat the egg whites with 2 tablespoons of the sugar until stiff peaks begin to form; set aside. With an electric mixer, cream the remaining sugar with the remaining butter until light in texture. One at a time beat in the egg yolks. Stir in the melted chocolate and the beer, and then gradually beat in the flour mixture. With a rubber spatula, fold in the egg whites. Scrape half the batter into each of the cake pans and bake in the middle of the oven for 30 to 35 minutes, until a toothpick inserted in the center comes out clean. Remove the pans from the oven and let the cakes cool while you prepare the frosting.

Chocolate Chip and Ommegang Frosting

1 pound semisweet real chocolate chips

2 tablespoons salted butter

5 tablespoons Ommegang Abbey Ale

5 tablespoons milk

Soften the chocolate chips and butter in a double boiler. (The chips should be soft, but still hold their shape.) Remove from heat. Using an electric mixer, beat the chocolate and butter until smooth, about 1 minute. Beat in the Ommegang and milk, one at a time, until the mixture is soft and shiny. Remove the cakes from the pans. Frost the layers.

COURTESY OF BREWERY OMMEGANG (P. 170)

Appendix:

Beer Lover's Pick List

Altbier, Rocky Point Artisan Brewers, Altbier, 86

Autumnation, Sixpoint, Pumpkin/Wet Hop Ale, 23

Beanhead Coffee Porter, Rushing Duck Brewing Company, American Porter, 123

Black Duck Porter, Greenport Harbor Brewing, Porter, 77

Blood Orange Pale Ale, Great South Bay Brewery, American Pale Ale with Blood Orange Extract, 74

Bourbon Barrel Flight Level 410, Cortland Beer Company, Bourbon Barrel–aged English Barleywine, 176

Bronx Pale Ale, The Bronx Brewery, American Pale Ale, 6

Brooklyn Sorachi Ace, Brooklyn Brewery, Saison, 8

Brown Ale, Newburgh Brewing Company, English Brown Ale, 119

Cafe Vero Stout, Adirondack Pub and Brewery, Dry Stout, 151

Chatham Porter, Chatham Brewing, American Porter, 113

Checker Cab Blonde Ale, Chelsea Brewing Company, Kolsch, 10

City Island Pale Ale, City Island Beer Company, American Pale Ale, 12

Country Shweat Imperial Wheat, Three Heads Brewing, Imperial Wheat Ale, 242

Cream Ale, Empire Brewing Company, Cream Ale, 178

Dark Mild, Roc Brewing Company, Dark Mild, 237

Delayle, Barrier Brewing Company, Berliner Weisse, 67

Dockside Amber Lager, Wagner Valley Brewing Company, Vienna Lager, 199

Double White, Southampton Publick House, Witbier, 88

Driftwood Ale, Montauk Brewing Company, ESB, 81

Flemish Red, KelSo of Brooklyn, Flanders Red Ale, 15

Flower Power IPA, Ithaca Beer Company, American IPA, 186

Frank, Community Beer Works, American Pale Ale, 227

Genesee Cream Ale, Genesee Brewing Company, Cream Ale, 235

Golden Delicious, Captain Lawrence Brewing Company, American Tripel, 111

Hammonds Porter, Finger Lakes Beer Company, Vanilla Porter, 179

Hop Manna IPA, Shmatlz Brewing Company, IPA, 137

Hop Sun, Southern Tier Brewing Company, Wheat Beer, 241

Hop Warrior IPA, Rooster Fish Brewing, American Double/Imperial IPA, 195

Hot-Jala-Heim Beer with Bite, Horseheads Brewing Inc.,
    Fruit/Vegetable Beer, 185

IPA, Oyster Bay Brewing Company, IPA, 83

IPW, Upstate Brewing Company, India Pale Wheat, 197

Irish Red Rye Ale, Bacchus Brewing Company, Red Rye, 167

Jan Olympic White Lagrrr, SingleCut Beersmiths, Pale Lager, 21

Junior IPA, Radiant Pig Craft Beers, IPA, 17

Long Ireland Breakfast Stout, Long Ireland Beer Company, Breakfast Stout, 79

Long Island Potato Stout, The Blind Bat Brewery, Irish Dry Stout, 69

Maple Porter, Blue Line Brewery, American Porter, 153

Moo Thunder Stout, Butternuts Beer & Ale, Milk Stout, 173

Mother's Milk, Keegan Ales, Milk Stout, 118

Near Varna, Hopshire Farm & Brewery, IPA, 183

Nitrous Hopcide, Ellicottville Brewing Co., IPA, 229

O'Defiant Stout, The Defiant Brewing Company, Dry Irish Stout, 116

Oatmeal Stout, Brown's Brewing Company, Oatmeal Stout, 134

Ol Gilmartin Milk and Oatmeal Stout, Bridge and Tunnel Brewery,
Sweet Stout, 4

Old Marcus, Middle Ages Brewing Company, ESB, 191

Old Slugger, Cooperstown Brewing Company, American Pale Ale, 174

Outrage IPA, Crossroads Brewing Company, American IPA, 114

Peacock, Birdhand Brewing Company, Golden Ale, 169

Pelham Bay IPA, Jonas Bronck's Beer Company, IPA, 14

Picnic in the Park, Fairport Brewing Company, Pale Ale, 231

Porter, Woodcock Brothers Brewery, Porter, 245

Rabbit in the RyePA, Good Nature Brewing, Session Rye IPA, 181

Railroad Street IPA, Rohrbach Brewing Company, IPA, 240

Red Wagon IPA, Fire Island Beer Company, American IPA, 72

Rockaway ESB, Rockaway Brewing Company, ESB, 19

Rusty Chain, Flying Bison Brewing Co., American Amber/Red Ale, 233

Ryely, Davidson Brothers Brewing Company, Seasonal, 155

Saratoga IPA, Olde Saratoga Brewing Company, IPA, 159

The Sauer Peach, Sloop Brewing Company, Berliner Weiss, 124

Schooner Ale, Port Jeff Brewing Company, English-style Pale Ale, 85

Simple Sour, Peekskill Brewery, Berliner Weissbier, 121

Sorghum Pale Ale, Steadfast Brewing Company, American Pale Ale, 138

Spring Fling, Blue Point Brewing Company, Copper Ale, 70

Sugar Hill Golden Ale, Harlem Brewing Company, American Blonde Ale, 13

Ubu Ale, Lake Placid Pub & Brewery, English Strong Ale, 157

Utica Club, Matt Brewing Company, American Adjunct Lager, 188

Vanilla Bean Stout, Yonkers Brewing Company, American Stout, 126

War of 1812 Ale, Sackets Harbor Brewing Company, Amber, 160

White Bite Wheat Ale, Spider Bite Beer Company, American Wheat, 89

White Hop Belgian IPA, CB Craft Brewers, Belgian IPA, 225

Witte, Brewery Ommegang, Belgian-style Wheat Ale, 171

Young Red Tart, Naked Dove Brewing Company, Flemish Red Ale, 193

Index

Miles Wine Cellars, 204

Mission Dolores, 61

Montauk Brewing Company, 80

Montauk Homebrewer's Association, 277

Mr. Goodbar, 254, 263

N

Nail Creek Pub & Brewery, 205

Naked Dove Brewing Company, 191

Newburgh Brewing Company, 118, 284

Newburgh Brewing Peated Porter,
    recipe, 284

New Haven Brewing Company, 79

New Holland Brewery, 167

New York City Beer Week, 268

New York City Brewers Guild, 1, 270

New York State Brewers Association, 177

North American Breweries, x, 233

Northeast Pizza and Beer Company, 208

North Fork Craft Beer, BBQ & Wine
    Festival, 272

NYC Beer Week, 1, 11, 45, 270

NYC Craft Beer Festivals, 267

O

Olde Saratoga Brewing Company, x, 12,
    79, 158

Old Toad, The, 221, 255, 264

124 Rabbit Club, 47

Owl Farm, The, 61

Owl House, The, 256, 264

Oyster Bay Brewing Company, 81

P

Pacific Standard, 61

Pantano's Wine Grapes & Home
    Brew, 277

Paper City Brewing Company, 11, 137

Pearl Street Grill and Brewery, 245, 293

Peekskill Brewery, 120

Peter Austin brewing system, 175

Peter Austin brew kettle, 173

Pine Box Rock Shop, 48

Pizza Plant, 257

Pony Bar, The, 49, 59

Porter and Caraway Mustard, 289

Port Jeff Brewing, 272

Port Jeff Brewing Company, 83

Privatbrauerei Hoepfner, 91

Prohibition, x, 68, 140, 165, 182, 188,
    221, 232, 251

Prohibiton, 20

Proletariat, 50, 55

Pub Crawl, Buffalo, 263

Pub Crawl, East Village, 55

Pub Crawl, Park Slope, Brooklyn, 59

Pub Crawl, Patchogue, Long Island, 105

Pub Crawl, Rochester, 264

Pub Crawls, New York City, 55

Pub Crawl, Syracuse, 218

Pub Crawl, Upper East Side, 57

Pub Crawl, Williamsburg, Brooklyn, 61

PUBFEST, 253

Pyramid Breweries, 15

Q

Queens Kickshaw, The, 50

R

Radiant Pig Craft Beers, 16

Rare Vos Cheddar Cheese Cake, 300

Rattle N Hum, 51

Red Brick Pub, 216

Reinheitsgebot, 198, 212

Revelry, The, 221, 258

Rheingold, 5

Riot Grrrl, 20